Ethics Vindicated

Kant's Transcendental Legitimation of Moral Discourse

Ermanno Bencivenga

OXFORD

UNIVERSITY PRESS

2007

OXFORD
UNIVERSITY PRESS

Oxford University Press, Inc., publishes works that further
Oxford University's objective of excellence
in research, scholarship, and education.

Oxford   New York
Auckland   Cape Town   Dar es Salaam   Hong Kong   Karachi
Kuala Lumpur   Madrid   Melbourne   Mexico City   Nairobi
New Delhi   Shanghai   Taipei   Toronto

With offices in
Argentina   Austria   Brazil   Chile   Czech Republic   France   Greece
Guatemala   Hungary   Italy   Japan   Poland   Portugal   Singapore
South Korea   Switzerland   Thailand   Turkey   Ukraine   Vietnam

Copyright © 2007 by Oxford University Press, Inc.

Published by Oxford University Press, Inc.
198 Madison Avenue, New York, New York 10016

www.oup.com

Oxford is a registered trademark of Oxford University Press

Library of Congress Cataloging-in-Publication Data
Bencivenga, Ermanno, 1950–
Ethics vindicated : Kant's transcendental legitimation of
moral discourse / Ermanno Bencivenga.
p.   cm.
Includes bibliographical references and index.
ISBN-13: 978-0-19-530735-1 (cloth : alk. paper)
ISBN-10: 0-19-530735-6 (cloth : alk. paper)
1. Kant, Immanuel, 1724–1804—Ethics.   2. Ethics, Modern—18th century.
3. Liberty—History—18th century.   I. Title.
B2799.E8B37 2006
170.92—dc22   2006040058

1 3 5 7 9 8 6 4 2

Printed in the United States of America
on acid-free paper

[T]he *Critique of Pure Reason* might well be the true apology for Leibniz, even against those of his disciples who heap praises upon him that do him no honor; as it may also be for sundry older philosophers, whom many an historian of philosophy—for all the praise he bestows on them—still has talking utter nonsense; whose intention he does not divine, in that he neglects the key to all accounts of what pure reason produces from mere concepts, the critique of reason itself (as the common source of all them), and in examining the words they spoke, cannot see what they had wanted to say.

(TA336 VIII 250–51)

PREFACE

Decades ago, as a young man, I entered Kant's conceptual territory. It was not easy, since there are no roads or pathways leading you there; you can only hope that somehow, magically, the duck will turn into a rabbit and everything will start looking different. I remember repeating to myself, like a mantra, "This table is only a representation" and "This representation is *of* a table," painfully trying to acquire a perspective from which both those statements would be true, and being frustrated when, as the perspective seemed to be at hand, any disturbing occurrence in the environment, however minimal, would immediately reconstitute, just because of its disturbing character, the point of view I was naturally familiar with. Nor were matters resolved when the Kantian point of view became itself more familiar, since at the end of the day I had to leave my transcendental ruminations and take care of ordinary objects and tasks in ordinary surroundings, in my ordinary empirical mode; thus my life became a perpetual shifting between incompatible views and, as strongly as I had come to believe that it was so much better that way, this belief did not make things any easier.

Kant's Copernican Revolution was my first report on what this life form is like—the revolutionary outlook *and* the constant oscillation between revolution and conformism. It could not be a report based on Kant only, of course: you do not face the most original, deep, and thorough mind of the Western tradition alone, or you would be swallowed whole and then spat back as a pathetic clone of the great man, reduced to parroting his language without understanding any of it. You need formidable intellectual tools to resist Kant and struggle with him; so that earlier book needed a lot of logic and metaphysics and epistemology, of metamathematics and set theory, of Plato and Aristotle and Descartes and Frege and Russell and Carnap—and Wittgenstein, naturally. Still, it was only a beginning; the real challenge here is the ethics, because no word Kant ever wrote is irrelevant to it, and because even the step from transcendental realism to transcendental idealism, epochal as it is, pales in comparison with the monstrous complications of thinking through freedom and responsibility, good and evil, respect and authority. This thinking through has required some twenty years: my dialogue on freedom and my article "The Metaphysical Structure of Kant's Moral Philosophy," which contained the essence of the story I wanted to tell, were both published in 1991, but then there would be passages in the corpus that would throw the project into disarray, and me into a condition of despair. Eventually, to make sense of them I had to address the very notion of making sense, and to bring out some of the most surprising and exciting consequences of Kant's revolution; but, again, that took time. And it took more and more tools: psychology and decision theory, history and politics, and more Plato and Aristotle as well as Bentham and Mill and Moore and Nietzsche and Rawls and Heidegger and Arendt and Levinas and Sartre. And, foremost, Hegel, to develop a clear sense of how things could look instead: of how far they could go wrong.

What I have come up with is a book of my maturity: a time of reflection and judgment, when one inevitably tries to appreciate the significance of one's life—among other things: what it means to be human, to behave rationally, to attempt to display goodness. Which brings me to the second point I want to make in this preface. Through most of my career, I have found myself writing two books at once, one in English and one in my native Italian; and it was intriguing to regularly find suggestive resonances between them, though their topics were often quite different. The present situation is a case in point, since at the time I was working on this book I was also writing in Italian about my conception and experience of America, and that amounted to a weighing and evaluating of a quarter century of confused and confusing occurrences, in both my own life and the life of this nation, and proved to be very much attuned to that other project of weighing and evaluating the towering figure of my intellectual life.

In one sense the resonance is obvious, because in the Italian book I talk about the America I value and cherish as a Kantian idea of reason, one in which humans are autonomous originators of their own destinies, and responsible for them, as opposed to delegating such responsibility to tradition or family or society or whatever. In another, slightly less obvious, sense the resonance is, however, even more important for me, since I have been arguing that the best representatives of the America I value and cherish are immigrants, people who have *chosen* this place, who have overcome a large part of their thrownness by taking their lives in their own hands, and of course America is a land of immigrants, and of course I am one of them. Ultimately, it is not essential that I was an immigrant *here*, because it is the very condition of being an immigrant that matters to me, in precisely the same way in which the Copernican revolution does: because an immigrant is always a person of two worlds, who cannot sit comfortably in either, who develops a critical attitude on both of them because of how much she can see missing there that others, perfectly at home in it, are not in a position to see. Just as with Kant: ideas are unreal abstractions, and yet real objects, the only objects there are, are but appearances—there is no safe, reassuring place anywhere. I would not want to have it any other way; but, then, I must recognize that others will feel differently. Kant, and America, are not for everyone, wherever they might be born.

This intricate nesting of personal and intellectual issues should make it clear, finally, that Kant, for me, is much more than a professional interest. He is, like any philosopher I ever cared about but more intensely than any other, a role model, a person of a kind I would like to be, an archetype of humanity. I have not met many of those. My wife and I spent a glorious afternoon with Konrad Lorenz, at his house in Altenberg; I have had a few times the privilege of admiring Noam Chomsky's brilliance; I once had lunch, all too briefly, with Norman Brown (I kept telling him about contemporary Italian philosophy—what little there is of it—and he kept asking me "But what about the politics?"). I have missed Marcuse and Sartre, and David Bohm. There isn't much else out there, you know. So, would I have wanted to be a guest in Königsberg once, maybe even be at dinner there? You bet: as everyone who is in this condition of awe, I feel very close to the object of my admiration; I feel (however delusively) as if I have a sense of the simplicity of his courage, the earnestness of his effort, the warmth of his humor, the supreme dignity of his conception of humans. So I would certainly have loved to sit in his wake and see my hero perform as I expected him to; but then I must ask myself, in a Kantian vein, if that satisfaction of a natural drive, whatever the pleasure derived from it, would have been for the better, and I must be skeptical of it. No confirmation of the truth of my interpretation could come "from the horse's mouth," Kant has taught me; what any interpretation must do is confront the same texts, scattered as many of them were by bloody wars and countless other vicissitudes. Any interpretation must take up these texts and become responsible for an autonomous reading of them. What reading I have to offer will say a lot about Kant, I hope; but, however that goes, I know it will say a lot about me.

CONTENTS

NOTE ON TEXTS

Most Kant quotes are from the *Cambridge Edition of the Works of Immanuel Kant*. The following abbreviations are used for volumes of this edition and for individual works within some of those volumes:

C: *Correspondence*
J: *Critique of the Power of Judgment*
LE: *Lectures on Ethics*
LL: *Lectures on Logic*
LM: *Lectures on Metaphysics*
N: *Notes and Fragments*
O: *Opus Postumum*
P: *Practical Philosophy*
G: *Groundwork of the Metaphysics of Morals*

PR: *Critique of Practical Reason*
M: *Metaphysics of Morals*
R: *Religion and Rational Theology*
RR: *Religion within the Boundaries of Mere Reason*
TA: *Theoretical Philosophy after 1781*
TB: *Theoretical Philosophy 1755–1770*

For Kant works not yet included in the published volumes of the Cambridge edition, I have used the following texts (and abbreviations):

AP: *Anthropology from a Pragmatic Point of View*. Translated by V.
Dowdell. Carbondale: Southern Illinois University Press, 1978.
E: *Education*. Translated by A. Churton. Ann Arbor:
University of Michigan Press, 1960.
PW: *Political Writings*. Edited by H. Reiss. Translated by H. Nisbet.
Cambridge: Cambridge University Press, 1991.

References to the first *Critique* are given by indicating the A/B number(s); for one note in Kant's own copy of the first edition I have given the A number followed by the volume and page number of the Akademie edition of the *Gesammelte Schriften*. Most other references include the volume (or individual work) and page number(s) of the translation and (when applicable) the volume and page number(s) of the Akademie edition. Thus, a typical reference would be M548 VI 424, to be read: page 548 of the Cambridge translation of the *Metaphysics of Morals*, corresponding to page 424 of volume VI of the Akademie edition. One reference includes only the volume and page number of the Akademie edition. I have uniformed all translations to American spelling, I have never italicized "a priori," I have never capitalized "idea," and I have always used italics when a translation uses boldface or small capitals. Square brackets are sometimes the translators' and sometimes my own; braces are always the translators'.

The only other works cited are the following:

Bencivenga, Ermanno. *Kant's Copernican Revolution.* New York: Oxford University Press, 1987.

———. Free From What? *Erkenntnis* 33 (1990): 9–21.

———. *La libertà: un dialogo.* Milano: Il Saggiatore, 1991. English translation *Freedom: A Dialogue.* Indianapolis: Hackett, 1997.

———. The Metaphysical Structure of Kant's Moral Philosophy. *Philosophical Topics* 19 (1991): 17–29.

———. Kant's Sadism. *Philosophy and Literature* 20 (1996): 39–46.

———. *Hegel's Dialectical Logic.* New York: Oxford University Press, 2000.

Euclid. *The Thirteen Books of the Elements.* Translated with introduction and commentary by Sir Thomas L. Heath. New York: Dover, 1966.

Hume, David. *A Treatise of Human Nature,* 2nd edition. Oxford: Oxford University Press, 1978.

Strawson, P. F. *The Bounds of Sense.* London: Methuen, 1966.

Ethics Vindicated

ONE

PROBLEMS FOR ETHICS

The alleged subject matter of ethics is human conduct. Not human behavior; not everything humans do. But, specifically, what they do of their own choice, because they *want* to do it; what they do *freely*. And here ethics faces a first monumental problem: its alleged subject matter runs the risk of vanishing into thin air, of turning out to be purely delusional.[1] For humans are natural beings, hence what they do, *everything* they do, is as much a necessary consequence of preceding events and conditions as the "behavior" of oceans and avalanches; and, one necessary step after (or rather, before) another, it is a consequence of events and conditions well beyond the scopes of their lives.[2] That I "chose" to write this book is a consequence of moves my parents made, and their parents, and their parents' parents, long before I ever came into the picture. Of course, I wanted to write it, but how much of a causal factor is that? That I want to do something, too, follows from things other people did and I could not have wanted to see done (since I was not there); hence, it cannot be a manifestation of my freedom. Thus, human conduct is nonexistent, indeed inconceivable; and ethics is left with nothing to deal with. Nor is the occurrence of indeterministic events (as, say, quantum mechanics sanctions it) going to provide any relief here; even if we are willing to admit that something A might happen as the result of pure chance, it would make no sense to claim that A is totally random *and also* the outcome of an individual's free choice.[3]

But assume that we successfully meet the monumental challenge above: that somehow we find room for genuine human actions—where an action is the unit of (human) conduct. Immediately we encounter another threat that is just as deadly. For what ethics is supposed to do with its subject matter is *judge* it, *evaluate* it, assess it on the basis of its own standards. If I do something freely, ethics will not content itself with relating it to other things I or others did equally freely, or with elaborating a taxonomy of what I or others typically choose to do, or even with bringing out how far I or others in fact (freely) approve of what I have done. Any such pursuit would belong to an empirical discipline like psychology, or sociology, or statistics; and ethics is no empirical discipline. Its concern is not with understanding what anyone does, but with determining how *good* it is: not good *for* someone, or *for* some purpose or other, but good, period, unconditionally good, good in a totally absolute sense—one that is independent of what happens and might well be in conflict with all that happens. How is this kind of judgment legitimate? How is it more than the expression of individual preferences? What is the place of values in a world of facts?

And it is not over. Aesthetics, too, is regarded by many as an evaluative discipline, and as one that might be based on equally ambitious (and unrealistic) expectations. Landscapes, people, and works of art are often assessed by comparing them with standards of beauty which, we might imagine, nothing fits perfectly, with ideals that everything falls short of. And we might occasionally feel nostalgic for such ideals, and desperately long for their realization; but it is unlikely we would go any further. Ethics, on the other hand, does not only evaluate conduct; it also *prescribes* it—when it regards something as good, it also judges it *necessary* that people do it. However beyond our resources good conduct might be, that is precisely what ethics imposes on us: what it says we *ought to* bring about. Ethics is a normative discipline, in a much stronger sense than any other. It is often claimed that scientific theories are normative because the world they "describe" is highly idealized: much more simple and elegant than the real world ever is. And yet, we do not ordinarily think that an astronomical theory tells the universe what to do, or that a sociological theory does that with communities, crowds, or institutions. Ethics, on the other hand, tells us—each of us—what to do; which makes its status, once again, uncertain (what kind of "discipline" is this, that pretends to shape what it applies to? does it amount to mere wishful thinking?) and leaves it totally mysterious where the *authority* that does the prescribing is to issue from. We are familiar with officers prescribing behavior to their subordinates, and with laws doing so in a state; in all such cases, we can think that the prescribing is authoritative because of the (physical or political) *power* the prescriptive agencies have. But what kind of power makes ethical injunctions authoritative? What sense does it make for ethics to claim, as it often does, that, unless they are consistent with its injunctions, even the officers' or the laws' commands carry no weight, have no real authority?

Ethics has more specific, local problems than the three I mentioned. As with any other human endeavor, its practitioners disagree in subtle and important ways on the details of their positions and arguments. But those three problems are its most basic ones, in the literal sense that, unless they are resolved in a positive way, ethics has no base at all. They are the preliminary to the entertaining of any substantive ethical views, the *conditio sine qua non* for the very legitimacy of moral discourse. Immanuel Kant's philosophy, as I see it, is a sustained, bold, and successful effort aiming at such resolution. In order to reach its goal, it is forced to many digressions, some of them enormously long and complex, and of enormous independent interest. But we do not want to miss the forest for the trees, because there is something of great consequence at stake.[4] The challenges to the credibility of ethics that Kant was facing in the eighteenth century had been raised before, in different languages using different metaphors, and are still being raised, in yet newer jargons; Kant himself would say, indeed, that there is no escaping their constant recurrence. They are an essential component of our form of life: of the irremediably conflictual existence we lead. But it is just as essential to our life that they be answered, and that the answer be loud and clear. The point of this book is to spell out Kant's answer,[5] in a language that speaks to our times, so as to, once again, patiently, attend to the interminable, unavoidable task of establishing the dignity and autonomy of our moral standards.

TWO

THE FRAMEWORK

In this chapter, I summarize the fundamental theses and results of my *Kant's Copernican Revolution* that are relevant to what follows. I do not argue for them, either textually or theoretically, since I intend to limit the amount of repetition to a minimum.[1] But I think that a brief summary is useful, as providing the basic presuppositions of my understanding of Kant's moral philosophy—the map within which this understanding is to be located, as it were.

1. Transcendental Philosophy

Most of Kant's predecessors thought that philosophy could and did establish factual truths; for example, that it could and did establish that God exists, or that the soul is immortal, or that the world is infinite (or finite). As established philosophically, such truths were proved by a priori arguments; hence in fact (one thought) *more* than their factual truth was proved. They were proved to be necessary; and that they were true was then supposed to follow as a trivial consequence.[2] Thus Anselm's and Descartes's ontological arguments proved that God must exist, that He *cannot but* exist, that His nonexistence is inconceivable; from which it was only (it seemed) a small step to conclude that He does exist.

Kant's transcendental philosophy, on the other hand, has no factual import whatsoever. It gives no information about the real world where we lead our ordinary, everyday life; it cannot add (or detract) anything to (or from) it. The existence and nature of what belongs to the real world is decided by our ordinary experience, inclusive of our empirical sciences. The philosopher is to receive this material and not to challenge it in any way.[3] His task is rather to understand it, to explain how it is possible.[4] More precisely: to provide a conceptual scheme, or logical space, within which the terms used in describing ordinary experience are given definitions generally consistent with that use.[5] It is not for philosophy to decide that, say, we know midsize objects like tables, chairs, and trees; that we do is part of life, and what particular experiences of tables, chairs, or trees count as cognitive is decided by ordinary people in ordinary epistemic contexts, by using their ordinary empirical criteria.[6] But philosophy needs to so determine what objects and knowledge are as to make it possible for us to sometimes know these objects—as to make sense of the claim that we sometimes do (and that the empirical criteria will sometimes attain their intended goal).[7] It is a scandal, Kant thinks, when philosophy cannot account for such claims and is forced to conclude (say) that we are not just empirically wrong in believing we know this or that, but conceptually wrong in believing we can know anything at all—or in believing we can know midsize objects, as opposed to the contents of our own minds.

The real world contains objects and events, and the most important relation among them is causality: how an event brings about another event, how the existence or the behavior of an object determines the existence or the behavior of another one. The logical space contains concepts, and the most important relation among them (as indeed was suggested above) is definition: how a concept is articulated in terms of other concepts, how an understanding of the former is provided in terms of (an understanding of) the latter. So the logical space is like a dictionary, where the concept of an oak is defined in terms of that of a tree, and the concept of an acorn is defined in terms of those of an oak and a fruit.[8] And the crucial demand to be put on this particular dictionary—it is worth repeating—is that its definitions be serviceable in our ordinary dealings, that they do not make it impossible for us to operate with them in ways that fit our general expectations. If I were to define an experience as cognitive, say, when it is particularly vivid, that would contradict my general expectation that many dreams are going to be much more vivid than most waking experiences while not being cognitive (whereas some of those experiences are).

To put it in yet another way, the logical space is like one of those computer programs that help you organize your finances. Whether you are rich or you are broke is not for the program to decide: that is decided by the empirical data of your assets and liabilities. But it is a condition of the program working properly that its instructions make consistent room for the empirical data: that by following them you do not find yourself running in circles, or getting contradictory outcomes, or being entirely mystified as to where a given asset or liability is supposed to be listed—or whether it is to be listed *anywhere*.

In Kant's own terms, transcendental philosophy is—like all philosophy, that is, all "cognition from concepts" (A837 B865)[9]—entirely constituted of analytic judgments (since "from concepts no synthetic propositions can be derived," N278 XVIII 298). Because this claim seems to contradict some of Kant's own statements,[10] and certainly does contradict a substantial amount of Kantian lore, it will be useful to articulate it further, with specific regard to the ethical works. Take the *Groundwork*, then, where we are told: "That . . . [the principle of autonomy] is an imperative, that is, that the will of every rational being is necessarily bound to it as a condition, cannot be proved by mere analysis of the concepts to be found in it, because it is a synthetic proposition; one would have to go beyond cognition of objects to a critique of the subject, that is, of pure practical reason, since this synthetic proposition, which commands apodictically, must be capable of being cognized completely a priori" (G89 IV 440). Leaving aside details to be discussed later, the general structure of the situation seems clear: Kant is concerned with a proposition of great significance for him, and one that he explicitly designates as synthetic. Fair enough. The whole issue, however, revolves around what it means for him to be concerned with it.

An earlier statement puts us on the right track: "[the] categorical imperative or law of morality . . . is an a priori synthetic practical proposition; and since it is so difficult to see the *possibility* of this kind of proposition in theoretical cognition, it can be readily gathered that the difficulty will be no less in practical cognition" (G72 IV 420; italics added). And later he insists: "*How such a synthetic practical proposition is possible a priori* and why it is necessary is a problem whose solution does not lie within the bounds of the metaphysics of morals" (G93 IV 444). So Kant has a problem, and the best way to understand exactly what that problem is will be to look at how he resolves it: "categorical imperatives are possible by this: that the idea of freedom makes me a member of an intelligible world and consequently, if I were only this, all my actions *would* always be in conformity with the autonomy of the will; but since at the same time I intuit myself as a member of the world of sense, they *ought* to be in conformity with it; and this *categorical* ought represents a synthetic proposition a priori, since to my will affected by sensible desires there is added the idea of the same will but belonging to the world of the understanding" (G100–1 IV 454). As we will see, the categorical imperative is independent of experience, hence a priori; and I have no difficulty accepting the claim that it is synthetic. What Kant is arguing here, however, is not that this imperative applies, but that it *can* apply. The argument he offers would have no hope of establishing the former, since the intelligible world he invokes to prove his point (whatever his point might be) is one about which (again, as will be detailed later) he must admit we have no knowledge. Therefore, Kant cannot even be attempting to prove the categorical imperative itself; what he is after is a modalized version of it, in which it is preceded by a possibility operator.[11] More precisely, since an imperative expresses the necessity of a certain kind of behavior, the characteristic modality, here as in a number of other crucial cases in Kant, is $\Diamond\Box$: *possibly necessary*.[12] It is *possible* that space *must* be three-dimensional; it is *possible* that every event *must* have a cause;[13] it is *possible* that one *must* act with total disregard for one's idiosyncratic makeup and situation. And this modalized version, as I pointed out in *Kant's Copernican Revolution*, is (with a qualification to be made in the next paragraph) well inside the scope of (analytic) cognition from concepts.[14]

And now for the troubling news. A consequence of Kant's characterization of (transcendental) philosophy is that the latter is not a cognitive enterprise: no knowledge can issue from it. Not in his view, at least, since for him a cognition (*Erkenntnis*—the unit of knowledge)[15] entails the interaction of concepts (or general representations—that is, representations that could in principle apply to more than one thing, though of course some *in fact* apply to only one thing or to none at all) *and intuitions* (or singular representations—constitutionally directed to a single thing); but intuitions do not enter in that reconnaissance of logical space transcendental philosophy consists of—though of course *the concept of* an intuition does. (Transcendental) philosophy can only establish *logical* possibility: it can prove that the description of something, as far as we can tell, is not incoherent. This proof, however, is a function of how detailed the description is and of how deeply we went into the analysis of the terms involved in it—or in what direction: Russell's paradox was close to the surface of Frege's set theory, except that Frege had chosen to look (very intently, and in great depth) away from it.[16] *Real* possibility, on the other hand (or

possibility, period: what is more than an *appearance* of possibility), requires access to a real (singular) example of what we are talking about
(to a corresponding intuition), and no such example is forthcoming
within the transcendental (that is, conceptual) reflection where transcendental philosophy is developed.[17] *Talk* of examples does; but this
talk is incapable of establishing its own consistency, however consistent
it might *sound*.[18] In critiquing itself, reason discovers its limits; rational
discourse is inspiring and edifying but incapable of proving the ve-
ridicality of its tenets. Which is not all bad, as these limits "make room
for *faith*" (Bxxx); that is, allow for a more nuanced and accurate understanding of the complexity of our form of life.

Three remarks are in order before moving on. First, admittedly, the
radical distinction implied here between ordinary concerns and philosophical activity seems artificial: ordinary people make constant use of
conceptual tools, even complex ones, and some have argued that what
tools those are determines what world they live in (Eskimos live in a
world in which there is no such thing as *just snow*, and so forth).[19] The
very notion of an ordinary person, one might insist, is a philosophical
abstraction. Which is a point well taken—except that it does not detract from the substance of Kant's position but only from its superficial
rhetoric. Changing some of the rhetoric but none of the substance, we
could then say: It is a scandal that our experience, inclusive of our
various attempts at making rational sense of it, should invariably make
so little sense; and what causes the scandal is one constant feature of
those attempts. They present themselves as final and all-inclusive: that
reason of ours which relentlessly motivates their recurrence cannot
help thinking of itself as self-standing and self-contained, as in need of
nothing external for a full resolution of its problems.[20] But such in not
the case: our reason is sharply limited precisely in how it can satisfy its
own demands, which is revealed in an obvious way by the poor
cognitive status of its pronouncements and in a less obvious but ultimately equivalent way by its necessity to always defer to an *other*—to
the nonrational or nonphilosophical as such; to what it itself must
characterize as nonrational and nonphilosophical—as a source of the
wisdom it is forever (and forever unsuccessfully) looking for.[21] As we
will see, this conclusion has no negative impact on reason's ambition
or on its nobility—the latter is indeed thought to be even higher here
because of reason's failure to attain its ambitious goal (because of its
faithfulness to its standards, hence to its vocation, in the face of such
failure). But it does set Kant in sharp contrast with all those other
rational thinkers who thought that intellectuals like themselves—

whether because they had seen the Forms, or because they knew the principles and causes of things, or because they had reached the stage of Absolute Spirit—exhausted the significance of the world in their intellectual activity, and hence should also rule it (or instruct its rulers).[22]

Second, since the other to which philosophy is supposed to defer has a temporal dimension, as well as a development along this dimension, deferring to it entails that philosophy may have to accept as given, and work hard to establish the possibility of, different material at different times; hence that its task may have to be repeatedly redefined, even to a dramatic extent. Which sometimes gets Kant in trouble because, for reasons I discuss in *Kant's Copernican Revolution*, he is constantly tempted to provide more detail for his conceptual accounts, hence to commit himself more to the (scientific or moral) views current at his time (in his terminology, to move from the critique to the system)[23]—as opposed to staying safely within the confines of such highly general statements as have most of a chance of remaining stable over time.[24] And, insofar as the views he refers to are no longer current, he exposes himself to the risk of being "refuted" by later developments that have nothing specifically philosophical about them and are entirely irrelevant to whether his transcendental arguments for the possibility *of the earlier views* are correct. Many of the actual refutations people have proposed over the years turn out to be, upon closer examination, way too hurried: that we are now in possession of abstract mathematical theories about more-than-three-dimensional, non-Euclidean "spaces," for example, does nothing to refute the (nonphilosophical) claim held by Kant that the space of our experience[25] is Euclidean and three-dimensional—in fact, it does not even prove that the objects described by those theories are legitimately called "spaces": that the use they make of this term is anything more than a suggestive metaphor. But, clearly, the risk is there; and I will not deny that I am far from sharing some of what Kant took from the "ordinary people" of his time—say, his unconditional approval of the talion law, of the death penalty, or of property rights based on first occupancy. In this regard, however, he is in no worse position than any other philosopher, who, whether he aspires to "comprehend his time in thoughts" or to be sharply critical of it, can certainly have nonphilosophical views many of his readers judge despicable, and can spend a large amount of his time and energy providing a justification for them—while still, perhaps, making philosophical moves that will benefit all future practitioners of philosophy. In fact, I would add, the very conception of philosophy that creates this problem for Kant also puts him in a *better* position to address it than most of his colleagues, in two ways. On the one hand, because of (his) transcendental philosophy's dependence on a nonphilosophical other, its verdicts cannot be considered absolute but must always be seen as open to revision if and when the nonphilosophical context changes—if and when, say (to consider some quite radical developments), we mutate into beings who visualize in an eleven-dimensional space, or who have intellectual intuition. On the other, this philosophy intends to prove possibilities, not necessities; and one possibility does not rule out another. Thus Kant's (both philosophical and nonphilosophical) views present themselves (despite his occasional statements to the contrary) as less definitive than most others'; and what falsehoods the man Kant may have believed in the sciences or in morality, or what mistakes the philosopher Kant may have made when rationalizing those falsehoods, can be corrected by the very listening attitude, and the very critical activity, which by all means he did not initiate from scratch but of which he first gave us a lucid and articulate account.[26]

My final remark builds on the previous ones and sets the stage for the next section. Kant was not just interested in describing the conceptual space of his time; he wanted to revolutionize it. And such revolutions often have empirical consequences—which once again makes the neat separation between transcendental and ordinary concerns look too simple. The first person who thought of equities as assets did not add a dime to anyone's wealth; but eventually, *because* people thought of equities as assets, many of them had more money to spend. Kant often tries to minimize the impact that his novel philosophical views can have on everyday life—most typically when he is defending himself against the censors' attacks.[27] But such defenses are disingenuous, and at other times he clearly manifests the hope that, in the long run, how we think of things will change how we live: "it could well happen that the last would some day be first (the lower faculty [of philosophy] would be the higher)—not, indeed, in authority, but in counseling the authority (the government). For the government may find the freedom of the philosophy faculty, and the increased insight gained from this freedom, a better means for achieving its ends than its own absolute authority" (R261 VII 35).[28] And yet, though these links complicate the relation between the two levels (in ways that will turn out to be crucially relevant to the Kantian analysis of morality), they do not deny their distinctness. That people come to have different basic conceptions is a fact, and as such it can certainly have causal influence in the empirical world, but what conceptions those are, and how they are related to one another, is independent of who holds them, or of whether anyone holds them at all.

2. Transcendental Idealism

Within transcendental philosophy, various positions are possible depending on what concept(s) is (are) considered primitive in logical space. The two positions around which Kant's Copernican revolution unfolds are *transcendental realism* (TR) and *transcendental idealism* (TI); that revolution is the transition from TR to TI, the "experiment" (Bxvi) of adopting TI instead of TR.

TR is the structuring of logical space *implicit* (for Kant) in the tradition: most likely, traditional philosophers would not have described what they were doing by using this language (or anything equivalent), but describing it that way best makes sense (Kant thinks) of their practice and of its outcomes. That is, it is most useful to characterize them as *thinking* in terms of objects: as taking the concept of an object (*res*) to be the fundamental one, and every other concept to be dependent on it—and most often definable (possibly after numerous steps) by an eventual reference to it.[29] Thus, a sailor is a human who works on a boat, and a human is a rational animal, and an animal is a self-moving living object; hence, a sailor is a rational self-moving living object who works on a boat (and rational is an object that can think and argue, and a boat is an object that holds humans and merchandise and crosses oceans, and an ocean is an object . . .). What an object is, on the other hand, a transcendental realist cannot say: he can use synonyms (a being, an entity, a thing, the bearer of properties), but an informative definition is out of the question, for no fault of his—primitive concepts cannot be defined.

TI, on the other hand, is the structuring of logical space that takes the notion of a representation (*Vorstellung*) to be fundamental, and every other concept (including the concept of an object—"what may be contained in my concept of a thing . . . [, what] belongs to its logical essence," TA89 IV 294) to be dependent on it—and most often definable in its terms.[30] Because TI is to this day a minority position, it is held to higher standards; and no sooner do people hear it described as I just did than they start asking, "What is meant by a representation?" or even worse, "*Whose* representations are we talking about?" And then they might even conclude that the position is not new after all, because a representation is nothing but a state (or a property) of a mind, which is an object like any other. Such irrelevant questions and criticisms must be resisted, while admitting the initial awkwardness of an unfamiliar way of thinking; one must firmly reject any tacit commitment to the very realist vocabulary that is being challenged while gently guiding interlocutors, by appropriate examples and rhetoric, to seeing things in a manner consistent with TI.[31]

Representations, here, are *no one's*; not, at least, to begin with. For at the stage where we are—at the very origin of logical space—there is nothing other than representations, hence nothing for them to belong to.[32] Eventually, after objects are defined, and some of them are characterized as minds, it will be possible to ascribe some representations to them; but it will take a lot of work to get there, if indeed we ever do. Which suggests that the word "representation" is an unfortunate choice, since it seems to imply that something is present to something else (indeed, something that *was* present once and is now present again—in this sense, "*Vorstellung*" is a little better, as it evokes no repetition), and what could both of these "somethings" be other than objects? But we cannot help that: there is no neutral language in which the various setups of logical space can be entertained and compared with one another. What language is available is always the expression of a given setup, and the current setup (current at Kant's time, and also at ours) is TR; so our language is reflective of this dominance, and the only possible tack for would-be revolutionaries is a translation (of their vision into the existing words and phrases) that is also (inevitably, like all translations) a betrayal—the forcing of new wine into old bottles, at risk of exploding them, and of spoiling the wine.

In TR, where representations are conceptually dependent on objects, they cannot, however, be regarded as conceptually dependent on (let alone as definable in terms of) the objects they are (allegedly) representations *of*, since (1) often there is no such thing and (2) whether or not there is one is often an empirical matter, which we cannot allow (not prima facie, at least) to have an impact on conceptual issues: if the dependence must be ruled out in *one* case, it must be ruled out in *all* cases that are only empirically different from that one (at least initially, and open to possible revision by the regimenting project to be mentioned later). So here it is crucial that, for example, one cannot understand my imagining a winged horse as a case in which an imagining relation occurs between myself and a winged horse (for nothing is a winged horse, hence an imagining relation with "it" is a relation with nothing—or not a relation at all); to give a conceptual account of this experience (as well as of the empirically different one of imagining the current Pope), the transcendental realist must regiment it in some way, and claim that its logical form is not what it appears to be.[33] In TI no such problem arises, and a representation is always of something: "All representations, as representations, have their object" (A108). It continues to be the case, however, that a representation cannot depend conceptually on what it represents (as the realist thinks of it)—this time because of the conceptual priority of representations. In fact, the very unfailing success representations have in "hitting upon" an object proves this "relation" to be a trivial, purely verbal, one: to speak of the object *of* a representation is only to bring out, in somewhat different terms, the representation's representational character.

Using more recent terminology than Kant's, the object *of* a representation, in TI's sense, could be called an *intentional* object[34] (and the representation's representational character could be called its *intentionality*); but we need to be clear that intentional objects here are not another *kind* of object as traditionally understood—they are not a species of the traditional genus *object* in the sense in which, say, red or round objects are. They are a step in a new understanding of objects altogether: of objects as conceptually dependent upon representations.[35] And, because of Kant's empirical conservatism (which, as related to the present issue, is relabeled *empirical realism*), they often end up being objects only in a manner of speaking, objects by courtesy. For, being an empirical conservative, Kant does not want to add any new objects to the world, hence in the final analysis he wants to say that the winged horse I am imagining, though an "intentional" object, is *really* no object at all: once again, *there is no such thing*.[36]

The conceptual "construction"—that is, definition—of (real) objects takes place by imposing requirements on representations.[37] Such requirements are best thought of as placed not on individual representations but on systems of representations. Kant calls them *categories*; equivalently, they could be called conceptual criteria of objectivity.[38] A system of representations cannot be called objective (that is, it cannot amount to knowledge, since a cognition is "an objective perception," A320 B376, or an objective "representation with consciousness," A320 B376) unless it is consistent and connected: the latter criterion, which replaces for Kant (in Hume's wake) traditional causal efficacy, amounts to lawlikeness or regularity—that representations follow one another according to rules.[39] Also, the objects of the representations must be identifiable and countable; since our means of identification are space

and time (they are the forms of intuition: the conditions at which only
we can represent anything singular—or, in more contemporary terminology, the necessary conditions for us to be able to provide any
demonstrative reference), objects must have a spatiotemporal location.[40]
And they must be irreducible to any conceptual specification of them,
and richer than any such; it must always be possible for us to extend the
relevant system of representations, to "synthesize" additional features
of their objects.[41] And so on. That a representation is objective *means*
that it belongs to a system of representations satisfying these criteria;
that the intentional object of a representation is a real object, or an
object *simpliciter* (an object, period), hence that there really (not just
verbally) is a relation between the representation and an object, means
that this representation is objective—or cognitive. Which is what Kant
expresses, famously, by inviting us to assume "that the objects must
conform to our cognition" (Bxvi).[42]

3. Appearances

So far, I have spoken vaguely of a system of objective representations.
The question naturally arises: how large is this system supposed to be?
And the most obvious answer, the only one that would satisfy reason's
drive to universality (more about this later), is: a global system, that is, a
set of representations to which nothing further could be (consistently)
added, that is no proper part of any other such (consistent) set.[43] If this
global, universal system were still to be regarded as objective, all representations belonging to it would have to be conceived as *unified*—not
as arbitrarily jumbled together but as objectively connected: as representations of elements and aspects of one and the same objective
world.[44] Kant, however, proves that the thought of an objective world
involves us in endless, irremediable contradictions; as a result, the
conceptual criteria of objectivity can only be applied meaningfully *in a
context*, that is, within a horizon that is not itself interrogated, to which
the same criteria are not applied—at least at the moment; they certainly
could be applied to it at some other time, provided that what is now
the context were to become part of another (uninterrogated) context.
To avoid absurdity, and make knowledge possible, overweeningly
ambitious reason must give way to *understanding*, that is, to its own
projection (the projection of its own criteria) onto a limited, dogged,
stepwise, myopic mode of operation.[45]

This is not an empirical issue; it has nothing to do with empirical limitations of ours, which we might think of eventually overcoming. It is a conceptual, or transcendental, issue; it has to do with a conceptual clash internal to the very criteria of objectivity—or rather, to the spatiotemporal conditions of their application. Take identifiability, for example, as translated into being assigned a definite spatiotemporal location. It turns out that such a location can only be assigned to an object relative to other objects, in a context in which other objects are supposed to have already received their own location. If we try to overcome this limit, the very search for identification becomes incomprehensible: it makes no sense to ask where or when an object is, period (in more dignified philosophical terms: where or when it is *absolutely*), or in relation to *the totality* of space and time (otherwise put, it makes no sense to ask where or when *the whole world* is, as opposed to asking where or when something is *in the world*). Similarly, the irreducibility of objects to concepts (of the ultimate subjects of predication to their predicates, as we could also say) clashes with the manifold nature of space and time: with the fact that spatiotemporal objects (what subjects of predication we do in fact encounter—and we can in fact know) are indefinitely divisible, hence there are no ultimate constituents of matter, no "objects" that could not also be seen as complicated (systems of) properties of, or relations among, simpler objects. Or take the lawlike (spatiotemporally determined) connectedness of objects (better: of the events in which they participate): it can only be meaningfully applied to some current objects (or events) if some antecedent objects (or events) are presupposed to which the former are connected. Therefore, we will never be able to reach an absolutely first antecedent for anything in the world (or in the chain of events) and we will never know, in an absolute, definitive sense, *why* that is (or happens)—but only relatively to something else that also is (or happens).

None of this would impress the transcendental realist. That criteria of objectivity have no meaningful absolute application is *our* problem, he would say, an epistemological one, and one that does not touch the metaphysical structure of the objects themselves, which are what they are whether they can be identified or not, whether they can be radically opposed to their properties or not.[46] So this contradictory outcome—this "antinomy of reason"—is no reductio of TR, as has often been claimed, but rather an important articulation of TI.[47] What it proves is that within TI the occurrence of knowledge necessarily depends on the act of choosing a context, and of holding on to it for as long as it is to be relevant[48] (conservation is continuous creation); and this act of choice[49] (of *synthesis*, [50] to use a Kantian term that has already emerged above; and now the significance of this word, of this "putting together," begins to come forth) can only be conceived as spontaneous, as itself not determined by anything else—because without presupposing it no determination is possible, because it is itself the origin of all determination. In TI we cannot think of knowledge as merely receptive, as the passive acceptance of a structure simply "given" to it: the world is (to be conceived as) being constituted as much as it is received, within the very same experience of receiving it; that "adequacy" to its object which is the ideal of knowledge ("[t]he nominal definition of truth, namely that it is the agreement of cognition with its object," A58 B82) is necessarily infected by an activity that makes the object what it is. "[E]xperience cannot be given but must be made" (O122 XXII 405).

Empirically, we distinguish objects from appearances, delusions, phantoms; and we do so by regarding the latter (but not the former) as partial, incomplete, unstable, and as dependent on our support for their very being (as well as for being what they are). If in a moment of confusion (or in the grips of a powerful desire) I see a tree as a person dear to me, that "person" will not sustain a prolonged inquiry: "she" will not display other angles (my perception of her will not be enriched) as I move around her (or rather, around the tree), in fact she might no longer be there if I look at her (that is, at the tree) again after getting distracted for a moment. Her existence is fragile, ready to collapse as soon as I stop offering it my cooperation. What is true empirically of this "object," Kant thinks, is true conceptually of all (empirical) objects: since a spontaneous act must be conceived as originating their being, they all lack the self-sufficiency, the independence objects *ought to* have. Nothing we ever encounter fully matches what we would expect of an object; we only ever encounter faulty objects, objects to a point. Transcendentally, empirical objects are all mere appearances, and it is a *transcendental illusion* to conceive of them as independently real—an inevitable, but still deceptive, mistaking them for what they cannot be. Or, to put it otherwise (and introduce more terminology), the concept of an object is an *idea* of reason, *that is*, a representation for which no adequate realization can be found in experience.

The other, more positive side to this coin is that within TI, where representations are primary (and because thoughts—or concepts—are a kind of representations), we can still *think* of objects in the proper sense, objects that are what they are entirely of themselves, independently of any external contribution or choice[51]—unreal as these objects are bound to be, thinking of them here (we know) is not thinking *of nothing*—and we may even claim that such thinking (of objects of pure thought, *noumena*) is a necessary consequence of reason's (frustrated) aspiration to fulfilling its standards (to realizing its ideas), and of its perpetual dissatisfaction with what world it is forced to recognize as real. Because of those features of the spatiotemporal framework which we found earlier to clash with our conceptual criteria of objectivity, none of these "objects in the proper sense" can be thought of as spatiotemporal (there are no things in themselves in space and time), hence we can never think of acquiring any information about them. They are nothing but fictions, and yet we do nothing wrong when entertaining them, or even (if appropriate) when judging what *can* be experienced in their light.

There is a tendency within Kant interpretation to overstate this positive side of the critical outcome, which it will be good for me to address here. People get carried away by passages asserting that "[a]s soon as ... [the] distinction [between appearances and things in themselves] has once been made ... , then it follows of itself that we must admit and assume behind appearances something else that is not appearance, namely things in themselves" (G98 IV 451), and conclude that the real world is made of things in the proper sense, which we can only know *as they appear to us.* Next thing you know, Kant is turned into an extreme case of Locke, and Schopenhauerian Nirvana is at hand: everything we have access to is a secondary property, but there is still something unspeakable that is the *true* basis of it all. And, in view of what crucial role synthesis has now acquired (and of moral considerations to follow), freedom looks like an attractive candidate for occupying this exalted metaphysical position; so one will declare that the noumenal subject is really exercising its spontaneous will, whatever the case might be for its unfortunate little brother that inhabits the delusive world of experience. In addressing this (exegetical, if not substantial) nonsense, we must remind ourselves of the transcendental nature of Kant's enterprise: all he means by such passages as the one quoted above, and all he *can* possibly mean, is that *calling* something an appearance amounts to also mobilizing *the concept* of something that would not be an appearance and in comparison with which our appearance talk can be made sense of. The thought of a thing in itself is the conceptual ground for thinking of appearances, and of spatiotemporal objects *as* appearances, much like the thought of a perfect,

archetypal human is the conceptual ground for thinking of any concrete human specimens as imperfect[52]—which is not supposed to
imply that, because there are imperfect humans, there must also
be perfect ones (which we only experience as imperfect?); or that,
because there are appearances, there must also be things in themselves.
All we can say, in all such cases, is that "our reason . . . [feels] a need to
take the *concept* of the unlimited as the ground of the concepts of all
limited beings" (R11 VIII 137–38).[53] Reason can provide a verbal
articulation for this need because its criteria of objectivity are, at
bottom, purely intellectual conditions—the criterion of causal connectedness is, at bottom, the purely intellectual condition of finding a
ground for something—and hence can be used independently of
spatiotemporal coordinates; though, of course, it is only when they are
applied in the context of those coordinates that they acquire as much
definiteness as makes it possible to say that *objects* are involved. And, in
conclusion, "[t]he thing in itself = x is a mere thought-object" (O184
XXII 421). "[When we] make the distinction between the representation of the thing *in itself* and that of the same thing as *appearance* . . .
[then] concepts, not things, are contrasted with one another" (O174
XXII 32–33).[54]

4. Apperception

In looking for a firm basis for their a priori arguments, traditional
transcendental realists were typically drawn to the experience of self-
consciousness. There, it seemed, one could make contact with something whose existence and properties were beyond doubt: however
questionable one finds the outside world, there is no question (or so
Descartes and others believed) that I exist, that I think some thoughts,
feel some emotions, and so on. I might or might not succeed in
building a bridge between such certainties and an equally certain
knowledge of what is other than me (Descartes believed this to be
possible, others did not); but, whatever the fate of this subsequent
operation, *that* I am and *what* I am is to be regarded as settled.

In TI, however, self-consciousness (in Kant's terminology, *apperception*) provides no knowledge. The first-person pronoun "I" must be
able to accompany all representations:[55] it is part of the logic of representations (of what representations are necessarily like) that they always have not only an object but also a subject[56]—understanding by
the latter: they can always be thought of as "representing" from a

specific point of view. But this point of view, which may be considered responsible for the mysterious act of synthesis that makes objective experience possible, is not itself an object—much as the horizon of experience *as such* never is, and indeed the two are but different angles on the same mystery. If I direct my attention to it, I end up either turning it into an ordinary empirical object ("it is this body, located in this position, seeing things consistently with its location"), which is just as dependent as any other such object on the original positing of a point of view, or being left with something totally indefinite, an "I, or He, or It (the thing), which thinks" (A346 B404)[57]—something to which I cannot attribute any quality; indeed for which I cannot even meaningfully pose any issue of identification or distinction, hence I cannot say *how many of it (them?)* there are. "The subject is not a particular thing but an idea" (O175 XXII 33). "The *consciousness* of myself is logical merely and leads to no object; it is, rather, a mere determination of the subject in accordance with the rule of identity" (O188 XXII 82). "No quantum of substance is possible in the soul. Hence also nothing that one could determine through any predicate and call persistent" (A183 XXIII 31).[58]

Thus, once again, TI ends up seeing things in reverse order from the tradition. The self "revealed" to consciousness can be no starting point for any epistemic construction: its unity is a purely formal one (it signals that experience always comes in a certain form) but is not substantial—it is not the unity of a substance, of an object.[59] If I want to move beyond this purely formal level, I must focus on the spatiotemporal *content* of experience: insofar as such content can be conceived as unified by the categories into a connected world,[60] it will be legitimate to think of that world as issuing from a single point of view. The unity of apperception can be nothing other than (categorial) coherence, hence it is dependent upon the coherence of the world that is apperceived. And, since I already know that the latter coherence can never be completely established (because the notion of "the whole world" is contradictory), I also know that *both* coherences will have to be thought of as always only "in progress": painstakingly constructed (by the understanding) one step at a time, invariably appealing to a context that must be taken for granted, constantly at risk of exploding into *in*coherence (as far as the I is concerned, into schizophrenia; as far as the world is, into an undifferentiated manifold) when the next step is taken.[61]

It sounds like a devastating outcome, and in some sense it is. In *Kant's Copernican Revolution* I described it by saying that my relation to the subject of self-consciousness is more akin to what we ordinarily call faith than to (anything Kant would consider) knowledge. But remember: knowledge must be limited, and faith is what it must make room for. The basis of knowledge is itself noncognitive; therefore, that I cannot know the self, that I can only think of it, believe that it is, have trust in its action, just makes the self one more *noumenon*—one more of those unknowable (hence unreal, though not for that reason insignificant) entities and processes I must invoke to make sense of what I do know. And, if this faith finds confirmation in some other, noncognitive experiences I also have, its noncognitive character will be no indictment of it, given how little knowledge is able to help itself.

THREE

FREEDOM

1. Overdetermination

The exemption of human actions from natural necessitation has traditionally been questioned and the irruption into the natural world of an entirely different sort of determination for events (that is, their determination by free human will), which seems to be a necessary condition if humans are to be responsible for (part of) what they do and consequently accessible to moral demands, has been regarded as doubtful. "[W]e cannot yet see how . . . [it] is possible" that we "regard ourselves as free in acting and so . . . hold ourselves . . . subject to certain [moral] laws," Kant says (G97 IV 450), in the usual modal formulation philosophical problems acquire for him: what is at issue is not our *being* free (or morally committed), but the possibility of our being so. The consistency that "constitutes . . . [the second *Critique's*] greatest merit" (PR142 V 7), that "*[c]onsistency* [which] is the greatest obligation of a philosopher and yet the most rarely found" (PR158 V 24), is threatened here: "there arises a dialectic of reason since, with respect to the will, the freedom ascribed to it seems to be in contradiction with natural necessity" (G102 IV 455). "[T]he necessity in the causal relation . . . [and] freedom . . . are opposed to each other as contradictory. For, from the first it follows that every event, and consequently every action that takes place at a point of time, is necessary under the condition of what was in the preceding time. Now, since time past is no longer within my control, every action that I perform must be necessary by determining grounds *that are not within my control*, that is, I am never free at the point of time in which I act" (PR215–16 V 94). And, if freedom is not "to be given up altogether in favor of natural necessity," then "this seeming contradiction must be removed in a convincing way" (G102 IV 456).

For Kant, the problem is especially troublesome, since for him reality (we know) *requires* inclusion into a naturally necessitated spatiotemporal context (that an event follows upon other events according to rules is a condition of its objectivity); hence, if any of my actions were to be exempted from universal causal determinism, they could not belong to world history. "On the other side, it is equally necessary that everything which takes place should be determined without exception in accordance with laws of nature" (G102 IV 455). "[N]othing really takes place which does not have a cause, and so has its determination in past time; this is the universal law of all occurrences in nature, and actions, as effects that in virtue of this cause succeed in time, stand under the mechanism of nature. For were the action not to have its determination in the preceding cause, by virtue of this law of necessity, it would have to be an accident, and this is impossible" (LE 269 XXVII 503). "[E]verything that we assume to belong to this nature (*phenomenon*) and to be a product of it must also be able to be conceived as connected with it in accordance with mechanical laws" (J290 V 422). "Whatever conception of the freedom of the will one may form in terms of metaphysics, the will's manifestations in the world of phenomena, i.e. human actions, are determined in accordance with natural laws, as is every other natural event" (PW41 VIII 17). Thus, "nothing in appearances can be explained by the concept of freedom and there the mechanism of nature must instead constitute the only guide" (PR163 V 30). "If . . . one wants to attribute freedom to a being whose existence is determined in time, one cannot, so far at least, except this being from the law of natural necessity as to all events in its existence and consequently as to its actions as well; for, that would be tantamount to handing it over to blind chance" (PR216 V 95).[1]

But, if the Kantian framework (and, specifically, his understanding of objectivity) makes this problem more serious, it also offers an effective way of addressing it. In the traditional model of causality as imposition, where events cause one another insofar as they force one another into being,[2] causal determination implies uniqueness: either an event (or collection of events) *a* forces another event *b* into being or it does not, and if it does then that is the whole story to be told about what causes *b*. We cannot expect some third event (or collection of events) *c* also to be doing the same forcing, unless perhaps *a* and *c* are doing it together, and the cause of b is in fact the conjunction of the two. Within this model, genuine *overdetermination* is ruled out: there cannot be several independent causal accounts of the same event. The situation is different in Kant's regularity model ("the concept of causality always contains reference to a law that determines the existence of a manifold in relation to one another," PR212 V 89); for here one can imagine inserting b into one regular pattern, and thereby causally explaining it, and then turning around and inserting b—the very same b^3—into another such pattern and thereby providing an additional, equally legitimate causal account of it. Overdetermination is possible, and one can even conceive of several distinct nature*s* as different ways of providing a structured, consistent parsing of the whole manifold ("nature in the most general sense is the existence of things under laws," PR174 V 43)[4]—however unrealizable and dialectical such a conception might be, the multiplicity of natures cannot be denied as a possible object of thought.[5]

Within the scope of natural explanation, the possibility of overdetermination offers a credible alternative to reductionisms and eliminativisms of all sorts. That a complete physical account of human behavior be (in principle) available, for example, is no argument for refusing *also* to provide a (potentially no less complete) psychological account of the same behavior. Different regular patterns will be brought forth in the two cases, but equally legitimate ones: the mind's existence and action are perfectly compatible with the body's.[6] But the compatibilism that figures most prominently in Kant's work is the one between *any* natural explanation and freedom:[7] however successful the former might be, no such success excludes the possibility of thinking that human behavior can be equally well accounted for as an exercise of free will, hence that it can be as much the object of a moral judgment as it is of scientific (physical, physiological, psychological, or what have you) understanding. And such thinking amounts to furnishing "the sensible world, as a *sensible nature* . . . , with the form of a world of the understanding, that is, of a *supersensible* nature, *though without infringing upon the mechanism of the former*"[8] (PR174 V 43; last italics added)—that is, not to *contradicting* the spatiotemporal regularities that make the sensible manifold into a world but to *adding* to them: to giving *the same* world *another form*. "The sensible nature of rational beings in general is their existence under empirically conditioned laws. . . . The supersensible nature of *the same* beings, on the other hand, is their existence in accordance with laws that are independent of any empirical condition"[9] (PR174 V 43; italics added)—laws that are going to prove as *constitutive* of freedom (as definitional of what freedom is) as natural laws are constitutive of (sensible) nature.[10]

Determinists, of course, think otherwise. "People who are accustomed merely to explanations by natural sciences will not get into their heads the categorical imperative from which ... [moral] laws proceed dictatorially, even though they feel themselves compelled irresistibly by it. Being unable to *explain* what lies entirely beyond that sphere (*freedom* of choice), however exalting is this very prerogative of the human being, his capacity for such an *idea*, they are stirred by the proud claims of speculative reason, which makes its power so strongly felt in other fields, to band together in a general *call to arms*, as it were, to defend the omnipotence of theoretical reason. And so now, and perhaps for a while longer, they assail the moral concept of freedom and, wherever possible, make it suspect" (M511 VI 378). But these "proud claims" would only be justified if reason in its cognitive, theoretical use were able to constitute a self-sufficient system. As things are (as the first *Critique* has proved), however "strongly felt" its power might be there, it is also sharply curtailed;[11] specifically, we have seen it depend for the realization of its (cognitive) goals on the reference to a spontaneous act of synthesis—an act that, being spontaneous, must represent an exception to the cognitive ideal of universal natural necessity. Therefore, though freedom cannot be understood (precisely because understanding is providing a natural explanation),[12] it cannot be denied either: the determinist is, paradoxically, the very last person who can deny it. And that is enough to have it survive another day. "[W]here determination by laws of nature ceases, there all *explanation* ceases as well, and nothing is left but *defense*, that is, to repel the objections of those who pretend to have seen deeper into the essence of things and therefore boldly declare that freedom is impossible" (G105 IV 459).

There are two elements to Kant's strategy of defense. The first one consists of the game of reciprocity hinted at above: determinism has no leg to stand on in his attack on freedom (not within TI, at least) because the very definiteness of the world depends on a free act of choice (of this particular world as opposed to any other). The freedom we defend in this way is the transcendental variety, that is: we defend the necessity of mobilizing the *concept* of freedom at some point in our philosophical account of the world. "[T]heoretical reason was forced *to assume* at least the possibility of freedom in order to fill a need of its own" (PR178 V 48), and "if ... [those who boast of being quite well able to understand the concept of freedom] had earlier pondered it carefully in its transcendental context they would have cognized its *indispensability* as a problematic concept in the complete use of speculative reason as well as its complete *incomprehensibility*" (PR142 V 7). *Whose* freedom that is, on the other hand, is entirely indeterminate at this stage: the world's "construction" could be attributed to individual humans as much as to their brains or their unconsciouses or their cultures or their political institutions. In fact, the logical space is opened here (though Kant makes no use of it) for any number of empirical theories that apply this concept in different (and competing) ways and give it different spatiotemporally viable articulations. Individual humans freely synthesize their world, one could say for example, when they are not totally brainwashed and indoctrinated by the education they receive into a single, monologic "system"; or cultures do so (over the heads of their individual members, hence necessitating their apparent free choices) as long as their mutual interaction does not issue in them swallowing one another—always keeping in mind that any such articulation will leave a residue of mystery: transcendental freedom will never be fully captured by any spatiotemporal construal, precisely insofar as the latter is spatiotemporal. "[T]he morally good [which, as we will see, is the same as the free, though the issue of whether this good is indeed *moral* must await chapter 6] as an object is something supersensible, so that nothing corresponding to it can be found in any sensible intuition" (PR195 V 68). "[N]o insight can be had into the possibility of the freedom of an efficient cause, especially in the sensible world: we are fortunate if only we can be sufficiently assured that there is no proof of its impossibility" (PR215 V 94; more about this incomprehensibility later).

The second element of the defensive strategy brings it down from the conceptual heaven to our everyday life: it makes transcendental reflection once more, and quite dramatically, reveal its dependence on the ordinary person's perspective. Whether or not cultures and brains and unconsciouses have original experiences of freedom, humans do,[13] and no conceptual account of our condition would be complete without taking such experiences into account. Humans hear the voice of the moral conscience; and, though (again) we are not yet prepared to discuss what is *moral* about this voice, we are certainly clear about the fact that it tells us what we *must* (not) do, and hence also what we *can*[14] (avoid to) do. About this *fact*, indeed, which Kant considers an "undeniable" (PR165 V 32) and an "apodictically certain" one (PR177 V 47), and which represents for him "the *ratio cognoscendi* of freedom. For, had not the moral law *already* been distinctly thought in our reason, we should never consider ourselves justified in *assuming* such a thing as freedom (even though it is not self-contradictory)" (PR140n V 4n).

When conscience issues its call, determinists will have to regard it as a delusion—as the result, say, of some kind of social conditioning.[15] They will not deny the fact that I heard the call, of course; but they will deny that there is any factual import to its *content*. In preparation for things to come, note that often my having an experience and the content of the experience belong to different registers of conversation, and that both may have their own independently legitimate claims to being regarded as factual according to the standards current in the relevant register. If I believe that $2 + 2 = 4$, for example, it is a fact that I believe so *and it is a fact that $2 + 2 = 4$*; the former is a psychological fact and the latter is a mathematical fact, and no one but the most extreme empiricist would dream of establishing the factuality of the latter on the basis of the factuality of the former (I might also believe that $2 + 2 = 5$, but my believing it would not make *it* a fact). Whatever they are prepared to say about mathematical facts, however, determinists are not going to display any benevolence toward the fact that, say, I ought not to kill my neighbor. They will admit the fact that I believe so (assuming I do), or that some agency within me is insisting that such be the case, or that I would feel very bad if I contravened the agency's claims and its consequent demands on my behavior; but this is as far as they will go. As for *what* I believe, or I am told by the inner agency, they will say that there is nothing there, nothing to be taken notice of or to be accounted for; and this judgment of theirs will not be grounded empirically (they will not argue that a particular instance of the call has proved delusional, as a particular visual or tactile experience could) but transcendentally: there is no room in their logical space for anything of the sort. And here Kant will stand firm. Conscience for him is not an intellectual capacity but a natural drive: "We have a faculty of judging whether a thing is right or wrong, and this applies no less to our actions than to those of others. This faculty resides in the understanding. We also have a faculty of liking and disliking, to judge concerning ourselves, no less than others, what is pleasing or displeasing there, and this is the moral feeling. Now if we have presupposed the moral judgment, we find, in the third place, an instinct, an involuntary and irresistible drive in our nature, which compels us to judge with the force of law concerning our actions, in such a way that it conveys to us an inner pain at evil actions, and an inner joy at good ones, according to the relationship that the action bears to the law.... [T]his instinct is conscience" (LE88 XXVII 296–97).[16] And, though it is certainly possible that we make empirical mistakes here (as with everything else that belongs to the natural realm)—specifically, that something we characterized as issuing from conscience will later be redescribed as (say) expressing a neurosis or understood as providing the wrong clues about good and evil[17]—the general legitimacy of the register invoked by this experience cannot be denied.[18] Whatever the empirical mistakes, "no sophistry will ever convince even the most common human being that . . . [the moral ideas] are not true concepts" (PR247 V 133–34)—that is, that no truth is to be found in the *standards* brought out in such cases and in the *tasks* they set for us. There is nothing in the name of which I could be convinced to forever discount this call, no higher dignity to which this voice should be sacrificed: the dignity asserted by the enemies of freedom has proven itself a giant with feet of clay, and in the void left by the explosion of their pretense the claims of conscience forcefully assert their right to be heard—just as visual or tactile impressions are.[19]

2. Autonomy

It is hard to avoid the recurrence of the prejudices that favor old, familiar ways of thinking, we know; so we must constantly, critically remind ourselves, when articulating a novel point of view, of how differently things look from there. The stage our discussion has reached can use such a reminder: we have established that overdetermination makes causality by freedom thinkable without contradiction, but we must make sure that everyone remembers how to take this "causality by freedom"—or, for that matter, causality in general. We are not to revert to thinking that, say, "I freely cause A" means that I kick A into being, maybe at the same time as something else (natural conditions of some sorts) also does the same kind of kicking. That I freely cause A can only mean here that, in addition to any number of other patterns in which A's occurrence falls, and which could then be offered as answers to anyone requesting an explanation of A, a pattern is also available that, in some sense yet to be clarified, is an expression of my freedom. Nothing and no one is *making* things be and events happen here, unless what *that* means is just what I said: that something is the case and something else is the case, and the something and the something else are a regular conjunction of occurrences, so much so that the latter could be predicted after observing the former. Kant, of course, often gives more sanguine statements of what is going on, because empirically that is how we speak; now, however, we know enough about the transcendental dictionary he is composing to tell how those conventional statements must be read.

Having thus hammered out the true significance of our first step, let us go one step further and ask ourselves: what sort of causality is freedom? A first answer might come by a negative route: an agent is *not* free as long as her behavior is *heteronomous*, that is, as long as its law is to be found in something other than the agent herself. I am not free as long as my behavior is explainable by reference to *external* influences by the physical world, or by tradition, or society. Which is precisely what any natural explanation of behavior does: an essential feature of it (we know already) is that its spatiotemporal scope cannot be limited, hence anything I do, if it receives an explanation of this kind, will eventually be explained in terms of events and causal factors lying well beyond the scope of my life. By contrast, then, an agent would be free insofar as the law of her behavior could be found entirely within the agent herself: free behavior (genuine action) would have to be self-determined, *autonomous* behavior. "*[F]reedom* would be that property of such causality [that is, of the will] that it can be efficient independently of alien causes *determining* it, just as *natural necessity* is the property of the causality of all nonrational beings to be determined to activity by the influence of alien causes" (G94 IV 446). "[F]reedom and the will's own lawgiving are both autonomy and hence reciprocal concepts" (G97 IV 450). A long tradition preceding Kant regarded autonomy as the sense of *God's* freedom: He could never do otherwise than He does, for whatever He does is a consequence (indeed a *necessary* consequence) of His nature, hence in Him freedom and *self-imposed* necessity coincide. Kant brings this sense into human life, inviting humans to literally think of themselves as godly, and of their (free) actions as just as much of an inevitable outcome of their own essence. "[The enjoyment of freedom] resembles . . . [beatitude], at least insofar as one's determination of one's will can be held free from . . . [the] influence [of inclinations and needs] and so, at least in its origin, it is analogous to the self-sufficiency that can be ascribed only to the supreme being" (PR235 V 119).[20]

What, then, is for behavior to be self-determined? Once again, it proves instructive to take a negative route. Though multiple causation is theoretically possible, we do not want to be fooled into taking as multiple causation something that is not multiple at all: if an alleged causal explanation E_1 can be incorporated without loss or residue into another causal explanation E_2, then E_1 has no independent explanatory value. It adds nothing to E_2 and can be discarded. For example, if E_1 explains the behavior of a fluid within classical thermodynamics, and

E_2 incorporates it without loss or residue within statistical molecular dynamics, then E_1 is providing no additional information and can be discarded—E_2 is all we need. In the specific context of human behavior, all sorts of alleged laws (that is, *maxims*) can be proposed for it;[21] often we propose such maxims ourselves, and say that we do X (for example) because we intend to achieve goal Y. It remains to be seen whether there is anything to such proposals: whether they can be fleshed out into independent explanations or instead what we do (inclusive of what goes through our mind as we behave in a certain way, and of what we would be prepared to say in case anyone asked us why we behave that way) is just another case of nature working itself out. If the latter is true, then any maxim we might proffer has only subjective significance, and does not acquire the status of an objective explanatory factor—a natural explanation is all we need. "A *maxim* is the subjective principle of volition; the objective principle . . . is the practical *law*" (G56n IV 400n).[22] "[B]ecause the impulse that the representation of an object possible through our powers is to exert on the will of the subject in accordance with his natural constitution belongs to the nature of the subject . . . it would, strictly speaking, be nature that gives the law" (G92 IV 444). In the *Lectures on Ethics*, Kant adds useful detail: "The formula which expresses practical necessity is the *causa impulsiva* of a free action, and since it necessitates objectively, is called a *motivum*. The formula which expresses pathological necessitation is a *causa impulsiva per stimulos*, since it necessitates subjectively. So all subjective necessitations are *necessitationes per stimulos*" (LE50 XXVII 255). We should not confuse the circumstances in which a maxim expresses a truly determining cause for an act, and hence provides us with a genuine *motive* for it, with those in which what necessitation is present is all coming from natural stimuli—and hence our behavior is in fact (whatever we might think of it) only passively ("pathologically") affected: "One who does something because it is pleasant is pathologically necessitated; one who does a thing that is good in and for itself, is acting from motives" (LE51 XXVII 257).

It is phenomenologically undeniable that I often will this and that, or that I do what I will. And some (most notably and relevantly, Hume) had thought of resolving the age-old problem of freedom by appealing to this undeniable fact. Freedom as spontaneity,[23] they would say, is simply doing what one wills to do. I am free to be sitting at this table now because I will to be sitting at the table and I do. But this is, Kant thinks, an evasion of the problem. To begin with, the freedom we are looking for should be a form of causality; so there should be more than a coincidence between the occurrence of a given mental content in my experience ("This is what I will") and the performance of a certain behavior on my part—the conjunction of the two should be a regular pattern.[24] Which automatically rules out all those quirky, pseudo-existentialist cases in which I do something "out-of-character" just in order to assert my independence of anyone's expectations (including my own): just then, Kant would think, I am likely to be most vulnerable to the vagaries of natural influences.[25]

Furthermore, even in the presence of a regular pattern, it is still possible that this be part of a *larger* pattern: that (as was suggested above) both my doing something and my willing to do it (however regularly associated they might be) be effects of a common cause. That a hypnotized subject raises his hand every time he wills to is certainly no evidence of his exercising freedom: both his raising his hand and his willing to raise it might be caused by what the hypnotizer told him. Or, to bring the matter closer to ordinary, everyday life, that I regularly will to buy a certain detergent and I do could both be explained as outcomes of effective advertising; hence their regular joint occurrence proves no causal connection. "It is a wretched subterfuge . . . [to call free] the actions of the human being, although they are necessary by their determining grounds which preceded them in time, . . . because . . . [they] are caused from within, by representations produced by our own powers, whereby desires are evoked on occasion of circumstances and hence actions are produced at our own discretion. . . . Some still let themselves be put off by this subterfuge and so think they have solved, with a little quibbling about words, that difficult problem on the solution of which millennia have worked in vain and which can therefore hardly be found so completely on the surface" (PR216–17 V 96).[26] So, as much as phenomenological will (the experience of willing, *Willkür*, often translated into English as "(power, or faculty, of) choice")[27] cannot be denied, any reference to it is irrelevant to establishing the reality, or even the possibility, of freedom. Which explains how Kant can unproblematically admit the experience of willing (and of doing what one wills) while claiming that no "consciousness of freedom . . . is . . . antecedently given to us [antecedently, that is, to the consciousness of the moral law]" (PR164 V 31).[28] The occurring of an episode of *apparent* consciousness of freedom cannot decide all by itself that what one is conscious of be *in fact* freedom.[29]

Willkür is defined as "[t]he faculty of desire in accordance with concepts" whose "ground determining it to action lies within itself and not in its object" and which "is joined with one's consciousness of the ability to bring about its object by one's action" (M374–75 VI 213);[30] so I am in presence of *Willkür* when, say, I desire this object before me *as a cookie, and* I am aware that I can extend my hand to get it, *and* the impulse I feel to extend my hand and get it originates in my mind (insofar as it is capable of desire) and not in the cookie (or, for that matter, in anything external to me)—but none of this can determine whether my *Willkür* is free or not. And only when freedom enters the picture are we in presence of something other than nature: of a *distinct* form of determination from what nature already provides. "[V]oluntary [*willkürliche*] action . . . belongs among natural causes as well. . . . [A]ll practical propositions that derive that which nature can contain from the faculty of choice [*Willkür*] as a cause collectively belong to theoretical philosophy, as cognition of nature; only those propositions which give the law to freedom are specifically distinguished from the former in virtue of their content" (J4 XX 196–97). "[T]he proposition which contains the possibility of the object through the causality of the faculty of choice [*Willkür*] may still be called a practical proposition, yet it is not at all distinct in principle from the theoretical propositions concerning the nature of things" (J5 XX 197–98). "That [*Willkür*] which can be determined only by *inclination* (sensible impulse, *stimulus* [at AP155 VII 251 inclination is defined more clearly as "[h]abitual sensuous desire"]) would be animal choice [*Willkür*]. . . . *Freedom* of choice [*Die Freiheit der Willkür*] is . . . independence from being *determined* by sensible impulses" (M375 VI 213). That we have experiences of willing is important, and importantly related to our experiencing the moral call; but, as we said about the latter, we need to discriminate veridical from delusive experiences here—to find criteria for determining when our sense of being the originators of our own moves is to be taken seriously. Conscience tells us (as we pointed out) that we ought to do certain things, hence implies that we can do them; now we must try to understand what conscience could possibly *mean*.

This is as far as we can go by purely negative considerations; to make further progress, we need to have some idea of what the "self" might be in "self-determined," or of how that essence of mine from which my autonomous behavior should necessarily follow is to be understood.[31] So try this: I am a human, and humanity is a form of rationality—the only form in which rationality surfaces in my experience ("[We do not know] rational beings other than human beings," PR146 V 12).[32] Autonomous determination on my part, then, could be rational determination. The suggestion is promising, for rational arguments do not seem liable to the unlimited "spreading" that characterizes natural explanation and makes heteronomy a necessary feature of the latter. The rational solution of a logical puzzle or a mathematical problem may take hundreds of pages, but is supposed to reach a definite end; in fact, if it did not, if it continued forever as the series of natural causes does, it would not count as a solution at all. Therefore, if some behavior of mine, in addition to whatever heteronomous account it receives, could also be accounted for as the conclusion of a rational argument, if it could also be seen as *rational* behavior, as a manifestation of reason, as reason showing itself to be *practical*, to have concrete currency in the world, then it could be judged spontaneous behavior on the part of a rational being like myself. There would be no superordinate explanation in which such a rational account could be incorporated; the account itself would be self-contained (again, independently of what *other* accounts of the same behavior could also be given). And, if what I did reflected what I willed to do, then my will would be for once a genuine causal factor—it would graduate from the subjective, phenomenological, noncommittal state of *Willkür* to the objectively determining state Kant calls *Wille*. "[T]he will is nothing other than practical reason" (G66 IV 412). "*Will* is a kind of causality of living beings insofar as they are rational" (G94 IV 446). "The feeling that arises from consciousness of this [moral] necessitation is not pathological, as would be a feeling produced by an object of the senses, but practical only, that is, possible through a preceding (objective) determination of the will and causality of reason" (PR205 V 80). "[The] concept of a free causality is without circularity interchangeable with the concept of a moral ground of determination" (C343 XI 155—as noted above, we must postpone discussion of what is "moral"; but I can say now that Kant takes it to be equivalent to "rational"). Or, in other words, we have found an answer for the question of when *Willkür* is free: "That choice [*Willkür*] which can be determined by *pure reason* is called free" (M375 VI 213). "Freedom is the causality of the pure reason in the determination of the power of choice [*Willkür*]" (N231 XVIII 181).[33]

3. Rationality

What is a rational account of a behavioral sequence (which, being thus accounted for, could also be called an action)? Note first of all that there is only one reason, both speculative and practical. "I require

that . . . [we] be able . . . to present the unity of practical with speculative reason in a common principle, since there can, in the end, be only
one and the same reason, which must be distinguished merely in its
application" (G47 IV 391). "[I]t is still only one and the same reason
which, whether from a theoretical or a practical perspective, judges
according to a priori principles" (PR237 V 121).[34] This one reason is
characterized by a demand for systematicity, understood as the necessary interconnectedness of all the elements in a given field—as their
coming together in a single, neatly organized totality.[35] "Systematic connection is the connection of various cognitions *in one idea*"
(LM300 XXVIII 533).[36] "[B]eing able . . . to derive everything from
one principle . . . [is] the undeniable need of human reason, which finds
complete satisfaction only in a complete systematic unity of its cognitions" (PR213 V 91). "Pure reason . . . requires the absolute totality
of conditions for a given conditioned" (PR226 V 107).[37] Therefore, it
can never find satisfaction in nature, since "[t]he determination of the
causality of beings in the sensible world can as such never be unconditioned" (PR178 V 48) and the very idea of a whole spatiotemporal world is dialectical—what spatiotemporal "world" we do in fact
encounter is destined to remain forever incomplete; it is never going
to match our *idea* of a world, much as its denizens are never going to
match our idea of objects. To find satisfaction, reason must disregard
empirical matters and focus on those that are a priori, that is, universal
and necessary ("rational cognition and cognition a priori are one and
the same," PR146 V 12; "universal cognitions, which at the same time
have the character of inner necessity, . . . one calls . . . a priori," A2).
The conceptual realm in which reason moves, Kant says in the *Jäsche
Logic*, is the result of an abstraction from all irrelevant (empirical)
traits;[38] and (for example) "anything at all empirical as a condition in a
mathematical demonstration degrades and destroys its dignity and force"
(PR158 V 25).

Artificial constructs like games or mathematical models provide the
best approximations to what would satisfy reason, because when attending to them one does indeed abstract from all sorts of external
considerations and focuses on a limited number of parameters, which
can then be controlled (at least in principle; but computers are turning
this principle more and more into a fact) with total effectiveness. The
right move in a chess game could in principle be conclusively determined (much like the right answer to a logical or a mathematical
question) because the physical shape or composition of the chess pieces
or of the chessboard, the physical or psychological nature of the players

or of the environment, and even the fact that the game takes place in space and time are entirely irrelevant to the determination. Such abstraction allows for universal application (of the parameters *abstracted out* of the context, to contexts in which the same parameters recur): if something is proved to be the right chess move (or the solution of a logical or mathematical problem is proved to be the correct one), this proof applies to all contexts in which a chess game is played (or the same problem comes up). *And* it makes it possible to answer certain why-questions (those raised at the same level of abstraction) by just citing the outcome of the proof: for every person in every context it would be legitimate to say, if she made that move (or gave that solution), and if we were speaking about her *purely as a chess player* (or as a problem solver), that she did *because it was the right one*. This answer would settle the issue forever, and if anyone insisted asking, "But why did she do it, *really*?" the only response we could add is: "Because she is a *rational* player."[39]

By analogy, if I am trying to provide a rational account (the sort of account that would satisfy reason) of a behavior *a*, performed by an agent *b* in a situation *S*, I must disregard all (other) specific features of *b* (including everything that identifies her as *that* particular agent) and concentrate on the simple fact that *b* is a *rational* agent (which, we know by now, is the same as an agent, period, since only rational agents can be regarded as true originators of their behavior—as something more than wheels in the mechanism of nature); therefore any conclusion I will thus reach concerning *b* will be equally applicable to all rational agents. I must play the artificial game of (rational) agency, as it were; and, if I play it successfully, then I will be able to answer the relevant why-question (to provide the account I was looking for) by pointing to the fact that doing *a* in *S* is the conclusion of a logical argument whose premises contain no distinctive reference to *b* but only general, abstract truths about what counts as a rational agent. "[B]ecause moral laws [that is, as I noted above and will discuss later, the laws that are definitional of freedom] are to hold for every rational being as such, [it is of the greatest practical importance] to derive them from the universal concept of a rational being as such" (G65 IV 412). "A practical law that I cognize as such must qualify for a giving of universal law: this is an identical proposition and therefore self-evident" (PR161 V 27).

Any condition limiting the import of the proof to particular circumstances (to the agent's physical or psychological state, to any desires or interests she might have, to any of her history or her feelings), hence turning the account the proof provides into a *hypothetical* one (one that only holds under the hypothesis that those circumstances take place), must be put aside, and nothing other than rationality must be referred to—thus making the explanation (as with chess games or logical puzzles) truly unrestricted, free from any provisos, *categorical*. "[G]rounds of reason provide the rule for actions universally, from principles, without influence from the circumstances of time or place" (TA135 IV 345). "Since I have deprived the will of every impulse that could arise for it from obeying some law, nothing is left but the conformity of actions as such with universal law, which alone is to serve the will as its principle, that is, *I ought never to act except in such a way that I could also will that my maxim should become a universal law*" (G56–57 IV 402; the prescriptive nature of this (meta)law that makes an "ought to" formulation adequate to it will also come to the fore later).[40] Not even the condition that the agent is a *human* one can be regarded as relevant here, not at least if we take it in any natural sense, as referring to those beings that are biologically classified as humans (or to any of their biologically determined features—for example, their drive to self-preservation): "we must not let ourselves think of wanting to derive the reality of . . . [the] principle [of duty] from *the special property of human nature*. For, duty is to be practical unconditional necessity of action and it must therefore hold for all rational beings . . . and *only because of this* can it be also a law for all human wills" (G76 IV 425). "I cannot presuppose this need [such as a sympathetic sensibility brings with it in human beings] in every rational being (not at all in God)" (PR167 V 34); *therefore*, it must be excluded from consideration when trying to determine truly practical laws.[41] And, by thus excluding and abstracting, we finally make contact with freedom "in the strictest, that is, in the transcendental, sense": "a will for which the mere lawgiving form of a maxim can alone serve as a law is a free will" (PR162 V 29).[42]

Depending on how the concept of a rational agent is articulated, some forms of behavior will be required (or ruled out) by the kind of logical argument indicated above; that is, this kind of argument will prove them (or the avoiding of them) to be a *duty*.[43] For example, if we expect a rational agent to be constitutionally concerned with maintaining the freedom that defines her as an agent, it will follow that it is contradictory (and hence ruled out) for her to sell herself into slavery, and (in most cases) to commit suicide (possible exceptions might include situations in which the only options are death and slavery).[44] If we expect a rational agent to be consistent over time, it will follow that it is contradictory (hence ruled out) for her not to fulfill her promises—and a duty to fulfill them. If we expect her to have a rational concern for truth, it will follow that it is contradictory (hence ruled out) for her to lie—and a duty to tell the truth.[45] If we expect her to be concerned with realizing and promoting her freedom, and we take (some amount of) financial independence and education to be an indispensable condition for attaining that goal, it will follow that, other things being equal, she must provide herself with (a certain amount of) financial independence and education. We might even think that a rational agent has "in certain respects . . . a duty to attend to . . . [her] happiness, partly because happiness (to which belong skill, health, wealth) contains means for the fulfillment of one's duty and partly because lack of it (e.g., poverty) contains temptations to transgress one's duty" (PR214–15 V 93).

As we go down the list of rational arguments above, we move from perfect duties (to perform, or not perform, certain specific actions) to imperfect ones (to pursue certain ends, which could be done in a variety of ways).[46] And it is certainly true of all duties, perfect and imperfect alike, that the arguments supporting them could be questioned: that different people might have different views on what is involved in the concept of a rational agent. This conclusion, however, should not be overstated, nor should it be used to devalue Kant's effort. People have different opinions concerning the structure of the physical world; worse still, all past scientific theories attempting to describe that structure have eventually been rejected and, if induction is any evidence, the same destiny awaits all present scientific theories. But none of this disqualifies the cognitive enterprise of accurately describing the world, nor its presupposition that there is a single, coherent world to be described. Kant's fundamental point here is a similar one and, though it is by no means uncontroversial, we must make sure that the nature of the controversy is well understood. Kant's position on freedom (or duty) does not stand or fall with the "derivation" he has provided of some particular duty; what is crucial to it is rather the (controversial) claim that there is an independent register of conversation based on the rationality of behavior, and that this register, much like the one based on natural explanation, presupposes the existence of a single, coherent, correct account (in this case, of what is rational) that the participants in the relevant conversations are trying to capture. That they (including Kant) have different opinions about what this account is in any or all cases, or that any or all of their specific views about it will eventually be rejected, does not disqualify their conversations or the register in which they are conducted; it has no relevance (for example) to the general claim that for someone "to have to say to himself 'I am a *worthless* man although I have filled my purse,' he must have a different criterion of judgment from that by which he commends himself and says 'I am a *prudent* man, for I have enriched my cash box'" (PR170 V 37). These two statements have different logical forms, which is quite independent of what *truth-values* they have.[47]

This is the appropriate place to address a sticky point in Kant's view: his firm denial of the existence of moral dilemmas—that is, of situations in which there is no legitimate moral choice for a given agent, and every course of action available to her is susceptible of blame (think of the Sartre character who is forced to give up either joining the war against the Nazis or caring for his mother; or of Sophie's choice in the book and movie by that title). Kant is adamant that in all circumstances (however differently things might *appear*) exactly one choice is rational, and that such is the choice we must make: "[I]t is impossible that duties themselves could contradict one another, since two *opposita* cannot both be necessary together" (LE261 XXVII 493). "[D]uty, as moral action, is morally necessary, and it is thus impossible that omission of the dutiful act could simultaneously be a duty as well" (LE273 XXVII 508). "[T]wo universal duties cannot contradict one another; it is only the grounds of duty, the *rationes obligandi*, that are in conflict here, because each of them would only be an insufficient ground for determining the act of duty. . . . The rule here is: *Lex fortior vincit; regulae si collidunt, a minore fit exceptio*. . . . [L]aws and rules can never contradict one another" (LE296 XXVII 537). The current discussion helps us see that what is at issue here is not an empirical conjecture about the occurrence or nonoccurrence of certain kinds of situations, but a transcendental condition of moral discourse. Scientists must operate *as if* there were always a single, unambiguous answer to any of their questions, whether or not they will ever convince themselves that they found it or that it can be found; scientific research as we know it would come to an end if this assumption were rejected. Similarly, humans involved in moral debate (perhaps with themselves) must conduct it *as if* there were a correct resolution of it, whether or not they will ever come to it and whether or not they will ever believe that they can come to it. *What* resolution of a given debate the man Kant may have considered correct is irrelevant to this point. We may or may not agree with him on the details of any specific moral matter; but, unless we accept the transcendental condition above, the whole conversation will turn out to be completely indeterminate and inaccessible to argument—hence there will be no room in it for reasoned agreement or disagreement, either: the various options (and the parties representing them) will not even meaningfully engage with one another. Which is not to say that we could not find ourselves *empirically* (as the Sartre and the Styron characters do) facing a moral dilemma: a situation in which we are empirically unable (however long we reflect on it) to decide what it is (or was) right for us to do. But it is to say that such a situation, somewhat paradoxically, would not even count as a dilemma if it were not entertained within the scope of the transcendental condition we are discussing: it is just because we act under the assumption that there should be an unambiguous answer that we agonize so much upon not finding one.

To bring out a different angle on the same point, consider Kant's frequent assertions that there can be no uncertainty in morals. The following is a good example: "One must *be fully certain* whether something is right or wrong, in accordance with duty or contrary to duty, allowed or not allowed. In moral things one cannot *risk anything* on the uncertain, one cannot decide anything *on the danger of trespass against the law*" (LL574 IX 70). From an empirical standpoint, these are extravagantly (even absurdly) strong statements; but that, I insist, is not the proper standpoint from which to judge them. What Kant is voicing here is the transcendental condition that, within moral as within scientific discourse, conceptual room must be available to make a distinction between opinions and knowledge—whether or not there is empirical reality to this distinction. Just as no one would dream of saying that her opinion of the correctness of heliocentrism is as good as someone else's opinion of the correctness of geocentrism, hence no one would dream of closing a discussion on this topic by an appeal to what the various parties believe, no one should dream (as moral relativists are fond of doing) that opinions can be the last word in a moral discussion. Even if (empirically) uncertain opinions are the best we will ever get, we must *think of* them as, at best, approximations to the kind of certainty moral knowledge would *have to* display; *and* we must continue to work toward that unattainable ideal, without resting content with what *feels* right at the time. Once again, this is precisely what is so agonizing about a moral dilemma: that there the insufficiency of our intellectual tools is especially apparent.[48]

Returning to our main train of thought, we must distinguish the nonphilosophical (moral) views Kant attempts to ground from the (transcendental) philosophical kind of grounding he can and will provide for any such views, and make it clear that disagreement with Kant can occur here at different levels, of different philosophical significance. One might not agree, say, that lying is unconditionally wrong—which will have no philosophical significance whatsoever. Or one might agree that lying is unconditionally wrong and that proving that it is should be carried out (within TI) as a proof of its irrationality, but disagree on what particular proof Kant gives—which will have some philosophical significance for a proper development of Kant's philosophy but no impact on it as a whole: Kant himself at times admitted that he had changed the proof of some (even more central) claim of his without seeming particularly impressed. Or (whatever one thinks about lying, or any other individual moral issue) one might disagree with the commitment to TI or with the special relevance Kant gives to rationality in moral contexts—and then it will be left to the critic to develop her own philosophical views, in substantial independence from Kant's. But the challenge that I find most relevant, and on which I am focusing in this chapter, is the one formulated by the determinist who claims that judgments of right and wrong make no sense at all: that people lie, or do not lie, when they are determined to do so—and there is nothing else to be said on the matter.[49] This challenge Kant meets by offering a logical distinction, not moral edification; and, though he will use the distinction to defend what *he* finds morally edifying, there is no reason to think of it as limited in that way.

Given how important this logical distinction is—specifically, how important it is for Kant to claim that judgments with the same grammatical structure may have distinct logical forms—it is useful to discuss it as it emerges in another context. "The judgment of taste," Kant says in the third *Critique*, "ascribes assent to everyone, and whoever declares something to be beautiful wishes that everyone *should* [*solle*] approve of the object in question and similarly declare it to be beautiful" (J121 V 237). Even more clearly, "[common sense] does not say that everyone *will* concur with our judgment but that everyone *should* [*solle*] agree with it" (J123 V 239).[50] These different attitudes are reflected in the ways in which we deal with people who judge otherwise. If I say, "This painting is rectangular," and everyone around me says, "This painting is not rectangular," since the logical form of my statement is, in fact, "Everyone looking at this painting will see it as rectangular,"[51] I will definitely have second thoughts about its correctness.[52] But if I say, "This painting is beautiful," and everyone around me says, "This painting is not beautiful," I will not be worried (or at least I will not *have to be*, which is all that matters when logical form is in question). Since the logical form of my judgment is, in fact, "Everyone looking at this painting *ought to* see it as beautiful,"[53] I will simply try to convince the others that they are not looking at the painting in the *right* way—and, if I cannot so convince them, I will (be able to) conclude that they are *all wrong*. That I *can* come to this conclusion in one case but not in the other is evidence that we are dealing with judgments situated at entirely different levels—as indeed Kant points out when considering a similar contrast between the agreeable and the beautiful at J99 V 214: with the former, "everyone is intrinsically so modest as not even to ascribe . . . assent to others (even though a quite extensive unanimity is often found in these judgments as well)," whereas with the latter, though one's taste "is often enough rejected in its claim to the universal validity of its judgment," one "can nevertheless find it possible . . . to represent judgments that could demand such assent universally, and does in fact expect it of everyone for each of its judgments."[54] Thus, it is the peculiar logical form of aesthetic judgments that "elevates them out of empirical psychology" (J149 V 266); and it is only by focusing on "the formal peculiarities of this kind of judgments, that is, only insofar as it is merely their logical form that is considered" that we can find "a guideline" to their deduction (J168 V 287)—that is, to justifying the entitlement they claim to universality and necessity, however correct such a claim might be in any specific case.

In *Kant's Copernican Revolution* I pointed out that Kant has a conflictual conception of human life: he sees it as pervaded by irreconcilable antagonisms, and even believes it to be better (for humans) that they be irreconcilable. The conflict was described there as one *of faculties*, and indeed I gave examples of the antagonisms between reason and sensibility, and between reason and understanding. But I also noted that having a faculty, for Kant, simply amounts to being able to operate in a certain way;[55] hence an irreconcilable conflict "of faculties" amounts for him to having distinct and independent ways of operating, without hope that any such way will ever be proven to be the (only) right one, or will be able to incorporate the others as its subroutines. This kind of incorporation is what Hegel was going to call "*Aufhebung*": an overcoming of diversity that makes it into different phases of the same (dynamic) reality. So here is what is genuinely controversial about Kant's position: he denies that an *Aufhebung* "of faculties" is possible, and would not even regard it as a good thing. Each of our distinct modes of operation will (have to) continue to spell out its characteristic logic, and there will never be a final resolution of this distinctness into a superlogic of it all. As each spelling out tends to acquire the imperialistic, "systematic" character we have associated with reason, it becomes apparent that there is nothing neutral or harmless about the quote with which I opened the present section: "one and the same reason...must be distinguished merely in its application"—this language should not lead us to think of a number of fields just sitting side by side and peacefully reconnoitered by an inertially self-identical intellectual agency. Limiting ourselves to the two "applications" that matter most to Kant's endeavor, we have seen that reason in its cognitive mode is intrinsically deferential to an Other, dependent on it for data (givens) that it can only passively receive; and we are beginning to see that reason in its moral mode is reason as practical, as active, as proudly asserting its autonomy.[56] Inevitably, these two applications establish their own values and, in the name of such values, incessantly indict each other, forever try to invade each other's territory and stake claims there, so that reason's unity turns out to be itself an antagonistic one. Reason is one and the same, yes, but as a war theater: it is traversed by an irremediable fissure, divided within itself, implicated in a perpetual internal confrontation. It is one because there is always going to be an issue of which is *the one*, universal way to proceed.

Hence, in the end, whatever one might think of Kant's specific construal of rationality (and whether or not one shares his specific moral views), one will remain true to Kant's general spirit, and to the general argument he has provided for the possibility of ethics against determinism, if one is ready to accept the following: when considering any given behavior *a*, and taking for granted that, if *a* is to be real behavior, a natural explanation must be possible for it (that is, one that characterizes it as heteronomously necessitated), each of us can *also* ask whether *a* is rational, *and* what it means for it to be rational, *and* can legitimately react to any attempt to reduce this inquiry to a natural (for example, a psychological) one by calling it a category mistake (a naturalistic fallacy)—and even by taking offense at this intrusion of irrelevant considerations, at this incapacity or unwillingness to maintain the discourse at the level where it belongs. That I do what I do because I am an animal conditioned in certain ways by my environment and genetic makeup does not decide whether what I do is right or wrong, indeed it is entirely orthogonal to that decision.

4. (Un)intelligible Mysteries

An important qualification must be added to the discussion above. Though I have spoken of a conflict there (and elsewhere), it must be clear from my description of it that one is not supposed to construe it in (anything like) an empirical manner—as different parties fighting for control of a given field. This is a conflict of overall interpretations, not of individual causal factors within a single interpretive context; and what is "conflictual" about it is that each interpretation continues to assert itself in its own terms, despite the presence or even the cogency of the others. Which entails something that is extremely important for the understanding and defense of human freedom and morality Kant provides, and that sharply distinguishes his position from what might superficially seem analogous ones. According to Kant, reason *never directly engages* the natural inclinations: "sensory impulses . . . stand in no connection with the moral law. The latter is simply an idea of . . . [man's] reason, and hence we no more find a necessary agreement of sensory urges and inclinations with the moral law, than we do a contradiction, since there is no linkage at all between them" (LE283 XXVII 520). What does get engaged with the natural inclinations are some other natural aspects of an empirical situation that we can *think of* as representatives of reason in the sensible world—and we will see how hard and frustrating it is to give that thinking any substance. "It is not the opposition of practical reason and sensibility, but of the appearances of the former" (TA424 XX 351). If reason faced the inclinations on their own ground, it would become one of them (a natural inclination to being rational), and there would be no more conflict in our sense: there would be a natural, empirical struggle, perhaps (like the one be-tween the driver and the two horses of Plato's chariot in the *Phaedrus*), and then either a winner or a compromise or even a state of suspen-sion, but not the kind of radical indeterminacy we are talking about. That freedom and nature articulate their respective discourses with different logics means that, however undeniable the former might be, it (and morality) will never make contact with the latter: each of them operates in its own sphere, and the confrontation (or conflict) is one *of spheres*.

In light of this qualification, it is time to reconsider the issue of overdetermination. So far, we have drawn positive dividends from it: that the same events can be conceived as both naturally and rationally necessitated—that is, as inserted in both natural and rational lawlike regularities—has opened the way to an attractive form of compatibility between determinism and freedom. But now we must remind our-selves of how (conceptually) fundamental lawlike regularities are from Kant's viewpoint. In TR, that the same things (or events)[57] belong to different regular patterns is just another harmless aspect of those things: they are what they are anyway, and it just so happens that, being what they are, they fall in different regular patterns. The patterns have no role in *constituting* the things—which also means that what really causes the things' behavior is independent of any particular regular pattern, and even such that it could take place, and have its causal impact, in the absence of all regular patterns (there could be miraculous effects).[58] In TI, on the other hand, what things are is to be spelled out in terms of regular patterns; hence different regular patterns make for different things, and different systems of such patterns make for different worlds altogether (nature, we know already, "is the existence of things under laws").[59] Therefore, the relation mobilized when we talk about "the same" events being both naturally and rationally necessitated is not straightforward identity, but rather identity (or identification) across distinct possible worlds (across incommensurable spheres)—a sensible one and an intelligible one. Which, as it turns out, is going to complicate matters a great deal.

There are two basic conceptions of a possible world, the counterfactual one and the descriptive one, and in my "Free from What?" I argued that they can be put in clear correspondence, respectively, with TR and TI. According to the counterfactual conception, a possible world is a way in which *these* objects, the objects existing in *this* (actual) world could have evolved; an indexical component is thus built into it, and identification across possible worlds is a nonissue—in every world, every object (if present) is just *itself, that* very object. According to the descriptive conception, on the other hand, a possible world is a structure our language can describe; and here, in the conception that reflects TI's point of view, identification across possible worlds is a serious, and often insoluble, problem—to resolve it, an indexical reference must be laboriously constructed, or held on to, which is anything but a matter of course. (Consider an extreme case: if Dante's hell is a possible world and the thicket behind my house is another, what sense does it even make to ask which devil in the former is the same as which shrub in the latter?)[60] So, when Kant says (for example) that "man considered solely as an intelligible being ... obligates man as a sensory being, and we thus have a relationship of man *qua* phenomenon towards himself *qua* noumenon" (LE275 XXVII 510), what is the force of this identity judgment? How legitimate is it to claim that in both cases we are talking about the self*same* man?

Imagine, to provide an element of contrast, that, after giving a physical explanation of something I did, I also try to explain it psychologically—within TI, that is, in a context where adopting a different causal account means moving to a different possible world. This task, in the case under consideration, amounts to looking for different regular patterns in the spatiotemporal framework, hence without losing contact with our spatiotemporal tools of indexical reference. I can still, that is, be talking about *this* thing I did, except that I relate it to *these other* (psychologically relevant) things, as opposed to *those* (physically relevant ones) I referred to before. Genuine identification across such worlds is feasible; hence, there is substance to the claim that in both cases I am providing an account of *the same* behavior. None of this can be done, however, when comparing the sensible and the intelligible worlds. Suppose that I consider a specific act of mine and ask myself if it can be regarded as falling within a rational pattern (in addition to a natural one). To do this, I must generalize upon it: I must provide an argument establishing that *an act of a similar kind would be performed by any rational agent in similar circumstances*. But that means comparing a spatiotemporal occurrence with a non-spatiotemporal, abstract entity,[61] hence forfeiting the indexical substratum that provides concrete content for any identity judgment and being constitutionally unable to establish that rationality could indeed belong to *this* act—in possible-world jargon, that *this* act *in* the intelligible world *is* indeed rational.

Here is where, finally, the analogy between artificial games like chess and "the game" of rationality breaks down. It does not matter to chess as such *who* makes the right move, or even if anyone does; nor does it matter to me as an individual, empirical chess player if I win a game only because my opponent got tired.[62] Rational accounts in this case can maintain an untroubled existence at their own level—untroubled, that is, by what happens in actual chess games. But, when it comes to my behavior, it matters a lot to me (and possibly others) that it be *me* who is rational, as opposed to an abstract agent. So here the issue of identifying objects at different levels (in different worlds) is a crucial one, and it is going to be perceived as a crucial limitation if it cannot be resolved. But that is just what happens: when spatiotemporal coordinates are left out, no sense can be made of the same thing turning up in different circumstances. There is something intrinsically defective to my thought of myself as an intelligence (or as free): insofar as it is a pure thought, I can never even be sure that it applies to me. The very operation of abstraction that makes it possible to find the definition of the right move relevant to all chess players (in a given situation on the chessboard) also makes it *impossible* to *distinguish* those players from one another, hence to determine *which is which*;

when I conduct a similar operation on myself, on the whole of myself, and reduce it to a *noumenon* (to something I can only think of) in order to establish the rationality of my moves, I also hereby lose any assurance I had of my identity and no longer know whom (or what) I am talking about. I concentrate on someone who shares certain behavioral parameters (abstractly conceived) with me, and the best I can say in the end is that I *hope* that that still be me: that it still make sense, a sense I cannot comprehend because I have given up on all the ways I had of making concrete sense of anything, to carry out the appropriate cross-world identification (I hope it makes some sense to say that this devil is the same as that shrub—though, if it does, I will never know it, or even understand it).[63] In conclusion, the intelligible world in which "I" am free is not one to which I can in fact say that *I* belong, let alone a "really real" one whose delusive shadow would surface in the spatiotemporal realm and in the empirical subject living there. It is a fiction inhabited by my rational ideas,[64] including the one I have of "myself"[65]—one which is so poor that I cannot really say, contra my wishes and my vocation, what it is an idea of. "Freedom . . . is a mere idea, the objective reality of which can in no way be presented in accordance with laws of nature and so too cannot be presented in any possible experience; and because no example of anything analogous can ever be put under it, it can never be comprehended or even only seen" (G105 IV 459).[66]

To further articulate this limitation consider the following passage, where Kant addresses the daunting task of thinking the end of the (sensible) world: "we will inevitably entangle ourselves in contradictions as soon as we try to take a single step beyond the sensible world into the intelligible. . . . But we also say that we think of a duration as *infinite* (as an eternity) not because we have any determinate concept of its magnitude—for that is impossible, since time is wholly lacking as a measure—but rather because that concept . . . is merely a negative one of eternal duration. . . . [I]f reason attempts this with the principle of rest and immutability of the state of beings in the world, . . . it would fall into total thoughtlessness, and nothing would remain for it but to think as the final end an alteration, proceeding to infinity (in time) in a constant progression, in which the *disposition* (which is not a phenomenon, . . . but something supersensible, hence not alterable with time) remains the same and is persisting. The rule for the practical use of reason in accord with this idea thus says no more than that we must take our maxims as if, in all alterations from good to better going into infinity, our moral condition regarding its disposition (the *homo*

Noumenon . . .) were not subject to any temporal change at all" (R226–27 VIII 333–34). Two important suggestions are offered here. First, if I want to provide any content for purely intellectual specifications (without "fall[ing] into total thoughtlessness"), I must still use (spatio) temporal references, if only in an analogical way; for example, I can use everlastingness ("proceeding to infinity (in time) in a constant progression") as a metaphor of atemporality.[67] I will focus on this suggestion shortly; now I note that, second, we are also told that we can entertain concepts defined in a purely negative way, so long as they do not "entangle us in contradictions" (which will inevitably happen as soon as we start asking more questions about them than their tenuous fabric can bear)—the concept of an eternity which is not (yet) everlastingness but only *the negation of* time,[68] or that of a disposition which is what is left of an action when all of its empirical features are deleted.[69]

In the intelligible world, "my" actions no longer have the outsideness that characterizes spatiotemporal occurrences; they are abstract states that I can only vaguely conceive as instantaneous choices (if instants are themselves conceived as out of time, as experiences approaching eternity). I do not have to be a philosopher to ascribe to myself states like that; in fact (Kant would say), any ordinary person does it whenever she attributes to herself—to her purely *internal* decision, the result of denying externality, or spatiotemporality, as such; hence no less an outcome of the *via negationis* than any legitimate thought about God—responsibility for what she has done. To be sure, as soon as I return into the sensible world (and especially if I am a philosopher), I will begin to articulate that instantaneous, internal state into a network of antecedent (external) events, and I might even convince myself in the end that there was nothing especially decisive or spontaneous about the course I took—that, considering the situation I was in, there was no *real* alternative to taking it. But none of this will prevent me from once again assuming the abstractive mode in the future: from disregarding all antecedent events and thinking of "my action" as an internal, eternal state—a choice made on purely rational grounds. "[T]he term 'deed' can in general apply just as well to the use of freedom through which the supreme maxim (either in favor of, or against, the law) is adopted in the power of choice [*Willkür*], as to the use by which the actions themselves . . . are performed in accordance with that maxim. . . . The former is an intelligible deed, cognizable through reason alone apart from any temporal condition; the latter is sensible, empirical, given in time" (RR79 VI 31). It is indeed a subterfuge (and one that at times Kant himself was tempted by) to use the language of internal decisions and dispositions to give philosophical substance to any claim of freedom, but it is no subterfuge to constantly return to this language despite the delusional character philosophy has attributed to it (or even to find inspiration there for additional philosophical inquiry)—on the contrary, this is one of many inevitable, endless oscillations Kant finds in our form of life. Once again, no harm is done by such talk if we properly understand its transcendental semantics, if, that is, we do not fall into the trap of thinking that internal dispositions belong in the same world as empirical behavior, that there is continuity between the two, and that indeed the former may cause the latter. All that belongs to the empirical world is external, because it is all in space; "internal" is a code word for reference to another world,[70] and no causal connection can exist between the two worlds. What I do in the empirical world is always caused by empirical (that is, spatiotemporal) conditions and circumstances; if I abstract from such conditions and circumstances, I can think of what I do as also being caused by a rational pattern—with all the limitations that were brought out here on the sense in which *I* can meaningfully think of the results of the abstraction as still being me and mine.

5. Relentless Criticism

In the next chapter, this abstractive stance will be the subject of further discussion, as we turn our attention to what responsibility I have for my *ir*rational behavior. Now instead I will pursue the first suggestion mentioned above: can the freedom I ascribe to myself in the intelligible world be given an analogical reconstruction in the sensible one? To a partial extent, yes; though not conclusively.

Intelligibly construed, freedom is autonomy: that an action is free is accounted for by providing a rational argument. Using the language we just introduced, I am free if my internal, eternal disposition to act is entirely determined (in the world to which such dispositions belong) by the rationality of the relevant argument. How could I rewrite this abstract condition in the spatiotemporal terms that apply to the empirical world?[71] Well, it would not be enough for an agent's single move to be found *in agreement with* a rational analysis of the relevant situation, since the agreement might be coincidental and hence establish no significant connection. Only if the agreement were a regular occurrence could we think of ourselves as entitled to say (within the regularity model of causality) that the move was made *because of* its rationality, or that its rationality accounts for it. "For, in the case of what is to be morally good it is not enough that it *conform* with the moral law but it must also be done *for the sake of the law*; without this, that conformity is only very contingent and precarious, since a ground that is not moral will indeed now and then produce actions in conformity with the law, but it will also often produce actions contrary to the law" (G45–46 IV 390). Note that Kant's language here contains at the same time a reference to intelligible dispositions or intentions (doing something "for the sake of the [moral] law") *and* an account of the latter in empirical terms: empirically, dispositions must be cashed out in terms of the logic of one's behavior—of how much this one thing we are looking at fits with everything *else* the agent does.[72] A disposition per se cannot be the *object* of any substantive analysis or judgment because, again, it does not belong to the world of (empirical) objects; so one can only study an empirical correlate of it,[73] and only (at best) one's entire life could count as such a correlate[74]—much as only everlastingness could be a sensible analogue of atemporality. A man's "immutable resolution" can only become known to him "from the progress he has already made from the worse to the morally better" (PR239 V 123). "[S]ince we can draw inferences regarding the disposition only on the basis of actions (which are its appearances), for the purpose of [moral] estimate our life is to be viewed only as a *temporal unity*, i.e. a *whole*" (RR111–12n VI 70n).[75]

What we need to find out is the "law of . . . [the agent's] causality," that is, his "*character*" (A539 B567): "We must judge a person from his character, not from his actions" (N409 XV 496)—and not his (atemporal, noumenal) *intelligible* character, whatever law he manifests in the intelligible world (for "[w]e are not acquainted with the latter" (A551 B579) and, as we have seen, we are not even sure how to find the agent in that noumenal world), but rather his *empirical* one,[76] "which is nothing other than a certain causality of his reason, insofar as in its effects in appearance this reason exhibits a rule, in accordance with which one could derive the rational grounds and the actions themselves according to their kind and degree, and estimate the subjective principles of his power of choice [*Willkür*]" (A549 B577). And, again, nothing less than an agent's whole career could provide enough evidence to determine what this character is, and to establish its rationality. "[C]haracter . . . [is] a consistent practical cast of mind in accordance with unchangeable maxims" (PR262 V 152).

What, then, *is* our empirical character? Is it ever possible to find out? Not quite. However deeply we have searched in an agent's behavior (including our own), we will never know what the law of that behavior is—or whether it has any law, other than the natural one that defines it as actual behavior. To begin with, our access to the logic of our own moves is seriously limited: the gradual process by which we come to know it is never going to be at an end, or to warrant any firm conclusion. "In fact, it is absolutely impossible by means of experience to make out with complete certainty a single case in which the maxim of an action otherwise in conformity with duty rested simply on moral grounds and on the representation of one's duty. It is indeed sometimes the case that with the keenest self-examination we find nothing besides the moral ground of duty that could have been powerful enough to move us to this or that good action and to so great a sacrifice; but from this it cannot be inferred with certainty that no covert impulse of self-love, under the mere pretense of that idea, was not actually the real determining cause of the will; for we like to flatter ourselves by falsely attributing to ourselves a nobler motive, whereas in fact we can never, even by the most strenuous self-examination, get entirely behind our covert incentives, since, when moral worth is at issue, what counts is not actions, which one sees, but those inner principles of actions that one does not see" (G61–62 IV 407). "[A] human being cannot see into the depths of his own heart so as to be quite certain, in even a *single* action, of the purity of his moral intention and the sincerity of his disposition, even when he has no doubt about the legality of the action" (M523 VI 392).[77] If, say, I have brought out a pattern of generosity in my behavior, I must admit that it is but a *partial* pattern, and that the next move of mine I examine might contradict the conjecture that I have a generous character. Perhaps I am only concerned with gaining a good reputation, or I like to have others depend on me, or I am trying to make amends for some other past behavior—and the next move I examine might well favor one of these less charitable explanations. "[O]ne . . . cannot show with certainty in any example that the will is here determined merely through the law, without another incentive, although it seems to be so; for it is always possible that covert fear of disgrace, perhaps also obscure apprehension of other dangers, may have had an influence on the will. Who can prove by experience the nonexistence of a cause when all that experience teaches is that we do not perceive it?" (G72 IV 419).

Besides, even assuming (*per impossibile*) that all my actual behavior be present to me and that all of it fit the rational demands, it is not clear that that would be enough. What if I have just been *lucky* never to encounter a truly agonizing choice; but, had I encountered it, my

virtue would not have been equal to the challenge? Isn't the nonoccurrence of such critical cases once again a coincidental matter, and
isn't therefore my supposed agreement with reason's standards, however extended to the whole of my life, not enough to refer to those
standards as genuine causal factors for my behavior? "[H]ow many
people who have lived long and guiltless lives may not be merely
fortunate in having escaped so many temptations?" (M523 VI 392–93).
"How many a man walks guiltless of such crimes, only because he
did not fall into similar circumstances; had he been brought into the
same temptation, he would also have been guilty of the same offence"
(LE192–93 XXVII 434). "We have only to ask whether we are certainly and immediately conscious of a faculty enabling us to overcome,
by firm resolve, every incentive to transgression, however great (*Phalaris
licet imperet, ut sis falsus, et admoto dictet periuria tauro*). Everybody must
admit that he *does not* know whether, were such a situation to arise, he
would not waver in his resolve"[78] (RR93–94n VI 49n)—hence does
not know how much his (supposed) virtue depends on his not having
faced such a situation.[79]

As a consequence of these limitations, rational analysis of (empirical)
behavior (as opposed to the issuing of those rational arguments that are
only relevant to the intelligible world—and as such can make a claim
to definitive closure) will have to be interminable,[80] and interminably
critical: never satisfied with a demonstration of autonomy (which can
only be provisional anyway), always suspicious, always unsympathetically concerned with establishing fault. What we will get from it is not
reassuring arguments to the effect that what we did was the right thing,
but perplexing counterarguments to the effect that it might not have
been—which is just as well, since "one is never more easily deceived
than in what promotes a good opinion of oneself" (RR109 VI 68).
Not even the most laudable behavior will be exempt from this severe
scrutiny, since "we can find satisfaction in the mere *exercise of our
powers*, in consciousness of our strength of soul in overcoming obstacles
opposed to our plans, in cultivating our talents of spirit, and so forth,"
and then we would have no reason "for passing . . . off . . . [such joys
and delights] as a different way of determining the will than merely
through sense" (PR157–58 V 24): for regarding ourselves as anything
more than highly sophisticated and clever *animals*. Reference to internal, eternal, intelligible dispositions will have one major practical,
negative consequence: because no sum of sensible occurrences (of appearances) is ever going to provide an exhaustive empirical correlate
for such a disposition, we will never be able to assert our freedom. "We

may be innocent enough *coram foro externo*, but not here" (LE193 XXVII 434).

Kant's mercilessly critical attitude toward human behavior provides a useful perspective from which to judge his apparently unreasonable, unqualified refusal of the moral legitimacy of any lie—as it surfaces, for example, in his "On a Supposed Right to Lie from Philanthropy."[81] The facts are well known and can be rehearsed quickly: a murderer comes to your house, in which you know that a potential victim of his took refuge, and asks you about that very person's current location. You answer that you have absolutely no idea where she might be. And, the common opinion goes, you do the right thing in thus protecting a human life—end of story. Whereas Kant would want you to tell the truth to the murderer; he would want you to *always* tell the truth, independently of the consequences. Which a long tradition of authors, beginning with Benjamin Constant, have regarded as an absurd stance.

This matter must be judged in the context of the crucial distinction articulated in section 3. What Kant would have chosen to do in the circumstances I described, or how he would judge anyone else's behavior, is an empirical (moral) question; and, of course, each of us could empirically disagree with him. But there is also a transcendental issue involved, which has to do with the clause "end of story" I used above. Kant would never want any such story to come to an end, and an agent to receive a final reassurance that her behavior was the right one. In the present case, he would unsympathetically remind you, as you perhaps begin to feel a little too content with yourself, that there is a cost to saving that life, that you have damaged—to a small extent, perhaps; but there is no telling where such exceptions will stop, once we allow one of them—the very texture of our civil coexistence and communication. "I ... do wrong in the most essential part of duty *in general* by ... [any] falsification ...; [for] I bring it about ... that statements (declarations) in general are not believed, and so too that all rights which are based on contracts come to nothing and lose their force; and this is a wrong inflicted upon humanity generally. Thus a lie ... always harms another, even if not another individual, nevertheless humanity generally, inasmuch as it makes the source of right unusable" (P612 VIII 426). "Whoever may have told me a lie, I do him no wrong if I lie to him in return, but I violate the right of mankind; for I have acted contrary to the condition, and the means, under which a society of men can come about, and thus contrary to the right of humanity" (LE203 XXVII 447). So the story is most definitely not at an end: there is guilt associated with any lie—however well

intentioned, and however good some of its consequences might be—
and Kant's extreme stance is a precious antidote to the complacent
hypocrisy that would have us avoid recognition of this fact.[82]

A similar point can be made about revolutionary action. We will
see in the next chapter that Kant rules out any use of political violence, even against a government whose power has issued from a
(possibly continued) act of violence; in all such cases, the only rational
behavior for him consists in responding to violence with *talk*—in
patiently (and, many would say, naïvely to the point of silliness) *arguing*
with the lawbreakers on the basis of the very legality they have vio-
lently established. Kant's uncompromising position in this and other
respects is best expressed by his most extreme deontological statement: "The proposition that has become proverbial, *fiat iustitia, pereat
mundus*, . . . sounds rather boastful but it is true; it is a sturdy principle
of right, which bars all the devious paths marked out by cunning or
force" (P345 VIII 378–79). However (self-)destructive the outcome
of my behavior, I ought never to contradict rational standards; in the
face of Hitler himself, I ought not to recur to "cunning or force."
Many, again, will find this position unreasonable—and perhaps it is,
empirically speaking. But, again, there is a transcendental angle to the
whole thing; and Kant is making us sensitive to it. People will use
cunning and force against the Hitlers of this world, and will fight hard
not to let the world perish; and they might well succeed, and this
might well be, ultimately, in the interest of reason itself. But the most
important thing these people will be giving up in the process—far
more important than their lives—is their rational integrity. Their
moves will not belong to the rational domain; and to claim (as many
are inclined to do) that in making such moves they would be applying
some kind of "superior" rationality (or, which is the same, morality)
is a Hegelian alibi: a pathetic attempt at having one's cake and eating
it, too. If I cannot convince you by argument that $2 + 2 = 4$, and in
frustration I resort to slapping you, and as a consequence you finally
become able to see the cogency of my proofs, I cannot deny that
slapping you is a move that has no course in a mathematical conversation; and I can only congratulate myself (and you) that an irrational,
unmathematical move could make you see mathematical light. Similarly, if I suspend rationality to deal with your irrational behavior, and
as a consequence you (or your successors) finally become able to join in
a rational conversation, I cannot deny that rationality was interrupted
by my behavior as much as by yours; and I cannot look for a *rational*
(that is, *moral*) justification for what I did.[83] In the terms I used before,

the least of evils is still an evil—its "least" character does not turn it into a good. And *fiat iustitia, pereat mundus* is a reminder of the radical conflicts that are constantly staged, in the Kantian framework, between incommensurable spheres: when we care about justice, what might happen to the world is irrelevant; and, when we care about the world, justice is forgotten. "[T]o expound morality in full purity is to set forth an idea of practical reason" (LE229 XXIX 604).

I noted above that it is a transcendental condition for the very existence of rational discourse that in all cases a single correct answer to a question be presupposed. We have now reached a conclusion that importantly qualifies the previous one: it is also a transcendental condition of this discourse, insofar as it applies to our lives, not just an empirical misfortune, that it never come to an end, hence that human agents never attain any certainty that that single answer (assuming they found it) is reflected in their behavior. To believe otherwise is wishful thinking: a childish, soothing delusion that everything is OK. *For all I know*, everything might *not* be OK, and this suspense is itself a good thing: "it seems never advisable to be encouraged to . . . a state of confidence but much more beneficial (for morality) to 'work out one's salvation with *fear* and *trembling*'" (RR109 VI 68).[84] "Professor Kant finds fault with *conscientia certa* . . . , insofar as this is taken to mean the objective certainty of the rectitude of the action" (LE362 XXVII 619).

We have already encountered the complementary, positive (or, rather, doubly negative) side of this unsympathetic attitude: no one will be able to deny the possibility of rational autonomy either. To be sure, freedom can never be shown to have instances, hence can never be properly understood; but, within the conceptual room provided by the bounds imposed on cognition, it will continue to be legitimate to consistently *think* autonomy—to conceive of ourselves as free beings. Our rational vocation will be expressed in this thought and, despite its unrealizability or indeed just because of it, the thought's persistency in the face of all contrary evidence (evidence, being empirical, could *only* be to the contrary) will be the strongest affirmation of our super-natural (or—to be less committal—other-than-natural) dignity.

A being that manifested autonomy, that was the origin of its own destiny, would fit reason's expectations about a true substance, a thing in itself, and would contrast sharply with the weak, ontologically de-pendent phantoms we have been forced to acknowledge ordinary em-pirical objects (including our empirical selves)[85] to be. We can think of ourselves as beings like that, I said: we can adopt a standpoint from which that conception follows—in fact, we must, if we are to respond to the call of conscience. And this other standpoint can (and must) coexist with the one we adopt when we think of ourselves as natural beings. "The human being, who ... regards himself as an intelligence, thereby puts himself in a different order of things and in relation to determining grounds of an altogether different kind when he thinks of himself as an intelligence endowed with a will, and consequently with causality, than when he perceives himself as a phenomenon in the world of sense (as he also really is) and subjects his causality to external determination in accordance with laws of nature. Now he soon becomes aware that both can take place at the same time, and indeed must do so. For, that a *thing in appearance* (belonging to the world of sense) is subject to certain laws from which *as a thing* or a being *in itself* it is independent contains not the least contradiction" (G103 IV 457). This purely negative absence of contradiction is all the foundation we have as we hold on to the rational register of conversation, and to the critical, suspicious attitude it forever promotes. Within the antagonistic, unresolvable form of life Kant has drawn for us, it is also, fortunately, all the foundation we need—since the opposition cannot do any better.

FOUR

VALUES

1. A Spectator

"It is impossible to think of anything at all in the world, or indeed even beyond it, that could be considered good without limitation except a *good will*" (G49 IV 393). Maybe so; but note that, prima facie, the difficulty (or impossibility) seems to rest precisely in conceiving of an *unqualified* (unlimited, unconditional) judgment of goodness. Qualified judgments approving of something raise no eyebrows: they are one and all, in Kant's terms, "technical" ("technical imperatives . . . always command only conditionally,"[1] M376 VI 221), and we need only understand the relevant field of activity (the relevant *techne*) to make sense of them—they do not trouble our ordinary, natural stance in any way. That a hammer is a good tool for driving nails into wood, and that being quick on one's feet is a good skill to have for attaining social success, are conclusions whose legitimacy and truth can be vindicated by extensive observation of, and reflection upon, ordinary, natural events. Any such judgment is relative, and is qualified (its scope is limited), in more ways than one: it is not only the case that a hammer is good *for driving nails* (not, for example, for preparing a dry martini), hence *relative to* that (former) task; a hammer is also good (at that task) in the sense of being better (at it) than most (possibly all) other implements, hence *relative to* the (existing) competition. But with such obvious limitations (indeed, because of them) none of these judgments sound strange: it takes a minute to figure out what they say, after which we are off using them in a perfectly relaxed manner—and justifiably so.

In the passage quoted above, however, Kant understands the "qualifications" to be added to technical judgments of goodness in yet a third sense: one that is related to those already cited, but also the one where serious problems emerge. For a hammer might be good for driving nails but also, say, for cracking my neighbor's skull open; and, though the former goal might be sometimes conceived as a good one, the latter hardly ever is. More generally, "[u]nderstanding, wit, judgment and the like, whatever such *talents* of mind may be called, or courage, resolution, and perseverance in one's plans, as qualities of *temperament*, are undoubtedly good and desirable for many purposes, but they can also be extremely evil and harmful if the will which is to make use of these gifts of nature . . . is not good. It is the same with *gifts of fortune*. Power, riches, honor, even health and that complete well-being and satisfaction with one's condition called *happiness*, produce boldness and thereby often arrogance as well unless a good will is present which corrects the influence of these on the mind and, in so doing, also corrects the whole principle of action and brings it into conformity with universal ends" (G49 IV 393).

The sense invoked here in which talents and gifts of fortune are only conditional goods is much more radical than their purely instrumental or comparative worth. They are good depending on the use to which they are put, *and* depending on how (unqualifiedly) good that use itself is. If the use is a(n unqualifiedly) *bad* one then, the better talents and gifts of fortune are at serving it (than anything else that could also be put to the same use), the *worse* the total performance will end up being: "without the basic principles of a good will . . . [moderation, self-control, and calm reflection] can become extremely evil, and the coolness of a scoundrel makes him not only far more dangerous but also immediately more abominable in our eyes than we would have taken him to be without it" (G50 IV 394). This notion of being bad (or good) applies to empirical matters as if from the outside and cannot be reduced to empirical distinctions among them: such distinctions can impact the degree to which the notion is applied, but not the substance of the application. Whereas technical judgments of goodness can be explained (away) within a horizon of facts—as generalizations upon classes of them: what the likely outcomes of various kinds of behavior are, and how conducive each of them is likely to be to attaining a certain preestablished goal[2]—here a brand new order of considerations opens up: one in which facts appear entirely irrelevant, and (independent) values enter the scene. Values indeed that, far from being reducible to facts, proudly assert their right to extend over all facts: to pass judgment on the whole of being, to approve or disapprove of anything that is (the case) in spite of its natural necessity (the natural necessity that *makes* it be). Hence, questions are bound to arise. On what are these value judgments based? Who (or what) is doing the approving or disapproving here?

Return again to the paragraph of the *Groundwork* from which I already quoted twice. Almost in passing Kant adds: "not to mention that an impartial rational spectator can take no delight in seeing the uninterrupted prosperity of a being graced with no feature of a pure and good will, so that a good will seems to constitute the indispensable condition even of worthiness to be happy" (G49 IV 393). His casual tone is deceptive, for we should least of all avoid mentioning the relevance of this spectator: one who is impartial, that is, uninfluenced by any personal interest, equitable in considering everyone's vicissitudes, fair in assessing deserts, and who is so *because* she is also rational—because she lets reason take control and speak inside herself, subjecting all other voices to it. This spectator is each of us insofar as she identifies with reason; indeed, she *is* reason judging and evaluating behavior, and approving or disapproving of it, and issuing verdicts that proclaim its worthiness or unworthiness, depending on how far that behavior can be regarded as an expression of reason itself. And that she is impartial as well as rational is a subtle reminder that (as we saw in the previous chapter) one's identification with reason is going to leave no room for asserting that what one thus identifies with is really *oneself*—as opposed to any rational being whatsoever.[3]

Thus, the emergence of the values we are talking about might not seem so extraordinary after all. A carpenter will judge the goodness of a hammer based on the standards implicit in his profession, and so will a social climber concerning the goodness of being quick on one's feet. In more exalted language, we could say that such judgments will be pronounced by the carpenter or the social climber *present in each of us*. Similarly, reason in us will look favorably upon any evidence of itself being practical, and unfavorably upon any irrational behavior; it too will apply its own standards. In doing so, it will be striving toward its self-affirmation, just like any other agency inside or outside us (the carpenter *as such* would want everyone to be thinking in terms of carpentry): toward seeing its law govern the whole world, and everything in the world be instrumental to such governance. That, by the way, is where the proper significance of the "formula of humanity" should be found: how we should understand "that the human being and in general every rational being *exists* as an end in itself, *not merely as a means* to be used by this or that will at its discretion; instead he must in all his actions, whether directed to himself or also to other rational beings, always be regarded *at the same time as an end*" (G79 IV 428). We know already that reason has no special regard for humans as a biological species, hence it is not featherless bipeds that must always be taken as ends and not merely as means: humanity here is but the garb—the only garb, as it turns out—in which rationality surfaces in our experience, hence in honoring it reason honors itself.[4] "*Humanity* . . . [is] rational being in general as pertaining to the world" (RR103 VI 60).[5]

But then, what does it mean to say that, in contrast with rational beings (and their rational behavior), "[a]ll objects of the inclinations have only a conditional worth" (G79 IV 428)? Isn't reason as much "inclined" to approve of itself and of the satisfaction of its own demands as, say, the sexual drive is? The short answer to this question is, yes; and yet it is an answer that does not limit the import of Kant's contrast between reason and every (other) drive. For reason is, precisely (we know already), the "drive" to the unconditional,[6] hence only an unconditional answer would count as satisfying it—a kind of answer that we do not seem to require (or strive for) in any other context. The sexual drive aims at sexual satisfaction, which depends on a high level of specificity in the objects and circumstances involved, to the point of not being meaningfully generalizable: of there being no general features of those objects and circumstances that could be abstracted and considered essential for everyone's "good" (as the sexual drive construes it). This individual's sexual satisfaction, this particular time, is very much her own—even more, her own *here and now*. Which means that, ultimately, she cannot quite say what is so special about it. It might take her a lot of effort to attain it, and she might have to travel a tortuous route in order to get there; and at every step of the way, if asked why she is taking that step, she might answer by pointing to her destination. But, if asked a similar question about the destination, she would have no answer, other than (perhaps) an inarticulate reference to her desire, which would seal rather than resolve her speechlessness. And anything else that is not rational would work the same way. Whereas something I do could be what my reason is looking for and approves of (hence it could provide me with rational satisfaction) only if I had available a complete logical argument establishing its necessity, a self-contained series of steps about which no further perplexities could be raised; and, if I had that much available, the goodness I would predicate of that kind of action (insofar as I identify with reason) would be without qualification, final, categorical. For "categorical" just means, logically speaking, that a judgment is independent of any condition, that it is simply issued, period, with no blanks to be filled; and only reason will ever even look for judgments like that—technical (value) judgments, insofar as they fall within the purview of theoretical, empirical inquiry, can only be made with any number of embedded hypothetical constraints.

I noted in the previous chapter that a rational analysis of human behavior is going to have primarily negative, critical significance: that, though we can think of ourselves as free and rational, and hope we might (sometimes) be, we will never know that we are—whereas we will often know that we are not. But the rigor required by this interminable analysis is ordinarily too much to sustain; hence, ordinarily humans will only listen to reason up to a point. They will ask, "Why did I do X?" and answer, "In order to attain Y"; then they will ask, "Why did I want Y?" and answer, "In order to attain Z",...and eventually, when they come to the end of their rope (that is, of their intellectual and moral resources), they will answer the last question they are willing to entertain, "Why did I want W?" by saying, "Because I liked it." This is a betrayal of reason, a reversing of the order of priorities that a rational being should follow if she is to be true to her own destiny:[7] it makes us think of reason as a slave of dumb desires, it reduces its role to that of providing clarification, and possibly instrumental advice, about a contingent, arbitrarily assumed end—one for which no additional request for justification is posed (or answered), hence one that can only be regarded as irrational (insofar as reason is the demand for a full explanation).[8]

There is no avoiding the constant occurrence of such unfortunate circumstances; as I will argue in detail beginning in the next section, we are not perfectly rational, we are also animals, and often reason is treated by the animals we are as nothing more than a tool (a convenient one, since "reason alone is capable of discerning the connection of means with their purposes," PR187 V 58) from whose use we derive no special status. "[T]hat...[the human being] has reason does not at all raise him in worth above mere animality if reason is to serve him only for the sake of what instinct accomplishes for animals" (PR189–90 V 61). But a further step can be taken down the road of this betrayal, and one that directly concerns the transcendental philosopher, not just the empirical human being. That is when philosophy itself is perverted in order to make us rest content with our limited resources: when chatter of a "rational choice theory" invites us to stop all questioning as soon as we get to our "preference profile," and confirms our natural tendency to do so (confirms nature in us), because it is the most "rational" thing to do. This is more than reason failing to take control of us: it is reason self-destructing. It is a genuine case of Hegelian *Aufhebung*: of reason being turned into its opposite, of "rationalization" becoming the acceptance and justification of irrationality, and hence of these two opposites, ultimately, identifying with each other and realizing dialectical harmony. In Kant's view, on the other hand, it is *just* a contradiction in terms, with no redeeming dialectical virtue; it is one more case of our "innocence" being violated by deluded, arrogant intellectuals. "[E]mpiricism . . . destroys at its roots the morality of dispositions . . . and substitutes for it something quite different, namely in place of duty an empirical interest, with which the inclinations generally are secretly leagued. . . . [T]he inclinations . . . (no matter what fashion they put on) degrade humanity when they are raised to the dignity of a supreme practical principle" (PR 197 V 71). "[There is] a propensity to rationalize against . . . [the] strict laws of duty and to cast doubt upon their validity, or at least upon their purity and strictness, and, where possible, to make them better suited to our wishes and inclinations, that is, to corrupt them at their basis and to destroy all their dignity" (G 59–60 IV 405).[9]

2. Evil

Reason approves all spatiotemporal occurrences that it can construe (if only provisionally) as its own manifestations in the world, and calls them (unqualifiedly) good; it disapproves any manifestations of regularities that contradict its conclusions, and calls them (unqualifiedly) evil. A state's painful effort to provide itself with a civil constitution will be judged favorably by rational, impartial spectators;[10] an "incessant drive toward a faith ever more estranged from reason" and the resulting "nonsense" (R 243 VII 10) will receive their most severe rebuke. Also, nothing can prevent reason from thinking of itself as leaving traces in human behavior, as being practical there; that is, nothing can prevent it from constantly rewriting its intellectual standards in terms of our empirical character, and from possibly finding the outcomes of such rewriting to be (temporarily, partially) satisfactory. Hence human behavior can be consistently conceived as (though never known to be) autonomous, or free. We can take our discussion so far to have established these statements; but they should not be confused with some other related statements that are (or rather, one of which is) far from unquestionable. To accept the above is *not* to accept the claim that humans can be understood as (possibly) freely performing some of their actions rationally *and* freely performing some of their actions *ir*rationally. That there is freedom to do good *and* freedom to do evil.

Consider someone *a* who coldly and deliberately plans and executes a neighbor's murder. Undeniably, he does what he wills to do; his behavior is an expression of his choice, and in the end he is happy that things worked out the way he wanted (assuming he does not get caught). If asked for an account of what motivated that choice, he could provide an elaborate scheme representing the crime as the most effective way of reaching some personal goal of his—he would have a maxim available that justifies his behavior and his choice. But, we know, that he willed the murder and that he has such a maxim available (hence that the murder was deliberately, rather than emotionally, perpetrated) can be explained as much in natural terms as the fact that he committed the murder in the first place: *a*'s early childhood experiences may have been such that he developed as a depressed loner and tended to internalize frustrations instead of reacting explosively to them, hence such that he became prone to fantasize obsessively about dramatic resolutions of them and eventually started seeing his behavior as the realization of his fantasies (however coincidental, or even nonexistent, the agreement of the two might have been). *And* he had the early childhood experiences he had because his parents had moved to a part of town where they had no connections and no friends, so the boy was brought up in an atmosphere of uncertainty as to how to communicate properly—he was not properly socialized. *And* his parents had moved to that part of town because the factory where Dad used to work had shut down. *And*...[11]

So the presence of a maxim and the relevance of will understood phenomenologically (*Willkür*) are no evidence that *a* can be regarded as the origin of "his" action: *a*'s behavior, his phenomenological will, *and* his maxim may all fall within the range of (and be exhaustively explained as) nature working itself out. The same of course would be true if *a*'s behavior had been perfectly rational: insofar as it was part of the real world, that behavior too would be explainable without residue by referring to natural laws (or rather, without any *other* residue than *every* natural explanation has: its being based on a mysterious, incomprehensible act of synthesis). But, in this case, something else

could be added to the natural explanation: a rational account war-
ranting the autonomy of *a*'s behavior, whatever its physical or psychological heteronomy—vindicating it as being *also* a manifestation of
Wille. If no such additional account is available, then *a*'s behavior is
not free. It is still bad behavior, by all means, but not spontaneous—
not an expression of autonomy.

Though this issue is an exceedingly complex one, and the balance of
the present chapter will be spent delving deeply into it, and delving
into it will force us to importantly qualify any straightforward statement about it, I find it useful, at this stage of the game, to issue precisely
such a straightforward statement. So here it is: There are no three
options in Kant's view concerning human behavior. It is not possible
for it to be free and good, free and evil, or unfree. Freedom is the same
thing as goodness: autonomous behavior is behavior reason approves
of, hence judges and values positively, period. "To think of oneself as a
freely acting being, yet as exempted from the one law commensurate
to such a being (the moral law), would amount to the thought of a
cause operating without any law at all (for the determination according to natural law is abolished on account of freedom): and this is a
contradiction" (RR82 VI 35). "Freedom is . . . not at all a faculty for
choosing evil, but rather the good, because our reason commands only
the good" (LM269 XXIX 903). If what we do is not such that reason
would approve of it, then *we* do nothing at all: we are not agents, not
players in the game in which we are involved, but only pawns in the
hands of irresistible nature. Reason will continue to exercise its judgment on those unfortunate occurrences and will firmly condemn them
as contradicting its standards; so clearly they will continue to be called
evil, since calling them that amounts to voicing a negative value
judgment. But we will not be the origin of this evil: nature as such will
be. "Radical evil" exists in us because we are dual beings, to which
two independent registers of explanation are applicable—the rational
one and the natural one—and because the latter is always threatening
to remain the only one available:[12] our rationality is always at risk of
vanishing into thin air, of proving itself a delusion.[13] "An evil heart . . .
[has] its origin . . . [in] the frailty of human nature, in not being strong
enough to comply with its adopted principles," Kant says at RR84
VI 37, giving what is for him a typical characterization of the conflict involved here as an empirical one—as a struggle between opposing
forces. Since we know that the conflict could not be empirical (we
know it to be a conflict of interpretations), we also know what is really
going on: in examining our behavior, reason cannot but root for

(something it can understand as conducive to) its own triumph, and be disappointed when we take a wrong turn, and wish that we had not—that we had had indeed enough strength to resist the particular inclination that led us astray. It cannot but identify with those other factors in us (education, tradition, a sense of shame, what have you) which were in fact opposing that inclination, and see them as its own counterparts in the phenomenal world, as a rewriting of its principles in spatiotemporal terms; though of course this identification is itself sustained by nothing but hope—there are not enough indexical resources to give it any substantial content.[14]

A perfectly rational individual would be a saint: she would always do the right thing, and reason would always approve of it. In a world of saints there would be no conflict, no disagreement, just as there is not when all the students in a class, each reasoning soundly on her own, find the correct solution of a mathematical problem.[15] Reason would have its usual effect of establishing consistency—as it does in its cognitive use, where "a universal law of nature makes everything harmonious" (PR161 V 28). But we do not live in a world like that: we can only conceive of it as a goal to be pursued, as the rational, purely intelligible, unrealizable idea of a *kingdom of ends* ("a kingdom of ends would actually come into existence through maxims whose rule the categorical imperative prescribes to all rational beings *if they were universally followed*," G87 IV 438).[16] In the (sensible) world we are familiar with—the *actual* one—things work much as they do in most classrooms: just as students' physiology and psychology often get in the way of their rational approach to mathematics (that is, of an approach reason would endorse) and make them not see the correct solution, so do our physiology and psychology often get in the way when it comes to any other aspect of our behavior and make us behave irrationally (that is, leave us with only a heteronomous account of what we did). And just as students' incorrect solutions are generally different from one another (there is only one reason, but there are many different empirical bodies and minds),[17] so are our heteronomously determined moves characterized by "the most extreme opposite of harmony ..., the worst conflict" (PR161 V 28). In both cases, reason cannot approve the outcome; it must judge it harshly and reject it outright.

The view that evil is not, that it is only a limit of being, had been formulated many times before. It was central to Neoplatonism and was at least intimated (if not always consistently) by Augustine. Kant's view reminds one of it, and yet in some sense it is the exact opposite.[18] For the only things that exist, for him, are natural ones: spatiotemporal things governed by deterministic natural causality. But those very things resist rationality, oppose what reason declares necessary; hence reason must deny them. Not deny their existence, though, since it cannot; deny their value. And conclude that when they are all there is, when no (additional) rational explanation can be given of them, then something crucial is missing: true agency, being a protagonist of one's own destiny, a spontaneous source of behavior. Pure nature devoid of goodness still *is*, of course, very much so; but it displays no freedom. Anything "acting" in it always calls upon a reference to something else, in a universal circulation of groundedness that ultimately leaves everything ungrounded.

What complicates matters is that (again) there is no denying the phenomenology of willing something irrational (or evil); so we must insist that phenomenology proves nothing about autonomy. As an additional illustration of this point, consider the following passage from the *Metaphysics of Morals* (M380–81 VI 226–27): "although experience shows that the human being as a *sensible being* is able to choose [*wählen*] *in opposition to* as well as *in conformity with* the law, his freedom as an *intelligible being* cannot be *defined* by this, since appearances cannot make any supersensible object (such as free choice [*freie Willkür*]) understandable." That is, we certainly see people sometimes obeying and sometimes disobeying the rational law, and doing both willingly; but that their will (phenomenologically understood) is indeed free is not decided by this empirical observation. It *cannot* be decided by it, since freedom (if present) would have to be superimposed on natural events and accounted for in terms that are independent of any naturalistic explanation, irreducible to what occurs in space and time—though of course, in order to be (conceivable as) real at all, such terms would then have to be translated into spatiotemporal conditions. "We can also see that freedom can never be located in a rational subject's being able to choose [*Wahl treffen*] in opposition to his (lawgiving) reason, even though experience proves often enough that this happens (though we still cannot comprehend how this is possible)." We witness the fact that irrational behavior is chosen by humans all the time, but we cannot judge that choice a manifestation of freedom.[19] "For it is one thing to accept a proposition (on the basis of experience) and another thing to make it the *expository principle* (of the concept of free choice [*freien Willkür*]) and the universal feature for distinguishing it (from *arbitrio bruto s. servo*); for the first does not maintain that the feature belongs *necessarily* to the concept, but the second requires this." What is the case does not decide definitional matters; on the contrary, before we can even describe what the case is, we need a consistent set of definitions for our terms—of what *must* be true of them. And no such consistency is to be expected by following the lead of empirical occurrences. "Only freedom in relation to the internal lawgiving of reason is really an ability; the possibility of deviating from it is an inability. How can the former be defined by the latter?" Irrational behavior can only argue for negative conclusions: show that reason had *no* causal import, hence that the alleged agent was really *not* the author of her behavior, that she could *not* help herself, could *not* display her autonomy—hence was *not* an agent at all.

An analogy might make things clearer. Imagine that rationality be like being awake, and that a purely natural (irrational) behavior be like being asleep. Whether I am asleep or awake, my behavior can be explained as the necessary consequence of natural events; when I am awake, however, I take it that it can also be accounted for in terms of my intentions (whose independence from natural events, for the sake of the current analogy, I will not call in question). Clearly, there are ways in which I can intentionally facilitate my falling asleep, by going to bed at the usual time, by drinking a glass of hot milk, or by counting sheep.[20] But it is also clear that my falling asleep is not itself under my intentional control; for it, *only* a natural account is possible. To make this point more forceful we can focus on the extreme case in which I fall asleep at the wheel of my car. I may be desperately trying to stay awake, and be conscious of myself and of the car and of the road until . . . I am no longer conscious of anything. Suppose the dozing off only lasts a few seconds; when I emerge from it I will be confused for a moment, and then immediately try to reestablish intentional control of the situation, and part of what that will amount to is regretting that I lost it and blaming myself for such an unfortunate and potentially dangerous occurrence. Thus, I will try even harder to stay awake, knowing full well that I will fall asleep again, and wishing that when it happens I do no damage to myself or others.

Now turn to the other side of the analogy, and remember that there is a main complication here: as opposed to the case of being awake, I will never actually know that my behavior is rational—I can only hope that it is. So imagine that, despite all my efforts, I lapse from a kind of behavior of which I can hope that it is rational (because so far I have found no evidence to the contrary) into one that definitely is not. Just as with falling asleep, I am not making myself do that; indeed, lapsing into irrationality amounts precisely to me no longer (even possibly hoping that I am) doing anything at all—no longer exercising any freedom. The lapse does not belong to me: its taking place shows that I am not even there, not actively participating in the living of "my" life. But I may emerge from this incident and resume my previous stance, at which point I will immediately try to reestablish a rational register of communication and action, as well as regret (pass a negative judgment on) what just happened.

An additional element of similarity with the case of falling asleep is that in both cases two modes of being are involved in a relation that is literally incomprehensible: such that it cannot be comprehended (comprised, included) anywhere. When I fall asleep, my waking, intentional mode is suspended and I move to my sleeping mode, and there is no neutral mode in which I can judge my stepping from the one to the other. I can do it as someone who is awake (I can, say, as soon as I am back on my intentional feet, review the data of my brain activity to find out what "went wrong"—or, maybe, right—at the crucial time) and I can also do it as someone who is asleep (I can dream I am doing it, which would be counted here as unintentional behavior), but not as someone who is neither (or both); which means that I am always already committed to (exactly) one of the two modes, and I am missing precisely what it is to move between them. Analogously, there is no neutral stance with respect to reason no longer speaking in me. There is reason condemning that occurrence (and, as we will see, insisting that I ought to, and could, have done otherwise); and there is a purely natural account of it, that describes it as what necessarily had to take place in the empirical world. But there is no mediation between the two, hence no independent judgment on the occurrence. Which is another way of expressing the irreducible logical distinctness of these two registers of conversation—or the nonexistence of a superordinate register into which they could both be translated. Once again, no *Aufhebung* is at hand: our form of life is radically and irremediably divided.

3. Responsibility

If no one is the free author of the evil he commits, how legitimate is it to judge him guilty, and even punish him, for it? To begin with, note that all behavior is part of nature, including the behavior of criminals, judges, and executioners.[21] A criminal represents a fall from the rational state of grace[22] precisely because only a natural explanation is applicable to it. We should not be surprised if, in a perfectly natural sense, other people respond to it in kind. Whether the latter's attitude is based on inducing deterrence, incapacitation, rehabilitation, or manifests simple vindictiveness, it is (at least) another case of nature working itself out—so much so that we can conduct empirical studies to establish whether a given punishment (say, the death penalty) really had the intended effect (say, deterrence). And, of course, transcendental philosophy has nothing to say about any of this: it must accept it as it does any other empirical fact. Empirical (or positive) law is no more part of its purview than empirical physics is—though the *possibility* of both very much concerns it. It is the general currency of judging and punishing practices that it needs to find (conceptual) room for, not any particular outcome of it; and that it does, in the present, positive sense, by subsuming them under (empirical) sociology, or psychology, or history.

This is hardly, however, the end of the matter, for positive judging and punishing practices can themselves be judged by reason: there are metaphysical principles to the doctrine of *Recht*.[23] Treating a criminal in a certain way is something one does; hence (like anything else that is done) it can be looked upon by a rational, impartial spectator and be regarded as what every rational being must do, or not do, to be properly sensitive to reason's concerns—as yet another case of reason being, or not being, practical. More specifically, one might argue that the application to a criminal of certain judicial and correctional procedures amounts to a (partial?) reestablishing of the rational level of interaction that was broken down by the criminal's own behavior; and then reason would undeniably approve of such procedures (consider them good)—just as it would disapprove of (consider evil) any policy that confirmed or even reinforced the purely natural stance adopted by the criminal, thus making reason's triumph even more distant and unlikely.

Kant does not say much about this possibility concerning individual crimes and criminals.[24] But from what he says about the exercise of right during a war we can extrapolate to the individual case. "Right during a war would . . . have to be the waging of war in accordance with principles that always leave open the possibility of leaving the state of nature among states . . . and entering a rightful condition" (M485 VI 347; see also P320 VIII 346–47). Similarly, there may be a "war" waged against an individual whose behavior reason disapproves of, but it must be conducted in such a way as for it to be conceivable that we can at any moment bring it to an end and enter a rightful condition of interaction with that individual (and among ourselves—for the breakdown of rationality implied by a crime usually has a larger scope than the direct dealings with the criminal). Reason would see this behavior as going in the right direction (that is, in reason's own direction): as being guided by (the individual equivalent of) the unachievable but still inspiring idea of perpetual peace.[25] Just as in the wars states conduct against one another they should never lose respect[26] of each other (and of themselves), in the (possibly aggressive, or punitive) confrontations we stage as individuals we have "a duty to respect a human being even in the logical use of his reason, a duty not to censure his errors by calling them absurdities, poor judgment and so forth, but rather to suppose that his judgment must yet contain some truth and to seek this out. . . . The same thing applies to the censure of vice, which must never break out into complete contempt and denial of any moral worth to a vicious human being" (M580 VI 463).[27] This, by the way, is a case in which duty fits well with pragmatic effectiveness: if the person we are trying to refute or censure really *was* entirely irrational, if there were not a grain of truth to what he is saying or a trace of goodness left in his heart, if he had entirely lost his humanity, then he simply could not understand our very refutation or censure of him. "It is foolish . . . when learned men call each other absurd and yet thereafter want to dispute with one another as to whether what they wrote is true or false. For by calling each other absurd, one thus denies to the other all true cognition whatsoever[;] and if I suppose that someone does not possess and is unable to possess any cognition at all, then how can he see my grounds for the falsehood of his cognition, or pride himself on a true cognition and believe himself to possess it? But then how am I in a position to dispute?" (LL81 XXIV 105–6). "We can convince someone only on the basis of his own healthy understanding. If I deny this to him, then it is foolish to reason with him" (N26 XVI 16).[28] Imputing rationality to each other is both a transcendental condition of a rational conversation and an empirical presupposition of such a conversation ever getting anywhere, so much so that "even in the judgments of a madman (however peculiar this remark may seem), on closer investigation there will always be at least a partial truth that can be found" (LL72 XXIV 94).

Since we are natural beings, we are in fact *always* in a state analogous to war: we can never attain that universal agreement in which everyone's reason would echo everyone else's; there is always going to be a residue of idiosyncrasy to our exchanges—an irrational, evil residue—and because of that there is going to be a recurrent belittling and abusing of each other in the name of our personal interests and desires. Reason stigmatizes any such moves, and demands that we always return to patiently weaving the fabric of a coexistence that fits its standards: one in which my reason responds to yours, in which we can think of ourselves as both citizens in a kingdom of ends. It demands that we return to such weaving after any interruption—and the interruptions will be constant, the conversation of reason will (have to) be (conceived as) one that is relentlessly halted, interpolated, intruded into by nature: a nature to whose modes of operation reason asks that we never stoop. Thus, for example, though there is no right to revolution, even in the presence of the most outrageous regime, it is also the case that "once a revolution has succeeded and a new constitution has been established, the lack of legitimacy with which it began and has been implemented cannot release the subjects from the obligation to comply with the new order of things as good citizens, and they cannot refuse honest obedience to the authority that now has the power" (M465 VI 322–33; see also P340 VIII 372–73).[29] There is no rational use of political violence: even when violence was used to obtain a given outcome (hence obtaining that outcome was illegitimate and immoral), the only behavior reason can approve of is one that sidesteps the violence and shows respect for rationality—and trust in it.[30] In the words of Kant's correspondent Biester, "it is easier to decapitate people . . . than courageously to discuss the rational and legal grounds of opposition with a despot, be he sultan or despotic rabble" (C467 XI 456); but it is this more difficult course that reason demands we follow.

Not everything is in principle susceptible to the call of reason for respect and trust, and this distinction will help us move from a purely legal to a properly moral sense in which we can be called responsible for our evil deeds.[31] Consider a crime and an earthquake. They are both irrational sorts of events; reason does not show itself to be practical in them, hence must judge them both negatively—regard them both as evil.[32] But there is a difference as to what is supposed to happen next (what reason would say *must* happen). The rational response to an earthquake will involve mobilizing ourselves and others to save human lives and human prospects for happiness, but the earthquake itself (or the earth) cannot be engaged at the rational level; therefore, insofar as that response involves the earth's tectonics, it will be only in an instrumental way—as something that is purely passive, hence can be manipulated at will. The rational response to a crime, on the other hand, will have to engage the criminal's own rationality: the rational level of discourse that we must try to reestablish after this lapse must

(I noted above) try to include *him*. (This is, ultimately, what it means to say that he is *responsible* for his crime. It is not enough for others to respond to him: *he* owes reason, and himself as a rational being, a response; he is an interlocutor in the rational conversation that is conducted, among other things, on what he did.) Therefore, a purely naturalistic treatment of the criminal would be perceived by reason as an additional failure: he has fallen into natural, animal behavior (which falling constitutes his *being* a criminal) and now continues to be handled like an animal, thus perpetuating reason's failure.[33] As soon as possible, formal considerations of mutual respect must be brought back into play,[34] even if it be only to make the criminal's execution a ritualistic act (no paternalism or sentimentality should have currency here:[35] the criminal *deserves* to be treated as an equal).[36] And, of course, all of this is still true when I am the criminal and the interaction I am talking about is one I have with myself: reason wants me to immediately start dealing with myself *as if I were free* and could freely disassociate myself from the crime I committed. Though the crime itself was a case of nature taking complete charge of my behavior, and of reason (hence freedom) being interrupted (of my turning a sleepy, deaf ear to its call), my retrospective attitude toward it will have to include a distancing from all natural factors that allows me to think of myself as an autonomous, spontaneous agent.

Within such a retrospective attitude, within the register of analysis it opens up, I will find myself facing a situation as formidable as it is unintelligible: one in which, that is, my thinking is subjected to clear, forceful constraints and yet the latter escape all canons of understanding. For I *must* think of myself (or anyone else) now as the kind of being who can be guided by rational principles, and more specifically as the kind of being who could *have been* guided by rational principles even at the time when I committed the crime—and as a matter of fact I was not so guided. Hence, I must think of myself as the kind of being whose lapse *then* was not necessary: who was just as free to fail then as (I must think) I am free to do good now.[37]

There are two aspects to this perplexing point of view. One is the denial of the obvious it brings about. Since *then* I did not behave rationally, all that was left to my behavior was a natural necessity whose outcome *contradicted* rational principles; hence thinking that I could have behaved rationally then amounts to thinking that I could have been exempt from natural necessity—that no collection of natural factors could have forced me to do what I did. In the *New Elucidation* Kant gives a forceful statement of the absurdity of this stance: "of what avail is it if the opposite of an event, which is precisely determined by antecedent grounds, can be conceived when it is regarded in itself, since the opposite still cannot occur in reality, for the grounds necessary for its existence are not present: indeed, it is the grounds necessary for the reverse which are present. The opposite of an event which is assumed to exist in isolation can, nonetheless, you say, be thought, and thus it is possible. But what then? It still cannot come to be, for the grounds which already exist are sufficient to ensure that it can never come to be in fact.... [J]ust as nothing can be conceived which is *more true* than *true*, and nothing *more certain* than *certain*, so nothing can be conceived which is *more determined* than *determined*" (TB21–22 I 399–400). And yet, he comes to realize later, I must take precisely this absurd stance, hold on precisely to the "isolation" (or abstraction) mentioned above, and in doing so I must regard myself as virgin of any empirical influence: "Every evil action must be so considered, whenever we seek its rational origin, as if the human being had fallen into it directly from the state of innocence. For whatever his previous behavior may have been, whatever the natural causes influencing him, whether they are inside or outside him, his action is yet free and not determined through any of these causes; hence the action can and must always be judged as an *original* exercise of his power of choice [*seiner Willkür*]. He should [*sollte*] have refrained from it, whatever his temporal circumstances and entanglements; for through no cause in the world can he cease to be a free agent" (RR86–87 VI 41). I know that, as a natural being, I could not have done otherwise, yet *I must believe differently*—I must think of myself as someone who could. And I must feel repentance for what I did, however vain this feeling might seem: I must experience "a painful feeling aroused by the moral disposition, which is empty in a practical way to the extent that it cannot serve to undo what has been done and would even be absurd...[b]ut..., as pain, is still quite legitimate because reason, when it is a question of the law of our intelligible existence (the moral law), recognizes no distinction of time and asks only whether the event belongs to me as a deed and, if it does, then always connects the same feeling with it morally, whether it was done just now or long ago" (PR219 V 98–99).

The second aspect of the viewpoint we are considering has already surfaced in the last quote: it is the denial of time itself, of the very difference between *now* and *then*—consistent with a judgment of the freedom of the *then* based on the freedom I must conceive myself as enjoying *now*. Judging something in the rational register is judging its necessity as the thing *to do*, not as the thing that must happen (be done) because something else happened (was done) *before*. So in this register time's rhythm is silenced:[38] the ground of what I do must be found in a rational argument detached from all empirical circumstances—those circumstances indeed that make my situation *then* distinguishable from my situation *now*. "Origin (the first origin) is the descent of an effect from its first cause, i.e. from that cause which is not in turn the effect of another cause of the same kind. It can be considered as either *origin according to reason*, or *origin according to time*. In the first meaning, only the effect's *being* is considered; in the second, its *occurrence*, and hence, as an event, it is referred to its *cause in time*. If an effect is referred to a cause which is however bound to it according to the laws of freedom, as is the case with moral evil, then the determination of the power of choice [*Willkür*] to the production of this effect is thought as bound up to its determining ground not in time but merely in the representation of reason; it cannot be derived from some *preceding* state or other, as must always occur, on the other hand, whenever the evil action is referred to its natural cause as *event* in the world. To look for the temporal origin of free actions as free (as though they were natural effects) is therefore a contradiction; and hence also a contradiction to look for the temporal origin of the moral constitution of the human being" (RR85–86 VI 39–40).

How shall we make sense of all of this? *Does* it make sense? Is it consistent with the fairly sanitized notion of freedom I reconstructed so far? Answering these questions requires an analysis of the very notion of *making sense*, to which I will attend in the next section. In closing the present one, I bring out a distinction that is of crucial relevance for getting clear about this extremely confusing situation.

When I consider my past behavior and judge that I ought to, and could, have done otherwise, there are *two* temporally distinct bits of behavior involved: there is the past behavior I pass a negative judgment on *and there is my present judging it*—and *both* of these bits can in turn be (atemporally) judged by reason.[39] It is still an open question what substance, if any, is to be found for my claim that I could have done otherwise; but, even assuming that no substance can be found for it, that I cannot articulate it in any defensible way (which in fact is the case, as we will see), issuing this claim now is precisely what reason requires of me. Taking the absurd stance described above, denying the inevitability of natural occurrences, asserting my freedom in the face of all contrary evidence, is itself something I do; and a rational spectator would have to approve of it. In doing it, I declare the nullity of the natural world and of the necessity that defines it; I state the priority of intellectual ideals over everyday experiences, and my openness to the universal point of view such ideals demand; I explode the pretense that nature be (conceptually) solid and firm. Nature, I am in effect implying then, is itself based on a mysterious act of synthesis: on a commitment that, just as it is made, can also be withdrawn. If it is freedom that ultimately grounds it, freedom can also unground it; if my current stance is absurd, the belief that nature be self-contained and self-sufficient is no less absurd. When hearing this pronouncement, reason must find itself vindicated, and its nobility forcefully (re)affirmed; therefore, whatever conclusion we may reach concerning the content of my retrospective claim, *the issuing of the claim* is exactly right—*more* right indeed because of its awkwardness, since the awkwardness signals that, in the conflict of interpretations constantly raging between nature and reason, I have taken reason's side. My insistence now that I was free then will be regarded by reason as evidence that I am rational, hence free, *now*: that I have resumed the rational level of discourse after its unfortunate interruption.

A time difference helps bring more clarity to this distinction, but is by no means essential—which makes the distinction even more crucially relevant. For, whenever I perform any behavior *a*, I can still distinguish my performance of *a* and my judging, *right there and then, simultaneously with that performance,* that I am performing *a* freely—that is, that while performing it I am being properly sensitive to rational standards—and once again such judging (however indefensible its content might be) is exactly the rational thing to do, and reason will approve it. Reason will look favorably upon someone who, as he is behaving badly, appropriates that behavior to himself by regarding it as an expression of his freedom, just as it would disapprove any self-description that was based instead on a cynical deference to "what the real world looks like" and to "how one *must* behave in order to survive in it"—quite independently of the *un*favorable view it will have of the very behavior that is at issue. As a matter of fact, a lot of this appropriation is *re*appropriation, a lot of what we admit responsibility for is past events; but it is not inconceivable or unheard of that it could be done in the present—that regret could be voiced at the same time as the behavior which is the object of it.[40] This is how I read Kant's statement that "every being that cannot act otherwise than *under the idea of freedom* is just because of that really free in a practical respect" (G95 IV 448): whatever else that being is doing, it is also subsuming what it is doing under the idea of freedom—which is itself a rational, hence a free, act. In the next chapter this notion of being free "in a practical respect" will be examined more closely; what will emerge then are a number of features of my behavior that could indeed be thought of as (collectively) constituting an additional act on my part.[41] For the moment, we can safely say that these features will be judged favorably by reason—however the latter proceeds to judge the behavior on which they are superimposed.

4. The Geography of (Non)sense

We need to turn our attention from the act of judging my behavior, both past and present, to the behavior itself that is being judged, and in doing so it will prove useful to look at one more passage from *Religion within the Boundaries of Mere Reason*: "The human being must [*muß*] make or have made *himself* into whatever he is or should [*soll*] become in a moral sense, good or evil. These two [characters] must be an effect of his free power of choice [*seiner freien Willkür*], for otherwise they could not be imputed to him and, consequently, he could be neither *morally* good or evil" (RR89 VI 44). This sounds like a flat denial of the thesis I proposed a few pages ago: that there is no third option here, that free and evil behavior is impossible. But it is not. The passage comes at the very beginning of a General Observation and simply states the terms of the problem: things must (*müssen*) be this way if we are to take at face value the ordinary judgments people pass on their own and everyone else's behavior (if we are to translate directly from the content of the judging acts to the behavior that is judged). In the following paragraph, Kant addresses the problem in his characteristic transcendental manner, asking how what is the case, what even *must* be the case, is possible: "How it is possible that a naturally evil human being should make [*mache*] himself into a good human being surpasses every concept of ours. For how can an evil tree bear good fruit?" (RR90 VI 44–45). That is, this frail being is irresistibly taken to reverse the order of priorities between sensuous incentives and the moral law: "the difference, whether the human being is good or evil, must not lie in the difference between the incentives that he incorporates into his maxim . . . but in their *subordination* . . . : *which of the two he makes the condition of the other*. It follows that the human being (even the best) is evil only because he reverses the moral order of his incentives in incorporating them into his maxims. . . . Now if a propensity to this [inversion] does lie in human nature, then there is in the human being a natural propensity to evil; and this propensity itself is morally evil. . . . This evil is *radical*, since it corrupts the ground of all maxims; as natural propensity, it is also not to be *extirpated* through human forces, for this could only happen through good maxims—something that cannot take place if the subjective supreme ground of all maxims is presupposed to be corrupted" (RR83 VI 36–37). So, how can any human being, frail and corrupted as she is, be regarded as having the autonomy that is necessary for her to be assigned responsibility for her behavior—good or bad as it may be? Kant's answer is: "in spite of . . . [the] fall [from good into evil], the command that we *ought* to [*sollen*] become better human beings still resounds unabated in our souls; consequently, we must also be capable of it, even if what we can do is of itself insufficient and, by virtue of it, we only make ourselves receptive to a higher assistance inscrutable to us" (RR90 VI 45). How what *must* be the case *can* be the case will only be seen (to a point) by moving to a different modality: there is no way of explaining how that behavior can be the case descriptively (hence actually); the "can" within reach here is one that is granted by the deontic necessity "ought to."[42]

The deontic character of rational necessitation will be addressed in the next chapter; here I only need to point out that the contrast between these two modalities is, once again, a contrast between the lawlike regularities that have currency in (and define) the two *distinct* sensible and intelligible levels of discourse. For, despite the fact that (as I will argue in the last chapter) even Kant's construal of knowledge is ultimately normative, he takes "ought to" to be an operator that does not apply to natural occurrences:[43] "The *ought* expresses a species of necessity and a connection with grounds which does not occur anywhere else in the whole of nature. In nature the understanding can cognize only *what exists*, or has been, or will be. It is impossible that something in it *ought to be* other than what, in all these time-relations, it in fact is; indeed, the *ought*, if one has merely the course of nature before one's eyes, has no significance whatever" (A547 B575). "[N]atural laws . . . never indicate that such-and-such ought to happen; they point merely to the conditions under which a thing does happen" (LE255 XXVII 485). So we can use (the relations between) those two levels of discourse to make sense of the present talk of responsibility for evil: to articulate the *response* I can be expected to give when I or others subject my evil behavior to rational scrutiny.

There is no question that we empirically talk that way, hence that transcendental philosophy should treat such talk as it does any other data: not discount it but rather legitimize it. And there is no question that what legitimation is forthcoming here will have to be based on the limitations imposed on knowledge, and on the conceptual space thus opened for faith (and hope). But there is also an important asymmetry between the amount of detail the legitimation will contain in this case, with respect to the contrasting case of moral behavior.

Say that I judge myself to have behaved immorally in some empirical situation S and claim that I could have behaved otherwise: that I freely chose to be immoral. What does that mean? In order to think freedom in S, I know, I have to abstract from the whole context of spatiotemporal regularities to which S belongs; and, if I do that, and I focus on the sketchy, near-empty thought of what is left of me after completing the abstraction process, it is vacuously the case that nothing could have determined that ghostly being to do anything. There is just not enough content there to make any determination possible; hence, no way anyone could refute my self-attribution of responsibility. But there is also no positive side to this negative outcome, no way I can now proceed to flesh out the "agent" resulting from my abstraction and say what *the law of its causality* is when it (I?) made the immoral choice of letting natural inclinations subordinate reason to them: what *else* determined its behavior, as opposed to the empirical factors I have discarded. Whereas I can provide this articulation for a moral choice: I can expand the relevant "act of will" into the notion of a whole world populated by rational beings whose choices are constantly guided by rational arguments; and I can think of such choices as in principle compatible with natural laws, even of the fundamental "choice" that grounds the empirical world as being made with this compatibility in view,[44] and of my own behavior as actively contributing to its implementation. However inconclusive my rewriting of intellectual conditions into empirical ones is forever going to be, there is something here that I can attempt to rewrite. But with *ir*rational, immoral behavior this project would be a nonstarter: absolutely nothing can get it going; no intelligible irrational world is available for me to use as a standard. "[T]here is actually no evil coming from principles, but only from the forsaking of them" (AP205 VII 293–94). "Evil is only the result of nature not being brought under control. In man there are only germs of good" (E15 IX 448).

Kant often issues perfectly conventional statements to the effect that we brought about our own moral destiny.[45] He has to, since the ordinary person he is getting his evidence from would certainly espouse such statements. And yet, they have a curiously repetitive character: they never build on one another; their collection never amounts to anything remotely resembling a theory; they essentially make the same conventional point over and over again. Nothing here compares with the subtle, substantive analysis of autonomy I discussed in chapter 3. Which, I am arguing now, is exactly as it should be. As I noted at the end of the previous section, it is a good thing (one reason approves of) if people, contradicting all evidence, regard themselves as the origin of evil, and this good thing can bring about other good, rational occurrences. Those who think that way will not invoke too many excuses for their behavior. You will tell them how many over-whelming physical and social factors were operative in making them do what they did, and they will shrug their shoulders and say that still they could have done otherwise;[46] they will even incongruously feel the burden of those very physical and social factors—incongruously identify with the synthetic act that made the whole world possible. "[H]uman beings are not permitted...to remain idle...and let Providence have free rein, as if each could go after his private moral affairs and entrust to a higher wisdom the whole concern of the hu-man race (as regards its moral destiny). Each must, on the contrary, so conduct himself as if everything depended on him" (RR135 VI 100–1). And, as a consequence of such an incongruous attitude, they will, more likely and more often than if they had a more self-serving, cynical one, *do* otherwise.[47] But that is all: no account is (or could be) given of *how it is possible* to be evil, hence we are not even sure of what we are saying when thus claiming responsibility for ourselves or others—in fact, we are not even sure that we are saying *anything*.[48] A nominal definition such as the one we are appealing to when making such claims never provides this kind of warranty: to say that I am free when (or because) I am not constrained is as informative as saying that a closed geometrical figure is a round square when (or because) it has four equal sides and angles and also no angle at all but a constant radius.[49] And yet, it is well enough to operate in this state of un-certainty: people do not really need to know more about *what it means to be evil*. It is fine if all they have in this regard is an empty, inarticulate gesture; they have no use for detailed (intellectual) *dia-bolical* conditions to be painstakingly rewritten in empirical terms.[50] To adapt from what Kant says in another context: "Just as, on the one hand, a somewhat deeper enquiry serves to teach us that the con-vincing and philosophical insight in the case under discussion is *im-possible*, so, on the other hand, one will have to admit, if one considers the matter quietly and impartially, that it is superfluous and *unneces-sary*" (TB358 II 372). Humans, however (insofar as humanity is a form of rationality), definitely have a use for articulating the opposite kind of condition: reason within them does, so how do you expect reason to speak, if not in its own name?

At R190n VI 170n Kant is addressing a criticism of his philosophy made by Rehberg, hence the context is likely to be especially illuminating as he feels challenged to make himself clear by an unsympathetic reader.[51] And this is what he says: "For those who believe that in the critique of pure reason they are faced by intrinsic contradictions whenever they stumble upon the distinctions between the sensible and the intelligible, I here remark that, whenever mention is made of sensuous means to promote the intellectual side (of the purely moral disposition), or of the obstacles which these means put in its way, the influence of these two so unlike principles must never be thought as *direct*. For, as beings of the senses, we can have effect only with respect to the *appearances of the intellectual principle*, i.e. with respect to the determination of our physical powers through the *power of free choice* [*durch freie Willkür*] as exhibited in actions, whether in opposition to the law or in its favor, so that cause and effect are represented as in fact of like kind. But as regards what transcends the senses (the subjective principle of morality in us which lies hidden in the incomprehensible property of freedom) . . . *we have no insight into anything* [*sehen . . . nichts . . . ein*] *in it which touches upon the relation in the human being of cause to effect apart from its law (though this is enough by itself)*; i.e. we cannot *explain* to ourselves the possibility of actions as events in the world of the senses from a human being's moral constitution as [something] imputable to them, precisely because these actions are free, whereas the grounds of explanation of any event must be drawn from the world of the senses" (second-to-last italics added). In large part, this text reiterates the point I made earlier that reason never directly engages the inclinations, and in general the sensible and the intelligible never overlap. What is new and interesting is that the one and only positive conceptual (insightful) specification we can take from "what transcends the senses" and try to understand in causal terms is the rational law, *which is enough by itself*. That is, as I would gloss this statement, it provides all the inspiration we need for better, freer behavior; as for behavior that is evil, we do not need to be told (or tell ourselves) anything more than that we ought to, and consequently could, have done otherwise. "The *cause* of the universal gravity of all matter in the world is equally unknown to us, so much so that we can even see that we shall never have cognition of it, since its very concept presupposes a first motive force unconditionally residing within it. Yet gravity is not a mystery; it can be made manifest to everyone, since its *law* is sufficiently cognized. . . . With respect to that which is universal human duty to have cognition of (namely anything moral) there can be no mystery" (RR165n VI 138–39n).

When accounting for a person's change of heart (from evil to good), Kant contradicts his own regulative principle that everything in nature happens by a continuous process[52] and states that this change "cannot be effected through gradual *reform* but must rather be effected through a *revolution* in the disposition of the human being. . . . And so a 'new man' can come about only through a kind of rebirth, as it were a new creation" (RR92 VI 47).[53] Clearly, it is not anything natural that he is talking about here, anything that can belong to an orderly network of natural necessities—anything that can *happen*.[54] But we can still lead our empirical lives in the wake of the injunction suggested by this intellectual ideal; we can comb the fabric of those lives searching for evidence compatible with the claim that our (alleged) intellectual counterpart did have such a rebirth. We have enough information to know what to look for as we do such combing. Reason, however, is not going to provide any clue for how we could think of ourselves as actuating an analogous conversion *to evil*, or of how a world could exist in which nature *and evil*—as an additional principle, as something over and above nature—are compatible. "An infinite progression in good can easily be thought, but not in evil" (LM409 XXVIII 770). And, if someone thinks otherwise, let them offer us a logic of evil that is as independent of natural necessity as Kant's logic of good is, and has as much explanatory dignity to it—that does not reduce to saying that people do evil *because they want to*, or *because it is evil*.[55] What we are facing here is the rock bottom of Kant's (meta)ethical convictions; we are confronting the ultimate challenge he launches to anyone who still wants to oppose him on this issue. Do better if you can; otherwise, resign yourself to admitting that, as that greatest of Kantian ethicists, Hannah Arendt, well understood and articulated in lucid detail, in the very face of a monstrosity beyond belief, evil is intrinsically banal.

Here, then, is how I would summarize Kant's resolution of the agonizing problem of how it is possible that we in fact be free agents:

1. naturally necessitated behavior belongs to the real, sensible world, indeed that it be naturally necessitated is part of what it means for it to belong there;
2. free, rational behavior belongs to an unreal, intelligible world, but we know what the law of its causality is and we can work

at a suitable rewriting of this law in sensible terms, in the hope
that such a rewriting will find its way in the sensible world
as well;

3. free, irrational behavior belongs to the same unreal, intelligible
level of discourse but never acquires enough structure to
make it into a world—we have no concept of what the law of
its causality might be[56] and hence no way of even beginning
to understand what a rewriting of it in sensible terms might
look like.

Therefore, we can conceive of the same spatiotemporal events as overdetermined by natural and by free, rational patterns, but not of them
as overdetermined by natural and by free, irrational ones: when we talk
of a free, irrational choice, we *abandon* all notions of causality.[57] And to
be sure we can (indeed we must) continue to blame ourselves for our
evil behavior, since in doing so we are only voicing a negative, abstractive possibility;[58] but we do not even know what sense it would
make to say that we are *really* (that is, in the sensible world) responsible
for such behavior.[59]

The conclusions we have thus reached can be generalized to an
instructive remark about Kant's overall logic. It has become common,
since P. F. Strawson's (justly) famous book, to think of Kant as concerned with establishing the bounds of sense. And, of course, Strawson
was critical of the particular way in which Kant proceeded to establish
such bounds—and in *Kant's Copernican Revolution* I defended Kant
from Strawson's criticism. But this whole discussion would seem to
presuppose that the bounds of sense be a clearly drawn line: that the
distinction between what makes sense and what does not be an all-
or-nothing one—one that sharply discriminates between full-fledged
meaning and total absurdity. And this simple picture does no justice to
the complexity of Kant's intellectual performance. The reason why he
can give Strawson and others the impression of inconsistently trying to
think both sides of that line is that, in fact, the line does not exist.[60]
There definitely is for him *the rational idea of* full-fledged meaning; but
this idea is (as all others) never realized, hence one way of describing
what Kant is doing is as an exploration of how much meaning can
be retained while some of its ideal conditions are lost. There is the
ordinary (non)sense of thinking of objects as perfectly determined
though, if pressed, we would be constitutionally unable to provide any
such determination; insofar as we are empirically used to it, we do not
even notice it.[61] And there is a lot more: what has surfaced here is

how rich and varied the spectrum of (non)sense is—how gradually humans lose their grasp of what they are talking and thinking about, and how desperately, in the absence of any clear criteria of significance, they remain attached to what small, fragmentary particles of meaning are still in their hold.

"[T]he greatest demand that one can put on a philosopher is always that he should define his concept," Kant says in the *Vienna Logic* (LL355 XXIV 912), and hence "[t]he endeavor of philosophers is of course to attain the greatest perfection through definitions" (LL359 XXIV 916); but then he hastens to add that "[w]e must not say . . . that that of which no definition has been given does not deserve any treatment. For there are many things of which we cannot give a complete concept" (LL359 XXIV 916–17). "To begin initially with the definition, then, as happens in most philosophies, and not to commit oneself to anything until one first has the definition, is actually to make all investigation impossible" (LL358–59 XXIV 916). "To aspire to a definition is to venture upon unnecessary difficulties. The mania for method and the imitation of the mathematician, who advances with a sure step along a well-surfaced road, have occasioned a large number of such mishaps on the slippery ground of metaphysics" (TB117 II 71).[62] Most often, I have to work with incomplete concepts; but that should not stop me, because "I can draw consequences from every mark of a thing[;] if I cognize only a few marks in the thing, then a few consequences can be drawn" (LL358 XXIV 916)—and to be able to draw a few consequences *is still something*: "there is still a great deal which can be asserted with the highest degree of certainty about the object in question" (TB117 II 71).

"[T]hat we understand what is meant by . . . [a religious mystery] does not happen just because we understand *one by one* the words with which the mystery is enunciated, i.e. by attaching a meaning to each separately, but because, when combined together in one concept, the words still allow a meaning and do not, on the contrary, thereby escape all thought" (R169n VI 144n). On the surface, this statement is a simple one; but only deceptively so. For when does a combination of separate meanings, indeed, "escape all thought"—on this side of the "*nihil negativum*" (A291 B348) of plain contradiction,[63] that is? We can come up with the notion of a rational world devoid of all those spatiotemporal conditions that give content and substance to any thoughts of ours (and without which, we know, "[t]houghts . . . are empty," A51 B75)[64]—yet this still counts as thinking.[65] We can even mention a free, irrational choice that happens in no world at all, and still we will be putting together words in a way that is not only grammatically appropriate but also has some level of logical legitimacy; we will be issuing sentences that cannot just be excluded from the range of meaningful expressions.[66] In the next chapter, I will show how all these different nuances of meaning (or, which is the same, of objectivity) are made possible by the commitment to a transcendental idealist framework; here I limit myself to pointing out that Kant does something more than playing (irresponsibly, according to Strawson) with the bounds of sense—he plays with the very notion that there be any such bounds. He plays at redrawing the bounds over and over again, as contexts shift and new tasks and standards come to the fore.

IMPERATIVES

1. Laws for Imperfect Beings

Humans are rational but (we know already) only imperfectly so. Reason is one among several factors (possibly, and indirectly) determining their behavior; it provides one among several patterns within which that behavior might fall. In fact, more than simple diversity is at stake here: granted the usual qualifications about the incommensurability of spheres, we are dealing with genuine opposition. "[E]very admixture of incentives taken from one's own happiness is a hindrance to providing the moral law with influence on the human heart" (PR265 V 156). If the law that explains some or all of my behavior is the maximization of pleasure, this law can manifest only local, coincidental agreement with (any suitable empirical rewriting of) the rational one, and will inevitably clash with it sooner or later—I will find myself doing things *because of it* that reason does not approve of. "[W]henever incentives other than the law itself (e.g. ambition, self-love in general, yes, even a kindly instinct such as sympathy) are necessary to determine the power of choice [*Willkür*] to *lawful* actions, it is purely accidental that these actions agree with the law, for the incentives might equally well incite its violation" (RR78 VI 30–31). This situation has important consequences for the internal logic of reason's utterances (as issued to humans):[1] they are *laws*, indeed, expressing the (unconditional) necessity of certain kinds of behavior, and yet those kinds of behavior do not always take place.[2] The Principle of

Necessity (PN) asserting that everything necessary is true does not hold for the necessity expressed by rational laws.

It is customary to distinguish those modalities for which PN holds from those for which it does not by calling the former *alethic* and the latter *deontic*; and we are all familiar with such mundane examples of deontic modalities as "One must not cross an intersection with a red light"—which is perfectly compatible with many people doing just that (and sometimes thumbing their nose at the law as they do). The necessity referred to in the rational/moral/legal register of discourse, then (as opposed to the one current in logic, physics, or metaphysics), is a deontic one: one for which auxiliaries like "ought to" and "should" are more appropriate than "must." "[W]hat is at issue here is not whether this or that happened; . . . instead, reason . . . commands what ought to happen" (G62 IV 408). Or, more elaborately, "in the case of the practical, . . . [reason] presupposes its own unconditioned (in regard to nature) causality, i.e., freedom, because it is aware of its moral command. . . . [H]ere, however, the objective necessity of the action, as duty, is opposed to that which it, as an occurrence, would have if its ground lay in nature and not in freedom (i.e., in the causality of reason), and the action which is morally absolutely necessary can be regarded physically as entirely contingent (i.e., what necessarily *should* [*sollte*] happen often does not). . . . [R]eason expresses this necessity not through a *be* (happening) but through a should-be [*Sein-Sollen*]" (J273 V 403).[3]

In ordinary speech, an alethic modality is often expressed by a simple statement in the indicative. "Nothing travels faster than light" is an acceptable rendering of the physical necessity of the relevant law, as is "Any object is identical with itself" of the relevant logical necessity. Deontic modalities, on the other hand, are often expressed in the imperative, thus signaling that they are not supposed to be descriptive (in the case we are interested in, of human behavior) but normative or prescriptive. According to Kant, they would be descriptive of the behavior of saints: "[T]his 'ought' is strictly speaking a 'will' that holds for every rational being under the condition that reason in him is practical without hindrance" (G96 IV 449). "The moral *'ought'* is . . . [a person's] necessary *'will'* as a member of an intelligible world" (G101 IV 455). But, as far as we, imperfect rational beings, are concerned, they do not state facts, they issue *commands*. Their content presents itself to us not as a report on what we (unfailingly) do but as a *duty* to be fulfilled, one we are *obliged* to fulfill—and yet also one that, quite often, we will not be able or willing to fulfill. "[T]he concept of *duty* . . .

contains that of a good will though under certain subjective limitations and hindrances" (G52 IV 397). "[I]mperatives are only formulae expressing the relation of objective laws of volition in general to the subjective imperfection of the will of this or that rational being, for example, of the human will" (G67 IV 414). "The dependence upon the principle of autonomy of a will that is not absolutely good (moral necessitation) is *obligation*. This, accordingly, cannot be attributed to a holy being. The objective necessity of an action from obligation is called *duty*" (G88 IV 439). "[F]or a being in whom reason quite alone is not the determining ground of the will, . . . [a practical] rule is an *imperative*, that is, a rule indicated by an 'ought'" (PR154 V 20). "[D]uty is the idea of a perfect will, as the norm for an imperfect one" (LE230 XXIX 606). It is time to ask: What (if anything) grounds the force of these imperatives? On what authority can they command that we act in certain ways? And why should we care?

There is no mystery in the force of technical or *hypothetical* imperatives (just as there is none in the significance of technical value judgments): they specify necessary conditions for achieving certain ends and are binding only for those who have chosen those ends. Reason will often be mobilized in determining their structure, but only (we know) in a subordinate role—as a slave to desires, hence as perversely distracted from *its own* ends. "Whoever wills the end also wills (*insofar as reason has decisive influence on his actions*) the indispensably necessary means to it that are within his power" (G70 IV 417; italics added).[4] If you want to kill your neighbor and to get away with it, take precautions not to be seen by potential witnesses, some such imperative might say, and it would be clear to all concerned that its force derives from the presumed intention of getting away with murder: leaving potential witnesses around (instrumental reason tells us) would make that goal unattainable, hence whoever wants to attain the goal *ought to* obey the imperative (which, on the other hand, *is* an imperative because he will not always succeed in obeying it—or even want to so succeed).

If there were ends we could impute to all humans (or all rational beings), we would be able to say of the corresponding hypothetical imperatives that they are binding for all humans (or all rational beings)—we could lift them from the hypothetical to the assertoric state. At first sight, happiness would seem to be a good candidate for such a universal end; but the assertoric character of the corresponding imperative ("Do whatever makes you happy") is largely a delusion, due to the vagueness of what "happiness" refers to. "Only experience can teach what brings us joy" (M371 VI 215), and that will be different things for different people; so the agreement on happiness as a goal is a purely verbal one. "[The] principle [of happiness] . . . does not prescribe the very same practical rules to all rational beings, even though the rules come under a common heading, namely that of happiness" (PR169 V 36). And, even if there were a factual agreement (if all existing humans agreed on what in fact makes them happy), this might still be only an accidental, contingent occurrence. "The determining ground would still be only subjectively valid and merely empirical and would not have that necessity which is thought in every law, namely objective necessity from a priori grounds, unless one had to say that this necessity is not practical at all but only physical, namely that the action is as unavoidably forced from us by our inclination as is yawning when we see others yawn. . . . This latter remark seems at first glance to be mere cavilling at words; but it defines the terms of the most important distinction that can ever be considered in practical investigations" (PR160 V 26). The important issue brought out here (which is indeed all but mere cavilling) is the distinction between genuine laws and empirical generalizations.[5] If all humans happened to agree that happiness consists of eating vanilla ice cream, one could still not use this agreement to ground a substantive assertoric (deontic) law ("Eat vanilla ice cream") because the next human who is born might contradict it—and thus prove, maybe, that what was going on with all the others is only that they had all been subjected to the same physical or psychological conditioning, from which the (fortunate) newborn is exempt. In the terms current in contemporary philosophy of science, genuine laws should support counterfactual reasoning.

The only imperatives that can be asserted unconditionally, then, are those promulgating the only values that are themselves unconditional: rational values. Imperfectly rational beings are subjected by their own reason to the obligation of being perfectly rational: "To make a rule for oneself presupposes that we set our intelligible self, i.e., humanity in our own person, over against our sensible being, i.e., man in our own person, and thus contrast man as the agent with humanity as the law-giving party" (LE330 XXVII 579). What obligation that is we know already: since no reference to specific circumstances can be accepted without limiting the import of the law, the content of a *categorical* imperative must follow from the purely formal notion of what it is to be a rational agent and a rational law of her behavior. Any human being will always have a particular goal in mind when she acts;[6] but from a rational point of view that must be regarded as entirely irrelevant, and her behavior must be accounted for, without residue, as following from the assumption of rationality—as being what it is because it is rational for it to be so. "This order of concepts of the determination of the will [that is, its being determined by the moral law] must not be lost sight of, since otherwise we mis-understand ourselves and believe that we are contradicting ourselves even where everything stands together in the most perfect harmony" (PR228 V 110). "[Epicurus's] chief divergence from the Stoics con-sisted only in his placing the motive in . . . pleasure, which they quite rightly refused to do" (PR233 V 115). Even when it comes to hap-piness, the proper relation of it with rationality is that the latter de-mands the former (generalized to everyone) as an end, not the other way around: "[T]here is . . . a law . . . to promote . . . [one's] happiness not from inclination but from duty; and it is then that . . . [one's] conduct first has properly moral worth" (G54 IV 399). "[T]he law to promote the happiness of others arises not from the presupposition that this is an object of everyone's choice but merely from this: that the form of universality, which reason requires as the condition of giving to a maxim of self-love the objective validity of a law, becomes the determining ground of the will; and so the object (the happiness of others) was not the determining ground of the pure will; this was, instead, the mere lawful form alone" (PR167 V 34). We will return to such priority issues later; now we need to take a closer look at the obligatory character of our relation to the rational law.

The conflict between nature and reason is a radical one, as we have seen; that we are natural beings is the source of radical evil. Natural inclinations are an obstacle to freedom;[7] our deference to them is the main manifestation of our frailty. A confrontation is constantly staged in us between those inclinations and reason; and what promotes one party will inevitably mortify the other. Insofar as reason is the basis of free, autonomous behavior, this confrontation implies that moves that are constraining (for the inclinations) will end up having a generally liberating effect. "Resistance that counteracts the hindering of an effect promotes this effect and is consistent with it. Now whatever is wrong is a hindrance to freedom in accordance with universal laws. . . . Therefore, . . . coercion that is opposed to this (as a *hindering of a hindrance to freedom*) is consistent with freedom in accordance with universal laws, that is, it is right" (M388 VI 231).[8] Reason often mani-fests itself as coercive, which has important consequences for how we feel about it because "the negative effect on feeling (by the infringe-ment upon the inclinations that takes place) is itself feeling" (PR199

V 73): when heeding the command issued by reason, humans cannot but feel their natural being denied, their animality rejected and humiliated—as both their drives are inhibited and any conception they might have of their personal worth, independent of the rational command itself, is refuted. "[T]he moral law . . . must by thwarting all our inclinations produce a feeling that can be called pain" (PR199 V 73). "[T]he moral law strikes down self-conceit" (PR199 V 73). "[W]hat in our own judgment infringes upon our self-conceit humiliates. Hence the moral law unavoidably humiliates every human being when he compares with it the sensible propensity of his nature" (PR200 V 74).[9] All claims that moral worth is to be found in one's own merit, as opposed to stern, uncompromising subjection to duty, must be regarded as foolish, and the allegedly (super)meritorious agents must be reminded of how much they owe to everyone else: "One need only reflect a little and one will always find a debt that he has somehow incurred with respect to the human race (even if it were only that, by the inequality of human beings in the civil constitution, one enjoys advantages on account of which others must all the more do without), which will prevent the self-complacent image of *merit* from supplanting the thought of *duty*" (PR264n V 155n). "[A]ll acts of kindness are but small repayments of our indebtedness" (LE210 XXVII 456).

The positive counterpart of this feeling of annihilation is *respect*, since what "humiliates . . . is an object of the greatest *respect* and so too the ground of a positive feeling" (PR199 V 73):[10] a feeling which is "not . . . *received* by means of influence . . . [but] *self-wrought* by means of a rational concept, which signifies merely consciousness of the *subordination* of my will to a law without the mediation of other influences on my sense," and which is "the representation of a worth that infringes upon my self-love" (G56n IV 401n). Mention of this feeling, Kant is keen on saying,[11] does not infect his pure morality with empirical matters: whereas the occurrence of any other pleasure or displeasure[12] is a simple (and passively received) fact of life, in the case of respect reason can prove to itself that an imperfectly rational being would have to experience it—whenever reason asserts itself and blows away the opposition. What this experience will *feel like* cannot be decided on rational grounds, of course; but that something like this will have to be felt can be. In other words, respect *as a feeling* does not fall within the purview of rational analysis—*only its concept does*.[13]

The proper object of respect is the rational law itself. "Any respect for a person is properly only respect for the law (of integrity and so forth) of which he gives us an example" (G56n IV 401n).[14] Here is deontologism with a vengeance (literally!): any goal a human being might set for herself, any state she might want to realize, even any person she might conceive as a role model must kneel shamefully before rationality as such, before the conformity to a law that is as supreme as it is abstract, uncaring, entirely self-referential. This law is the only possible bearer of dignity, "that is, ... [of] unconditional, incomparable worth" (G85 IV 436).

And yet, though "[t]he feeling of the inadequacy of our capacity for the attainment of an idea *that is a law for us* is *respect*" (J140 V 257)—though, that is, what we feel this way is our impotence—there are two sides to our discomfort, and one of them is ennobling, indeed can be exhilarating. Because, in making us unhappy with what we are, with our *nature*, respect also shows us able to transcend *the whole* of nature, to recognize ourselves as denizens of another, *un*natural, world, and entitled to assert the superiority of the latter (and of its law) over everything that is real. If respect is humbling, it is a humbling of ourselves *by ourselves* (the positive counterpart of our feeling of annihilation is once again a feeling of ourselves, this time as the annihilating agent);[15] hence it manifests a *sublime* presence that belongs in our own mind[16]—though it can find useful and inspiring reminders, analogues, symbols in natural phenomena. Or, I should say, it does so manifest our sublimity—and the analogical relation of sublime nature to us—modulo the constitutional vagueness of any reference to "ourselves" in the intelligible world, and of any identification we might want to carry out with the reason speaking "in us." For, to feel that way, we must give up every characteristic that would define us as specific empirical individuals—hence also as individuals at all: as *this* person as opposed to any other. "[I]t is just in ... [the] independence of maxims from all ... [natural] incentives that their sublimity consists, and the worthiness of every rational subject to be a lawgiving member in the kingdom of ends" (G88 IV 439). "[N]ot so much the object as rather the disposition of the mind in estimating it [is] to be judged *sublime*. ... [T]rue sublimity must be sought only in the mind of the one who judges, not in the object in nature, the judging of which occasions this disposition in it" (J139 V 255–56). "[T]he feeling of the sublime in nature is respect for our own vocation, which we show to an object in nature through a certain subreption (substitution of a respect for the object instead of for the idea of humanity in our subject)" (J141 V 257). "[W]e gladly call ... [fearful] objects sublime because they elevate the strength of our soul above its usual level, and allow us to discover within ourselves a capacity for resistance of quite another kind, which gives us the courage to measure ourselves against the apparent all-powerfulness of nature" (J144–45 V 261). "[T]he sublime in nature is only improperly so called, and should properly be ascribed only to the manner of thinking, or rather to its foundation in human nature" (J160 V 280).[17]

We are now ready to address the problem posed (in various forms) earlier: what is the source of the authority moral commands have on me? And, in addressing it, I will begin by posing another one: what authority issues from physical or political power? Ultimately, commands based on the latter are binding for me because of the connection they establish, directly through the use of force or indirectly through the reference to a social contract, with my empirical integrity—which is going to be challenged unless I obey them. But my empirical integrity is not all there is to me: as indeed the ambivalent feeling of respect shows, I have a rational integrity as well.[18] Or, rather, I can conceive of myself as possibly having one; and in the name of that conception I can come to disregard whatever appeal to my empirical integrity cannot be rewritten as rational. I can come to judge, and even feel, any such appeal as reduced to nothing, hence as having no purchase on me, if reason does not sanction it. *And* I can think that the authority to which I thus defer originates in myself, that I am myself the seat of a rational power which I thus recognize as higher than any empirical one. Whereas the claim an officer or the state has on me depends upon my giving way to my natural drive to self-preservation, hence upon my being reduced to an obtuse wheel in nature's irresistible mechanism, the claim reason has on me is one I have on myself.[19] I heed reason's commands because *I want to*; indeed because it is precisely by heeding them that *I*, for the first time, *want*.

Why, then, ought I to identify with reason? What exactly is wrong with "perverting" it into an instrumental use? If such questions are meant to ask for more than just a reiteration of reason's intrinsic normativity, if the "wrong" evoked here is one that is supposed to impress someone who positions herself outside reason and is considering whether she wants to enter its territory, then the answer can only be: nothing is wrong, not in the categorical sense that is relevant to reason (the one Socrates is challenged to elucidate in the *Republic*, as opposed to the hypothetical one that Glaucon and Adeimantus bring up as a common, *natural*, but for them unsatisfying alternative: being immoral is wrong because it is socially unacceptable), for when one gives up on reason (or stands outside it) only technical, hypothetical laws are going to be applicable to one's behavior.[20] One will be missing a whole register of conversation, judgment, and action; and will not understand when others speak, judge, or move in ways relevant to this register. One will not be human in the Kantian sense, but only in the biological, natural sense. And that, we might say, is all right (as it is for cows and pigs, for stones and planets), if it were not that this positive way of putting it (as opposed to "nothing is wrong") involves a use of the word (and concept of) "right" these "people" have no access to. They can only say "right *for something*," and they can stop inquiring what that something is whenever they "like"—except that none of this behavior (whatever they might think or say about it; indeed *inclusive* of what they think or say about it) will really belong to them; it will be nature doing its usual (heteronomously necessitating) job on them. Therefore, if one understands the unconditional "right" that is implied here—if one is asking "why ought I to be rational?" with this categorical sense in mind, expecting some kind of *final* answer—one is already in reason's territory,[21] and her question has already, automatically, been answered. For then one is not a stone or a planet, a cow or a pig: one has proven herself sensitive to reason's demands,[22] though one might also try her best to silence them and to think of herself as not at all different from an irrational object. That she thinks that way, however, does not make it so, as it does not when people believe logically contradictory statements. In both cases, we need to help them see how things (including *they themselves*) are—and hence see that they *could not* be as they presume. Which might or might not work, of course: no guarantee is forthcoming here that anyone will see the light.[23]

In the *Groundwork*, Kant puts this matter starkly and straightforwardly: "for us human beings it is quite impossible to explain how and why the *universality of a maxim as law* and hence morality interests us. This much only is certain: it is not *because the law interests us* that it has validity for us . . . ; instead, the law interests because it is valid for us as human beings" (G106 IV 460–61). That is, we cannot explain why we should find ourselves bound to morality, other than by saying that what is expressed in this bond is our commitment to our own humanity—or rationality. That I *do* identify with reason and I do feel the force of the categorical imperative is, Kant thinks, unquestionable: "[t]he concept of duty . . . is not only incomparably simpler, clearer and, for practical use, more readily grasped and more natural to everyone than any motive derived from happiness . . . ; it is also . . . far *more powerful*, forceful, and promising of results" (P287 VIII 286). But it is just as unquestionable that no philosophical account can be provided of this force. Philosophy can say what it is to be human, that is, rational;

it cannot tell any of us why being human should matter to her, let alone provide arguments that will convince her otherwise in case she *felt* it did not matter—and it is feeling that is needed here. "[T]he moral law has precepts, . . . but no motives; it lacks executive authority, and this is the moral feeling. The latter is no distinction between good and evil, but a motive in which our sensibility concurs with our understanding. Men may indeed have good powers of judgment in moral matters, but no feeling" (LE138 XXVII 361). "Moral feeling is the capacity to be moved by the moral as an incentive" (N499 XV 336).[24] Which is but another angle on that radical evil (or frailty) of the human condition we discussed in the previous chapter: "[A]lthough the understanding is well aware of . . . [morality], such a motivating ground still has no driving force. Moral perfection meets with approval, to be sure, in our judgment, but since this motivating ground of moral perfection is produced from the understanding, it does not have a driving force so strong as the sensory one, and that is the weakness of human nature" (LE85 XXVII 293). The classical issue of *akrasia* resurfaces here, with a complex Kantian twist that turns it from an occasional experience into a transcendental necessity: if indeed the will is, as we have seen, "nothing other than practical reason," then the will is constitutionally unable to have any (direct) effect on our behavior. What reason can judge as willed behavior is always behavior that belongs to nature, hence to something other than (our) reason, *other than us*. We can struggle to *identify*, not regard ourselves as simply *identical*, with it.[25]

To provide additional detail for this negative outcome we must go back to the delicate, frustrating relation between the real world in which we conduct our ordinary affairs and the ideal one in which we *hope* to be present. If the claims of rationality that we conceive as completely vindicated in the latter world are going to have any re-levance to our behavior in the former, it is because something existing there—that is, something natural—does the real job of bringing about real behavior consistent with them: because, say, the education I have *in fact* received and the self-discipline I have *in fact* developed as a consequence[26] offer successful real resistance to the temptation I feel to get out of some particular trouble by uttering a lie. "The foundation of this practice [of being content with conforming with duty] lies . . . in the negative and positive discipline of the body, by cultivation of . . . [man's] mental powers, enlargement of his knowledge, removal of his errors, limitation and refinement of his capacities for desire; a resist-ance that, by toughening of the body, he puts up to all contrary incli-nations, and to flabbiness" (LE392 XXVII 656). "On the approval and assenting judgment of... [the] intellectual man, the worth of the sensory man depends; the latter will retain this approval if he has been able, by sensory cultivation, to further acquaint himself with the laws of the intellectual man, and to pay attention to them in his actions, and test his own worth accordingly" (LE423 XXVII 695). But the connection between these two conditions taking place in the two different worlds—between the moral judgment issuing from consideration of what would be the case in the kingdom of ends and the "corresponding" natural process leading me (possibly) to faultless behavior in the spatiotemporal domain—is going to remain just as mysterious and undecidable as the one between the noumenal and the phenomenal me, and for just as inescapable conceptual reasons: there are, in this case too, no adequate demonstrative tools available for carrying out a successful identification, and no empirical rewriting of intellectual standards is going to attain the required completeness.

I have articulate, substantive views about what ought to be done, and about what is done; and I can use the former to pass judgment on the latter. I can even say how certain things that are done (or happen) are more conducive than certain other things that are done (or happen) to the doing of things that ought to be done.[27] But I do not have the faintest notion of how my views about what ought to be done could relate to, let alone determine, anything specific that is done—*including* those very things that are done and are more conducive than other things that are done to doing things that ought to be done. For, once again, determination can only take place in the same world; and, as for the "correspondence" mentioned above between the two worlds, I am not in a position to construe it as anything more than an hopeful gesture. "The causal relation of the intellectual to the sensitive and the determination of sensibility in accordance with merely intellectual principles or vice versa cannot be understood by us at all" (N147 XVII 611)."When I judge by understanding that the action is morally good, I am still very far from doing this action of which I have so judged. But if this judgment moves me to do the action, that is the moral feeling.[28] Nobody can or ever will comprehend how the understanding should have a motivating power; it can admittedly judge, but to give this judgment power so that it becomes a motive able to impel the will to the performance of an action—to understand this is the philosophers' stone.... When... sensibility abhors what the understanding considers abhorrent, this is the moral feeling. It is quite impossible to bring a man to the point of feeling the abhorrence of vice, for I can only tell him what my understanding perceives, and I do indeed bring him also to the point of perceiving it; but that he should feel the abhorrence, if his senses are not susceptible to it, is impossible. Such a thing simply cannot be produced. . . . Yet we can indeed produce a *habitus* . . . through imitation and frequent exercise. . . . Education and religion should therefore set out to instil an immediate abhorrence of evil in actions, and an immediate delight in their morality" (LE71–73 XXVII 1428–30).[29]

2. Virtue and Goodness

Two important, related qualifications are in order, before we proceed—indeed as useful steps in developing what follows. First, though respect for people is only subordinate to respect for the law, it is also true that concrete examples of moral behavior are of great value in the course of moral education—and in general in sustaining our hope that such behavior is indeed possible. "[The] predisposition to the good is cultivated in no better way than by just adducing the *example* of good people (as regards their conformity to law)" (RR93 VI 48). Since the only things or events whose real possibility we can establish are the actual ones,[30] and the actuality of rational behavior can never be established beyond doubt, humans could easily be led to despair. So here cases that appear to be taken from ordinary life will be of help. "A good example (exemplary conduct) should not serve as a model but only as a proof that it is really possible to act in conformity with duty" (M593 VI 480).[31] To be sure, these cases will reveal themselves, when carefully scrutinized, to be as abstract as our earlier references to artificial games or mathematical models: it is not with the complexity of a whole human experience that we deal here (for then we would be subject to the same uncertainty concerning "motivations" as we are in our own case), but with a stylized narrative that foregrounds the most obviously edifying elements.

"One tells . . . [a ten-year-old boy] the story of an honest man whom someone wants to induce to join the calumniators of an innocent but otherwise powerless person (say, Anne Boleyn, accused by Henry VIII of England). He is offered gain, that is, great gifts or high rank; he rejects them. . . . Now threats of loss begin. Among these calumniators are his best friends, who now refuse him their friendship; close relatives, who threaten to disinherit him (he is not wealthy); powerful people, who can pursue and hurt him in all places and circumstances; a prince who threatens him with loss of freedom and even of life itself. . . . [R]epresent him . . . firm in his resolution to be truthful, without wavering or even doubting" (PR264–65 V 155–56). There is no question that this is a much fictionalized Thomas More, turned from a real person into a character of a morality tale:[32] into a too-good-to-be-true instance of that *virtue* which is defined as "the capacity and considered resolve to withstand a strong but unjust opponent . . . with respect to what opposes the moral disposition *within us*" (M513 VI 380).[33] And yet there is also no denying the tale's inspirational value, Kant thinks, to the extent that it adds flesh and blood to what would otherwise remain a purely formal injunction[34] and can direct a well-meaning but still somewhat rudimentary pupil to the sorts of actions in which his good will may find more proper manifestation.[35] Such tools are not to be discarded, then, as long as priorities are straight: as long as the law is seen as the decisive factor in establishing respect and humans are honored only as the (hypothetical) carriers of it—and do not become objects of independent veneration, thus bringing morality down to an empirical level. "[I]t is not comparison with any other human being whatsoever (as he is), but with the *idea* (of humanity [that is, of rationality]), as he ought to be, and so comparison with the law, that must serve as the constant standard of a teacher's instruction" (M593 VI 480).[36] When looked upon in this light, indeed, the very fictionalization of the examples (as well as Kant's lack of concern with, or even positive discouragement of, finding out what their actual details were—and whether they were in fact as good as they are made sound) can be seen as an important signal that their value is entirely dependent on the value of the law. Generating examples of this sort is a main component of the activity of rewriting intellectual conditions in ways that show their relevance to our ordinary, spatiotemporal experience, as a guide to what *ought to* take place there; so, if the intellectual conditions overthrow the literal truth of that experience, that is just as it should be. As we already noted above, when goodness trumps reality, reason cannot but issue its approval.[37]

The second qualification has to do with Kant's extreme deontologism. The obvious alternative, as a moral philosophy, would be teleologism, where morality is defined by its search for a *telos*, a goal, an ideal object or state.[38] That Kant is a deontologist does not mean, however, that objects and goals have no role in his view; here as always, it is a matter not of ruling out important elements of our experience but of being clear about what comes conceptually first and what has only a dependent status. Thus consider the following passage from the second *Critique*: "The only objects of a practical reason are . . . those of the *good* and the *evil*. For by the first is understood a necessary object of the faculty of desire, by the second, of the faculty of aversion, both, however, in accordance with a principle of reason"

(PR186 V 58). We know from the previous section that our will is always directed to an object, and that the question is what the basis of this directedness is.[39] Is it some feature of the object that attracts us, or is it rather that, being independently led in a certain direction, we cannot help seeing the object situated at the end of the road we are traveling on, and describing what we are doing as tending toward it? Kant's answer is: definitely the latter—if the will is to have any genuine significance and our behavior is to count as free.

"By a concept of an object of practical reason," he says, "I understand the representation of an object as an effect possible through freedom. To be an object of practical cognition so understood signifies, therefore, only the relation of the will to the action by which it or its opposite would be made real, and to appraise whether or not something is an object of *pure* practical reason is only to distinguish the possibility or impossibility of *willing* the action by which, if we had the ability to do so (and experience must judge about this), a certain object would be made real. If the object is taken as the determining ground of our faculty of desire, the *physical possibility* of it by the free use of our powers must precede our appraisal of whether it is an object of practical reason or not. On the other hand, if the a priori law can be regarded as the determining ground of the action, and this, accordingly, can be regarded as determined by pure practical reason, then the judgment whether or not something is an object of pure practical reason is quite independent of this comparison with our physical ability, and the question is only whether we could *will* an action which is directed to the existence of an object if the object were within our power; hence the *moral possibility* of the action must come first, since in this case the determining ground of the will is not the object but the law of the will" (PR186 V 57–58). As the moral law is an imperative, an object of practical reason whose concept depends on the concept of that law will also be one that *ought to* exist and might well *not* exist (just as the law might not be realized). So far, nothing much is new, but mention of these objects suggests a general remark that constitutes the substance of the current qualification and that was in fact relevant all along, while (to make sense of Kant's position) we talked about such strange things as my counterpart in the intelligible world or the result of abstracting from all the empirical determinations of some behavior of mine, but becomes especially appropriate now, as we encounter obvious Kantian examples of that kind of talk.

In the transcendental realist's logical space, objects are the starting point. And by that I mean: complete, full-fledged objects, of which we can have only partial knowledge, of course, but that is our problem, not the objects'—an epistemological, not a metaphysical one, to rehearse the realist's typical ploy. For every property that it makes sense to predicate of an object, in the realist's framework, the object will have either that property or its negation; indeed, that an object not be complete in this sense (that, say, it be metaphysically, not just epistemologically, indeterminate whether Sherlock Holmes had a mole on his left calf or not) is good indication that it does not exist—that it is not an object after all. The situation is quite different in the post-revolutionary, transcendental idealist framework. Here we certainly have the *idea* of complete, perfectly definite objects; but nothing we encounter will ever be adequate to it. Within our conceptual itinerary (our conceptual construction, or definition, of objects), we will start with sketches of objects, approximations to objects, objects by courtesy (intentional objects), and we will gradually narrow down our field aiming at objects *simpliciter*, until we realize that objects by courtesy, approximations to objects (however detailed they might be), are all we will ever get. Even disregarding this negative conclusion, however, it is clear that from this point of view the objects we intend to eventually reconstruct are meant to be a subset of a larger class of what we could still call objects—perhaps in scare-quotes. It is to this larger class that the "objects" of practical reason belong (as well as my intelligible rational counterpart, and the entity I blame for my free, irrational behavior). The realist would have no room for them: they are too fuzzy for him, *constitutionally* fuzzy (not just in our representation of them), definite only to the extent that the moral law itself is definite—only to the extent of being the imaginary, and blurred, foci of pursuing lawlike behavior. Which is to say: not very definite at all.[40]

Think of asking yourself, before a race, who will win it, and of answering: "The winner." Objects of practical reason are "objects" in the same sense as the reference of this definite description:[41] just as the latter has no specificity beyond the race itself, and beyond the fact that someone will win it, so do those other objects receive what (little) structure they have from the law, and add no further, independent content to the information it provides. Statements referring to them provide only another, "object-based" manner of expressing the law—as "The winner in this race will be the world champion" is but another, perhaps catchier but not independently informative, way of saying "This race is the decisive event in the world championship." They extend beyond the most basic formulation of the law, but only by rephrasing it in ways that are more sensitive to our empirical structure, not by really adding to its content. We are empirical realists, we *live* in a world of objects regardless of how we *think* of them (and of whether or not we have gone through Kant's Copernican revolution), hence we are also empirically guided by objects (goals) whenever we act in that world—and it is no wonder that we find it so natural to come up with objectual reformulations of our normative statements, even if such reformulations add nothing to the statements themselves. "[T]his [reaching beyond the law] is possible because the moral law is taken with reference to the characteristic, natural to the human being, of having to consider in every action, besides the law, also an end (this characteristic of the human being makes him an object of experience)" (RR6on VI 7n).

The way I articulated this second qualification confirms the conclusions I reached concerning the first one and provides both an additional, useful angle on the ever recurring problem of our responsibility for evil and a preview of the relations between knowledge and morality that I will be addressing in the next section. So consider evil first. Within TR, whatever I do I am either free to do or I am not; and, as I consider any behavior of mine, I must make up my mind which of these two options I want to assert. However edifying it might be to claim responsibility for an evil act, if in fact I believe that freedom coincides with rationality and hence a lapse in rationality coincides with a lapse in freedom, then I must also admit that claiming responsibility for an evil act would amount to contradicting myself. But in TI the situation is quite different. What is conceptually primary here is representations, and objects only surface as the intentional relata of such representations—with as much definiteness as the representations will grant them. So I may well (and in fact, as I have argued, I do) have good reasons for *both* believing that freedom is rationality and hence my irrationality manifests a lack of freedom *and* for taking charge of what evil I do. While I call both the objects thus referred to "me," I cannot begin to establish an identity between them—I have no resources available to constructively conceive of this identity. And yet, I do not have to, for such "objects" to play a legitimate and even a highly significant role *within* the relevant representations and the fields of discourse and activity in which those representations enter. After all, no objects whatsoever—not even ordinary empirical objects—can be fully detached from the representations they are objects of; that is what it means for them to be appearances. The opaqueness of reference, within TI, is a common destiny.

Turn to morality and knowledge. In the confrontation between nature and reason, the former will have objective reality on its side: it will be able to claim that something can only be taken really to exist or to occur if it fits natural, spatiotemporal laws. Therefore, only what we have (natural, spatiotemporal) experience of is proven (by that experience) to be *really* possible; in order to establish that something (including some morally required behavior) really can be, we have to produce an actual example of it. Reason, on the other hand, will insist on the priority of its ideal standards, and will want to subordinate the very criteria of objective reality to them; specifically, it will use a natural, spatiotemporal fleshing out of those standards to give them a certain amount of empirical content, stopping precisely where the addition of any *further* content might weaken, rather than strengthen, its case. And, of course, in thus ruthlessly exploiting the natural point of view, it will derive reassurance from its established conviction that the reality and real possibility alleged by the latter are ultimately delusive: that the rock bottom allegedly reached by the presentation of an actual example is but an unsteady, phenomenal one—hence there is only a difference in degree, not in kind, between a material entity and a conceptual abstraction (between, say, the concrete organism constituting my empirical self and the *noumenon* to which I attribute my "internal dispositions"). The conflict of faculties is never going to be at an end; in particular, faculties are forever going to play this game of judging each other by their own standards and turning each other into their own tool—no recourse is possible to a neutral, "higher" agency that might decide the issue once and for all.

3. The Dynamics of Hope

So Kant's denial of teleology is a denial of its *foundational* role, and is perfectly compatible with teleology still showing up in his conceptual story—provided that, when it does show up, it be subordinate to the primacy of law. Now we need to work out the details of its appearance and subordination.

There is a sense in which "ought" implies "can," we noted already. It is not a cognitive sense; it cannot be. It cannot be the case that, because I consider myself subject to the moral law, I also know that I am able to obey it.[42] It is supposed to be a practical sense; to manifest itself in my practice. "[E]xperience, by exhibiting the effects of morality in its ends, gives an objective, although only practical, reality to the concept of morality in having causality in the world" (R6on VI 7n). But such vague statements require considerable unpacking.

Specifically, what is it to have "only practical reality"? What kind of reality is that? Or, to return from a different angle to a passage already quoted in the previous chapter (at the end of section 3), how shall we read Kant's statement that "every being that cannot act otherwise than under the idea of freedom is just because of that really free *in a practical respect*" (italics rearranged)? We have developed some notion by now of what it might mean to "act under the idea of freedom"; but what does "being free in a practical respect" amount to?

When I respond to the call of the moral law,[43] I act as if I were able to obey it. Someone (including myself) observing my behavior would inevitably come to the conclusion that one of its presuppositions is for me to rely on this ability, to regard myself as being in possession of it—such is the only way they could make sense of what I do. Intellectually, I might even be convinced that I am always totally determined; that I never have any choice or any alternative option. But my attitude gives me the lie; the commitment I continue to evince despite my intellectual conviction, the passion I continue to exude as I go about my duty, the effort I continue to put out as I face resistances are to be taken at least as seriously as the tales I spin in my speculative mode[44]—especially when one considers that those tales are not self-sufficient and self-standing. Once again (as was noted in chapter 3) it is the logic of my behavior that matters, not the (often complacent) accounts I give for it or the maxims by which I would declare it to be determined; it is this logic that a rational, impartial spectator will try to fathom. So there are, in general, implications of my practice, contents whose truth is demanded by (any plausible interpretation of) it, much as the beauty of a loved object is demanded by the love itself, or the worthiness of an achievement is demanded by my desperate striving for it; and never mind whether I could *prove*, in a theoretical sense, such beauty or worth. Insofar as my practice is rational, there are still implications of it: practical postulates.[45]

Freedom is such a postulate, as indeed the above made clear: however unknowable and even incomprehensible it might be, whenever I act responsibly (that is, so as to be able to think of myself as responsive to reason) I move in its wake, its presence colors everything I do. I could deny it in words, but I assert it in deed. Whereas transcendental freedom—the concept of freedom as it surfaces in our cognitive reconstruction of the world—is indispensable but problematic, no such problem arises for practical freedom, the freedom expressed by my practice, invoked by it, the one I bring out (even despite myself) as soon as I stop thinking and start acting. "[T]he concept of an empirically unconditioned causality is . . . theoretically empty (without any intuition appropriate to it) but it is nevertheless possible and refers to an undetermined object; in place of that, however, the concept is given significance in the moral law and consequently in its practical reference; thus I have, indeed, no intuition that would determine its objective theoretical reality for it, but it has nonetheless a real application which is exhibited *in concreto* in dispositions or maxims, that is, it has practical reality which can be specified" (PR185 V 56). "Even the most obstinate skeptic grants that, when it comes to acting, all sophistical scruples about a universally deceptive illusion must come to nothing. In the same way, the most confirmed fatalist, who is a fatalist as long as he gives himself up to mere speculation, must still, as soon as he has to do with wisdom and duty, always act *as if he were free*" (P10 VIII 13).[46] I argued in the previous chapter that one can disregard all natural constraints and *take oneself to be free* ("act under the idea of freedom"); and that reason will judge such behavior approvingly, as consistent with the conception of a free act—whatever it might say of what *else* one does. But taking oneself to be free, if we are to look at what people do and not just listen to what they say, amounts to acting in a way that displays a commitment to freedom—or, to switch from an adverbial to a nominal language, to also perform the act of displaying this commitment (this passion, this effort, this irrepressible drive): of having the commitment show up in one's (other) behavior, of forcing a judgment of that behavior that makes it incompatible with a cynical attitude. So, when one behaves like that, one is indeed free in a practical respect.

There is more. Whenever we behave in a goal-directed manner, we are implying that we trust things will work out in the end. We might not (consciously) *believe* it,[47] we might indeed be totally pessimistic about the outcome; and yet anyone will think that we act as if what we do not believe will in fact be the case—otherwise, again, it would make no sense for us to act that way. Along similar lines, the scientist's theorizing and observing activities are based on trust that nature be rationally constituted, hence that reason can discover its laws, however implicit or unconscious (or even consciously denied) such trust may be: "Could Linnaeus have hoped to outline a system of nature if he had had to worry that if he found a stone that he called granite, this might differ in its internal constitution from every other stone which nevertheless looked just like it, and all he could hope to find were always individual things, as it were isolated for the understanding, and never a class of them that could be brought under concepts of genus and species[?]" (J18n XX 215–16n). "[T]he reflecting power of judgment . . . could not undertake to *classify* the whole of nature according to its empirical differences if it did not presuppose that nature itself *specifies* its transcendental laws in accordance with some sort of principle" (J18–19 XX 215).

Now consider an imperfectly rational being who is (to be thought of as) trying to obey reason's injunctions. Her imperfect rationality is *not* rationality, just as an incomplete circle is not a circle and a roofless house is not a house: to say that something other than rationality must be referred to in order to explain her behavior is to say (given reason's self-contained character) that her behavior is not rational. As a natural being, she will always fall short of her goal; nature will always be in the way. But, as one who also moves in the wake of rationality, she must move as if the latter will eventually triumph: as if she trusted that the conflict staged within her between nature and reason will be eventually resolved in reason's favor, and nature will become an instrument of reason. "It is a priori (morally) necessary *to produce the highest good through the freedom of the will*" (PR231 V 113). And realizing this necessity is not possible unless *all of* nature is made consistent with reason, "because any practical connection of causes and effects in the world, as a result of the determination of the will, does not depend upon the moral dispositions of the will but upon knowledge of the laws of nature and the physical ability to use them for one's purposes" (PR231 V 113): to trust that she will be able to behave rationally in the end *is* to trust that *the world* will become rational—in light of the limitations of her finite being, she can hope for no favorable outcome unless everything else is cooperating in the same enterprise. Therefore, a presupposition of her behavior is that a universal teleology be intrinsic to nature: a plan guiding all of its concrete, empirical workings toward a final agreement with reason. Which in turn requires a perfect rationality having enough power to determine rational ends for all of nature and willing to exercise such power—and that is just our ordinary understanding of God. "[W]hence have we the concept of God as the highest good? Solely from the *idea* of moral perfection that reason frames a priori and connects inseparably with the concept of a free will" (G63 IV 408–9).

This perfect being would guarantee the possibility of the perfect combination of virtue and happiness virtue deserves—a possibility which cannot be the *motive* of virtue, or that would be no virtue, but which is inevitably presupposed by virtuous behavior. "[I]n practical principles a natural and necessary connection between the consciousness of morality and the expectation of a happiness proportionate to it as its result can at least be thought as possible (though certainly not, on this account, cognized and understood)" (PR235 V 119). Indeed, that this connection be finally established is required not just by the person struggling to assert her morality but "even in the judgment of an impartial reason" (PR228 V 110; see also PR240 V 124): consistently with the understanding we have reached of the impartial witness, it is reason itself here that is projecting its own success, and subjecting nature to it (more about this later). And "the postulate of the possibility of the *highest derived good* (the best world) is likewise the postulate of the reality of a *highest original good*, namely of the existence of God" (PR241 V 125). Our previous analysis of "objects of practical reason" makes it clear that this talk of God is only an object-based formulation of what could be said with no reference to God (or any other object); hence to say that one trusts that God exists is only another, more colorful and possibly more attractive, way of saying that one trusts that things will (rationally) work out.[48] But then it is also a perfectly acceptable way of saying something whose truth the agent's behavior shows her to be committed to.

We can take another step. Since my past and present states are characterized by imperfect rationality, hence (again) by *no* rationality, acting in the wake of reason/freedom means acting in the wake of a future where my attempt will succeed: acting as if my future were to be rational, *demanding* a rational future for myself. "*Teleology* considers nature as a kingdom of ends, *morals* considers a possible kingdom of ends as a kingdom of nature. In the former the kingdom of ends is a theoretical idea for explaining what exists. In the latter, it is a practical idea for the sake of bringing about, in conformity with this very idea, that which does not exist but which can become real by means of our conduct" (G86n IV 436n). But no state I will ever reach after a finite progress can be conceived as a total realization of reason's demands: I will continue to be a natural being, hence imperfectly (that is, not) rational. Therefore, it makes no sense to consider any finite progress as one *toward rationality*: what it is instead is a progress toward its final (still irrational) destination. The only way I can make sense of my development as directed toward rationality, hence the only way I can make sense of my striving for this goal, is by thinking of the development as *infinite*. "[A]s an ideal of holiness ... [the moral disposition in its complete perfection] is not attainable by any creature but is yet the archetype which we should strive to approach and resemble in an uninterrupted but endless progress" (PR207 V 83). And "[t]his endless progress is possible ... only on the presupposition of the *existence* and personality of the same rational being continuing *endlessly* (which is called the immortality of the soul)" (PR238 V 122). So I must be able to think of myself as never coming to an end—as immortal. And note that no such requirement surfaces concerning the other extreme of my being: I cannot construct a similar argument to the effect that I ought to have no *beginning*.

Thus, the existence of God and my immortality are too (in addition to freedom) necessary practical postulates of reason: practical implications of any human behavior that reason would approve of.[49] I cannot claim knowledge of the relevant statements—or, for that matter, of their negations. Reason has concluded that, from a purely theoretical point of view, I am to remain ignorant about such matters. But reason in me also values the rationality of my behavior and, given the limitations it finds in me, it translates this valuation into a prescription: my behavior ought to be rational. Which entails: it ought to be such that it can be described as guided by those beliefs that are practical implications of rational behavior. "[G]ranted that the pure moral law inflexibly binds everyone as a command (not as a rule of prudence), the upright man may well say: I *will* that there be a God, that my existence in this world be also an existence in a pure world of the understanding beyond natural connections, and finally that my duration be endless; I stand by this . . . and I will not let this belief be taken from me" (PR255 V 143). In a suggestive summary statement at TA438n VIII 397n, Kant says that "to *believe* in . . . [a world-governor], from a moral and practical viewpoint, . . . *means* [*heißt*] . . . to act . . . as though such a world-government were real" (last italics added).

The exact quality of our commitment to the postulates is one of those finely balanced issues Kant's philosophy is so full of. To begin with, they have the logical form of theoretical statements, of descriptions (in the indicative) of states of affairs; but they derive whatever force they have from rational imperatives.[50] "[B]y . . . [a postulate of pure practical reason] I understand a *theoretical* proposition, though one not demonstrable as such, insofar as it is attached inseparably to an a priori unconditionally valid *practical* law" (PR238 V 122). "These postulates are not theoretical dogmas but *presuppositions* having a necessarily practical reference and thus, although they do not indeed extend speculative cognition, they give objective reality to the ideas of speculative reason in *general* (by means of their reference to what is practical) and justify its holding concepts even the possibility of which it could not otherwise presume to affirm" (PR246 V 132). They are what "a righteous man" would have to "assume . . . from a practical

point of view, i.e., in order to form a concept of at least the possibility of the final end that is prescribed to him by morality" (J317–18 V
452–53); that is, in order to get a sense of the objective he is working
for—he *ought to* be working for. To work for something is to posit it as
attainable, whether or not it is in fact attainable and whether or not we
even (intellectually) admit that it is: "in virtue of the moral law, which
imposes . . . [the] final end upon us, we have a basis for assuming, from
a practical point of view, that is, in order to apply our powers to realize
it, its possibility, its realizability" (J320 V 455).[51] "I should [*soll*] act as if
there are a God and a future life" (N389 XVIII 678). So, again, the
only basis for what is *stated* here is what *ought to be* the case.

A second (related) aspect of this fine balance has to do with *how*
forceful these statements are. On the one hand, they do not have the
arbitrary character of something that depends on individual desire:
there is necessity to them. "[I]t was a duty for us to promote the highest
good; hence there is in us not merely the warrant but also the necessity,
as a need connected with duty, to presuppose the possibility of this
highest good. . . . [T]hat is, it is morally necessary to assume the existence of God" (PR241 V 125). On the other hand, Kant understands
the relevant necessity "as a *need* connected with duty" (italics added),
and similar statements occur elsewhere ("[it is] a *need having the force of
law*, to assume something without which that cannot happen which
one *ought* to set unfailingly as the aim of one's conduct," PR140 V 5).
Furthermore, in the continuation of the same passage from PR241 V
125, while insisting that the "moral necessity" of the assumption of
God's existence is a need, he contrasts its "subjective" character with
the "objective" one of duty itself. And later he says in no uncertain
terms: "It might almost seem as if this rational belief [*Vernunftglaube*] is
here announced as itself a *command*, namely to assume the highest good
as possible. But a belief [*Glaube*] that is commanded is an absurdity"
(P255 V 144).

The belief in God (or freedom, or immortality) is only ever con-
jectural: it is only ever a reasonable (even if *the only* reasonable)[52] way
of making sense of what we ought to do. It is "the only way in which it
is theoretically possible for . . . [reason] to think the exact harmony of
the realm of nature with the realm of morals as the condition of the
possibility of the highest good" (PR256–57 V 145), but it never turns
into a true law: the only law here continues to be the one to behave
rationally. "What belongs to duty here is only the striving to produce
and promote the highest good in the world, the possibility of which
can therefore be postulated, while our reason finds this thinkable only

on the presupposition of a supreme intelligence" (PR241 V 126).[53] A need is an empirical condition, and that the duty to obey the moral law issues for us in a need to believe in God is a consequence of our empirical goal-directed nature. *We* are empirically so constituted that we cannot think of an action if not as directed to an attainable end, hence *we* have a need to postulate that God exists if we are to understand what we are doing when we try to behave morally; but, in giving satisfaction to this need, we never overcome our limits or reach a clear (let alone veridical) conception of what we are talking about. "Faith [*Glaube*] . . . is trust in the attainment of an aim the promotion of which is a duty but the possibility of the realization of which it is not possible for us *to have insight into* [*einzusehen*]" (J336 V 472). And, it might be useful to reiterate, when satisfying our need by the use of the singular term "God" we are not giving any more substance to our achievement. Once again, this term is in no better shape than "the winner" before the race is run; the object-based grammar of our sentences should not make us think of them as having richer logical implications. "God . . . is the moral law itself, as it were, but thought as personified" (R409 XXVIII 1075–76; see also R421 XXVIII 1091). "From the practical point of view, it is one and the same thing whether one founds the divinity of the [moral] command in human reason, or founds it [in] such a person [as God], since the difference is more one of phraseology than a doctrine which amplifies knowledge" (O232 XXI 28).

In Euclid's *Elements*, definitions and axioms are formulated in the indicative ("A point is that which has no part"; "Things which are equal to the same thing are also equal to one another"), but postulates are in the imperative: "Let the following be postulated: To draw a straight line from any point to any point." They do not state truths about space; they contain instructions about *what to do* in it. Kant is sensitive to this distinction: "Pure geometry has postulates as practical propositions which . . . contain nothing further than the presupposition that one *could* do something if it were required that one should do it" (PR164 V 31). But his postulates are not like Euclid's: they do not tell us to "draw" freedom or God; they tell us that freedom and God *are*— because of what else we *are* told to "draw." Such (alleged) statements of fact will never acquire the objective status that either physical laws or moral injunctions have, each in their own realm. They rather sit somewhat uncomfortably between the two, straddling their distinction: they negotiate a relation between theory and practice in which the latter becomes the controlling factor (and Kant's term "practical cognition," we can see now, is an expression of that hierarchy: of how knowledge itself is to be humbled before our moral concerns).

One main problem with determinism and other kinds of reductionism is that they do no justice to the nuances, the multifarious, heterogeneous variations present in our form of life. Kant's "conflictual" vision performs much better in this respect; specifically, here, it allows for an alternative way in which a propositional content can relate to the world—other than by mirroring it, that is. This content can articulate the consequences of a task we have vis-à-vis the world (and ourselves): of a prescribed behavior that, for being phrased as a command, will not have to lack a rich and complex logical structure, but might well allow for interesting arguments and suggestive conclusions. All originating in the normative register, of course; but no less "real" than what belongs to the descriptive one—indeed such that reason in its descriptive, speculative use must defer to them and put itself at their service: "accept these propositions and, although they are transcendent for it, try to unite them, as a foreign possession handed over to it, with its own concepts [that is, try to elucidate them and systematize them]"[54] (PR237 V 120), thus ultimately acknowledging the primacy of what we ought to do on what we can know.

The postulates of practical reason constitute the essential claims of a religion founded on reason (that is, on morality) alone, entirely independent of the empirical occurrence of revelation—a religion that we, by extending our analysis of the term "God," could characterize as being in its entirety nothing other than an object-based reformulation of rational discourse, devoid of any additional content. "[The assumption of the existence of God] can be called *belief* [*Glaube*] and, indeed, a pure *rational belief* [*Vernunftglaube*] since pure reason alone (in its theoretical as well as in its practical use) is the source from which it springs" (PR241 V 126). "[T]he Christian principle of *morals* itself is not theological (and so heteronomy); it is instead autonomy of pure practical reason by itself, . . . since it places even the proper *incentive* to observing . . . [the moral laws] not in the results wished for but in the representation of duty alone" (PR243 V 129). "The concept of God . . . is one belonging originally not to physics, that is, to speculative reason, but to morals, and the same can be said of the other concepts of reason which we treated . . . as postulates of reason in its practical use" (PR252 V 140).

It is important to stress that this religion "within the boundaries of mere reason" is but a stylistic variant of morality.[55] For, if it had its own cognitive status and provided its own source of motivation, it would also inevitably become yet another *impediment* for morality—as much as natural inclinations are, indeed as allied to them in encouraging *evil*. It would make morality (not just very difficult, but even) impossible to sustain. "[H]ence most actions conforming to the law would be done from fear, only a few from hope, and none at all from duty, and the moral worth of actions, on which alone in the eyes of supreme wisdom the worth of the person and even that of the world depends, would not exist at all. As long as human nature remains as it is, human conduct would thus be changed into mere mechanism in which, as in a puppet show, everything would *gesticulate* well but there would be *no life* in the figures. . . . [I]t is quite otherwise with us" (P258 V 147). *Fortunately*, it is otherwise with us, as Kant proved when "deny[ing] *knowledge* in order to make room for *faith* [*Glaube*]" (Bxxx), that is, when belaboring, on his way to the vindication of morality, that monumental digression that was the *Critique of Pure Reason*.[56] "It is good that we do not know but only believe that there is a God" (N204 XVIII 55). "[O]ur faith is not knowledge, and thank heaven it is not!" (R415 XXVIII 1083).

Kant's attitude toward philosophical theology can be extended to his view of the whole of philosophical activity, thereby providing a useful articulation of the stance from where, as I noted at the beginning of *my* path here (at the beginning of chapter 2), his transcendental journey takes its departure. If conceptual analysis were able to establish some *facts* with the *necessity* that it promises, we would be best advised to let ourselves be guided by it in our everyday life. But no such promise is going to be fulfilled: transcendental reflection can only come up with tales attempting to flesh out the merely logical possibility of ordinary modes, and use them as defensive weapons against other tales, destructive of those very modes.[57] Our cognitive endeavors as well as our moral commitments will have to stand on their own, never deluding themselves that they can find supernatural justification in a philosophical argument, more than they can in a divine ordinance. Human affairs are shaky and uncertain, and so is human philosophy: a constant struggle for a final comprehension that will not be obtained, for a real possibility that will not be established. To this possibility, and to its relations with such other modalities as actuality and necessity, so often evoked in what precedes, it is time now, as our journey draws to a close, to turn more concentrated attention.

SIX

ORDINARY MORALITY

1. Analytic and Synthetic Methods

We know from chapter 2 that transcendental philosophy is entirely constituted of analytic judgments. It could not be otherwise: as a form of philosophy, it is a purely conceptual discipline, and no synthetic judgments are possible without involving intuitions. But this discipline can be developed by two distinct methods, for which Kant continues to use, somewhat confusingly, the same terms "analytic" and "synthetic."[1]

The distinction is given its clearest formulation in the *Prolegomena*, which are supposed to offer "a *plan* . . . laid out according to the *analytic method*, whereas the *work* itself absolutely had to be composed according to the *synthetic method*, so that the science might present all of its articulations, as the structural organization of a quite peculiar faculty of cognition, in their natural connection" (TA60 IV 263). The basic element of contrast between the two methods is that, when proceeding analytically, we "rely on something already known to be dependable, from which we can go forward with confidence and ascend to the sources, which are not yet known" (TA70 IV 275), whereas, when proceeding synthetically, we must be "inquiring within pure reason itself, and seeking to determine within this source both the elements and the laws of its pure use, according to principles" (TA70 IV 274).

The analytic method looks easier, and the reason is that it relies on the implicit adoption of PN—a vastly popular principle among

philosophers and lay people alike.[2] For the method's logical structure is
as follows: Pure mathematics (say) is actual, hence it is possible (first
application of PN—in the equivalent form: everything actual is possible).[3] But such and such *must* be the case for it to be possible; hence
(second application of PN) such and such are actual (and possible).
Kant remarks that this strategy has an important limitation: it cannot be
applied to metaphysics because "we cannot assume that metaphysics
as science is *actual*" (TA70 IV 275). There are, however, more serious
problems with it. First, that anything be actual has no currency in
philosophy: it is a simple matter of fact which it is not legitimate for
philosophers to import into their conceptual arguments.[4] Second, and
most important, PN, despite its popularity, is, when properly scrutinized, a highly questionable "law." That such and such be declared
necessary provides no assurance that they are real (unless we also independently know that they can be):[5] the whole context in which
these necessities arise might be delusive, as witnessed by the sad case of
rational psychology—a discipline based on deriving conclusions by
logically cogent arguments from the absolutely certain presence revealed to self-consciousness, and itself proven to be the consequence of
a collective (conceptual) hallucination. Therefore, it is quite appropriate that the *Prolegomena* be described by Kant as mere "preparatory
exercises . . . [which] ought more to indicate what needs to be done in
order to bring a science into existence if possible, than to present the
science itself" (TA70 IV 274)—as just whetting our appetite for the
real thing.

The real thing (that is, in this case, the first *Critique*) proceeds by
defining (from scratch) enough of TI's logical space to be able to prove
that, within it, it is possible for us (say) to know necessary laws of
nature. This is a progressive effort, as opposed to the regressive one
manifested in an application of the analytic method:[6] it does not move
from the given existence of something to what (only) can bring it
about, or from the grounded to its ground, but from the ground to the
grounded. And it is a constructive one: there is no cheating here; the
possibility at issue is not implicitly assumed before the work has even
started, but is painstakingly established by mobilizing considerable
theoretical ingenuity. In pursuing this strategy, the philosopher behaves much like the mathematician, who decides what is to count as a
circle or a square and then proceeds to inquire on what follows from
her definitions—a similarity that Kant resisted admitting to, for reasons
that will become apparent shortly.[7]

The distinction between the analytic and the synthetic methods is of crucial relevance to the structure and significance of the present book. Its first chapter proceeded analytically, by drawing a number of necessary consequences from the presumed existence of morality. It was quite clear in this case (more so than, say, in the case of mathematics) that, for all their being necessary, such consequences were far from immediately plausible; and that articulating their plausibility (that is, their conceptual coherence, in the face of what else we presume to be actual) was a highly challenging task, open to a number of serious objections. In addressing the task, I (or, rather, Kant) proceeded synthetically, and the final outcome of the process is a complex conceptual construction that meets all the objections originally considered. One might still ask, however, whether this construction can be thought of as indeed establishing the possibility of what we *ordinarily* understand as morality.[8] This question has been suggested and sidestepped before, and can no longer be postponed. To some extent, it goes beyond the scope of (transcendental) philosophy, because the result of any conceptual analysis depends on what "component concepts... were already thought in... [a given concept] (though confusedly)" (A7 B11) and different people might well (as a matter of fact, on which philosophy has no purchase) conceive morality (perhaps confusedly) in mutually inconsistent ways. Still, a stand on this issue is in order—however corrective, rather than direct, our answer to the question might end up being. I will present such a stand in the last section, after giving, in the next one, a brief summary of Kant's solutions of the original problems.

2. The Problems Resolved

The same event can receive multiple accounts; the question "why?" asked in regard to it has multiple legitimate answers. Some of these answers will insert it in patterns that reach indefinitely far, where the same "why?" question keeps being asked in regard to any answer given, and every new answer is given in terms of something *else*, in an interminable chain where the law of *A* is always provided by something *other than A*. But none of this prevents us from also thinking of the possibility of a different kind of answer: one that inserts the event in a rational pattern and thus finds a definitive account for it, a full stop for the search. This would be a case of reason showing its presence and efficacy in practice, showing itself to be practical; and it would also be a case of true autonomy, of the law of the event originating from the agent herself, insofar as she is rational. That even a single case like this ever occurs cannot be established, in fact cannot be properly understood; but (again) no one can deny its status as a legitimate object of thought. Much less can causal determinism issue any such denial when one considers that *its own* status is highly uncertain: that the conceivability of the very world it pretends to know and account for rests on positing a mysterious *act* of choice—a spontaneous, free act. Freedom is unknowable and even incomprehensible; but its possibility can be successfully defended.

What the above declares to be possibly free is reason: the autonomy to which events can possibly testify is rational determination. Therefore, reason would look with approval at any manifestation of this autonomy, conceiving it as a sign of itself. Reason would judge all such manifestations *good*—*unconditionally* good because reason itself is the search for the unconditioned, and can only be satisfied by an unconditional realization of its own standards. That it *is* ever satisfied we will never know, of course; but we do know *what it means* to say that it is, which is enough for our purposes. The place of values in a world of facts is no mystery as long as value judgments are understood as reason's commentary on facts; what makes possible "the view from nowhere" expressed by these nontechnical, categorical pronouncements is the nontechnical, categorical nature of the agency that utters them.

Humans are rational beings, but only imperfectly so. Reason fights (must think of itself—or, rather, of its "agents" in the sensible world—as fighting) an uphill battle within every human against natural drives. The independent register at which reason speaks is often suspended, and human behavior is left with only naturalistic, heteronomous accounts of itself. Reason will disapprove of these developments, will blame them on the people "responsible" for them (however thin the meaning of such blame and responsibility might be), and will look with favor at the patient rebuilding, retexturing of the rational level of interaction. Therefore, reason will prescribe behavior to humans, indeed prescribe them to behave as if they held certain beliefs: those which are necessary practical presuppositions of the execution of reason's commands. And the authority such prescriptions have derives from humanity itself, the only example of rationality we have access to. We can certainly disregard them, at the cost of losing what distinguishes us from windows, tomatoes, and bacteria—hence of no longer even understanding what we are missing.

3. Philosophy and Freedom

The man Kant was definitely of the opinion that the conceptual construction summarized in the previous section matched perfectly ordinary people's understanding of morality, and that only deluded thinkers could claim otherwise. Just before offering the somewhat fictionalized biographical account of Thomas More I quoted earlier, he says: "[I]f one asks: What, then, really is *pure* morality, by which as a touchstone one must test the moral content of every action? I must admit that only philosophers can make the decision of this question doubtful, for it is long since decided in common human reason, not indeed by abstract general formulae but by habitual use, like the difference between the right and the left hand. We will, accordingly, first show in an example the mark by which pure virtue is tested and, representing it as set before, say, a ten-year-old boy for his appraisal, see whether he must necessarily judge so of himself, without being directed to it by a teacher" (PR264 V 155). And, after giving the example, he concludes that "duty, not merit, must have not only the most determinate influence on the mind but, when it is represented in the correct light of its inviolability, the most penetrating influence as well" (PR265 V 157). Moving from examples to general statements, he acknowledges at PR213 V 91 that "that pure reason, without the admixture of any empirical determining ground, is practical of itself alone: this one had to be able to show from the *most common practical use of reason*, by confirming the supreme practical principle as one that every natural human reason cognizes . . . as the supreme law of its will." But he quickly satisfies himself that "the justification of moral principles as principles of a pure reason could . . . be carried out very well and with sufficient certainty by a mere appeal to the judgment of common human understanding."[9]

What Kant himself believed (maybe self-servingly) will not decide the present issue, however, since opinions differ here[10] and many will think that, in trying to save ordinary morality from devastating philosophical attacks, Kant has finally given us something no longer worth saving. His freedom will be judged an undesirable feature of behavior, for in order to be free in that sense I have to cancel out whatever makes me the particular individual I am, and reduce "myself" to an abstract pattern indistinguishable from anyone else who is also similarly "free." His utter disregard for emotions and happiness (even the emotions and happiness of those dear to me) will be considered absurdly demanding—even inhuman. His conception of natural inclinations (indeed of nature, or being, as such) as intrinsically leading to evil (since evil just *is* being led by them), and of respect for the moral law as a feeling of humiliation, will be taken to have a clear nihilistic slant. And his whole picture of things will be explained as the outcome of a harsh Pietist education,[11] and of the consequent internalization of too high a dose of (Western, paternalistic, bourgeois) Super-Ego. Some notion of the *telos* of human nature will be invoked as providing a saner reconstruction of moral commands—whether it be virtuous Aristotelian *eudaimonia*, the greatest amount of pleasure for the greatest number, or simply the attainment of one's idiosyncratic goals. In short, it will be argued that, whatever the cogency of Kant's "synthetic" reconstruction of morality and of his consequent vindication of its possibility, what has thus been reconstructed and vindicated has little to do with anything most people would recognize as, indeed, morality. In choosing (albeit half-heartedly) to proceed like a mathematician, he has fallen prey to an objection often raised against mathematicians: there are (say) no Euclidean triangles in nature, those triangles are only idealizations, and forcing them onto reality amounts to a violation of the latter's complexity and detail.[12]

I am not about to argue here for Kant's view of ordinary morality, or against any alternative one(s); I am not writing that kind of book. I am trying to account for his specifically philosophical contribution to this discussion, and that can only be, given his conception of philosophy: here is a view of morality people (like me) have, here are some conceptual problems raised concerning this view, and here is a consistent conceptual framework in which the problems are resolved. If others have different views of morality, let them come up with their own resolutions of what conceptual problems their views must face. But this is not all that can be said on the matter, for, while addressing the conceptual problems posed by his view of morality, Kant, just because of how extreme that view was, made general moves from which everyone (whatever their views of morality or anything) can learn. Liberating moves, as it turns out: such that they help us think "outside the box" and look at things and events in novel ways.[13] Which is, I claimed elsewhere, the best philosophy can do, and the main reason why this activity continues to flourish.

One major liberating move is as follows: It is not hard to understand the success of TR, I said in *Kant's Copernican Revolution*. This conceptual framework is but the result of extending to our transcendental mode thinking strategies that are familiar to us when we exploit our ordinary empirical realism. Since Kant would never give up the latter, the oscillation between realist and idealist attitudes is inescapable for him—as is the transcendental illusion that constantly issues from this oscillation: from viewing ordinary objects as independently real and then switching to the acknowledgment that they cannot be. That we can thus find no position of rest is, I argued in my earlier book, a great spur to creativity, precisely insofar as it is critical of any alleged resting position, and of the complacency and laziness that go with it. The same situation arises (not surprisingly) in Kant's treatment of morality. Empirically we are goal-directed beings, he admits without hesitation; hence within transcendental reflection we are naturally inclined (it could not be otherwise, given what our *nature* is) to adopt a similar stance, to move in the same direction, as it were, and to think of some goal to be achieved as what *defines* good behavior—in addition to it being the (desired) attainment of some goal that *causes* us to do whatever we do. Thus, one "natural" step after the other, we might end up making the goal that carries the definitional burden a generalized, "rationalized" version of our everyday-life purposes; at which point ethics would have nothing to add to our worldview that is not already offered by prudential wisdom, hence ultimately by experience, and reason would be passively enslaved to that very experience, instead of subjecting it to the most persistent questioning.[14]

Kant's conceptual recommendation, on the other hand, is characteristically onerous: he wants us to make sense of moral terms and moral judgments by conceptual moves that are directly antagonistic to our empirical habits. Empirical psychology and sociology will continue to study regularities in what people want to achieve and how they try to achieve it; but the *logic* of (human) action will have to find what *makes it* action by turning the motivational hierarchy upside down, away from objects, hence (once again) by having us think along unfamiliar lines, and move awkwardly around new conceptual associations and dependencies, and consequently feel strangely out of place all the time. Just as one feels when learning a foreign language, or getting adjusted to a foreign environment (except that here the learning and the adjusting will go on forever); and, just as in those other cases, the situation will often be terrifying, but will also have an enormous enriching potential.

This is not, again, an independent defense of Kant's view. There is no such thing: those who appreciate the thrilling challenge of a life form perpetually out of balance are already intimately Kantian; and there is no denying, of course, that many others like their philosophy, and their morals, to be conciliatory and reassuring. All I can say is that it is an undeniable feature of the Kantian scheme of things that people operating in it become apt at using conflicting registers and contradictory stances. Less apt at using any of them, perhaps, than if they had been totally dedicated to it; but able to play one against the other, and to see (and critically evaluate) from each the blind spots that are inevitably present in the other. This is (I repeat) a *feature* of the Kantian framework, which it is worth being clear about; whether it is a *valuable* one will be decided differently by different judges.

In a similar vein, here is another thing Kant has to offer: The most intractable problem for any system of thought is how to deal with what denies the system's very principles. Can we reason logically about illogical objects? (What, for example, is necessarily true of the round square?) Can we apply the laws of physics to the "singularity" of the Big Bang? The temptation arises, in all such cases, to throw up one's hands and say that the system has reached its limit: that our logical or physical account of the world stops there, hence anything beyond it makes no sense—or maybe it is our account that does not, and should be replaced. The same problem and the same temptation are present when dealing with normative systems. In deontic logic, the problem takes the dramatic form of a paradox. From the tautology

$$p \rightarrow (\sim p \rightarrow q)$$

there follows, by Necessitation and Distribution,

$$Op \rightarrow O(\sim p \rightarrow q);$$

that is, if something p is deontically necessary—or obligatory—then it is also obligatory that, if p does not happen (is not done), anything at all happen (be done). If it is obligatory that I stop at a red light, then it is also obligatory that, if I run a red light, I eat my hat (*and* I do not eat it).[15]

The best that standard (realist) logic can do with such paradoxes is to prevent the cases in which principles are contradicted from "infecting" the entire system. By accepting "relevance" inferential patterns, for example, we can keep the contradictions "local" and continue to reason soundly in noncontradictory environments.[16] It is still the case, however, that we do not seem able to reason, soundly or otherwise, in the contradictory environments themselves. Which is especially troubling for ethical reasoning, given how imperfectly moral (hence how contradictory of moral principles) our world is taken to be, and provides a powerful incentive for people trying to give their ethics a "scientific" basis, for them wanting it to forget "unreasonable" demands and make its injunctions "realistic"—make them generally descriptive of what people (tend to) do, as opposed to utopically normative of what they ought to do, but rarely in fact do.

What we are facing here is one more consequence of TR. If logic is, essentially, *ontology*, a doctrine or theory that presupposes one or many realms of objects and takes itself to be *describing* their most abstract, formal properties, then we cannot expect it to say something informative about the "objects" or "realms" that contravene such a description—the most it will be able to say, perhaps, is that *anything goes* there. But, in Kant's TI, ontology is at best an elusive target (an imaginary focus), and what governs our thinking is not descriptions but *norms*: ideals that anything existent or even possible not only *can* and *does* fall short of, but indeed (we prove to ourselves) *must* fall short of. Our everyday experience, within TI, is a constant rewriting of data in the light of those unrealizable norms, constantly challenged by its inadequacy and yet constantly expressing, in its striving *and* in the inadequacy of its outcomes, the norms' profound significance.[17]

As I see it, TI does the most justice to the kind of knowledge human beings can make a reasonable claim to: a succession of conjectures aiming at the faithful description of a consistent, connected, all-inclusive universe, which are invariably shown to be faulty as the "objects" they posit turn out to be delusive appearances, as the "laws" that substantiate them turn out to be ridden with exceptions. And it does so because, even in its treatment of knowledge, it is essentially a deontic logic: not as the TR brands of formal systems that illegitimately go by that name while extending realist modes of thought to imperatives,[18] and in sharp contrast with the TR definition of knowledge *on the basis of objects*, which is bound to leave us helpless prey to the skeptic's sneer. It is deontic as it is itself founded on imperatives, on commands that can *never* be rephrased in the indicative mood and yet whose dignity still colors the pale approximations to their absolute standards we are able to manage—the forever contextual, dependent objects and laws the understanding can offer in partial satisfaction of rational demands. Just as constitutionally defective spatiotemporal implements can be called *tables* because of their resemblance to the Platonic idea of a table—except that here the mysterious ontology of Platonic ideas and of the resemblance relation (that is, the realist residue present in Platonism) is replaced by a clear *de*ontology.

A fundamental aspect of my interpretation of Kant, as this book has made abundantly clear, is that I attribute to him a view of the human

form of life as constituted of independent, irreducible, mutually conflicting registers. When the deontic character of even his analysis of
cognition is brought out, this view appears much more sensible. For,
as long as we admit that we can know necessary laws of nature and
we concede to the reductionists the realist construal of a(n alethic)
necessity based on objects (according to which what a law claims to be
necessarily true of the latter can only be so because it is in fact true,
necessarily, of them—which is to say: PN holds), it will be hard to
oppose to the *facts* our opponents thus claim to have established the
apparently wishful-thinking character of norms. If, on the other hand,
the conflict of faculties is a conflict *of norms, including* cognitive ones,[19]
if our scientific activity is itself only the perpetually frustrated effort to
match rational requirements (that is, laws stating a *deontic* necessity),
then there is no asymmetry—and no privilege for epistemic projects
over ethical ones. Still, given TI's characteristic emphasis, it makes
sense that this kind of transcendental philosophy should do justice most
directly to what in our ordinary experience bears its normative character on its sleeve: to that morality which invariably recalls a guilty
conscience, an admission of wrongdoing, a sense of original fall—of
a fall *which is our very origin*. To that aspiration to infinity which will
forever make us rest uneasy with our conditioned, bounded being,
with our dependent status concerning "what . . . [we require] for
complete satisfaction" (PR207 V 84), and will forever invite us to
think of ourselves, *counter*factually, as self-sufficient and autonomous.
Morality is, within TI, the context where our condition emerges most
transparently, the plain, object-language version of what we might
otherwise fail to detect through the mists of semantic ascent; and,
insofar as philosophy is a reflection on that condition, it is itself but
moral philosophy—such reflection is most obviously hitting the mark
when it concerns itself with the moral life.[20]

In morality (and moral philosophy) as much as in the sciences, the
understanding will tirelessly contextualize reason's demands, and come
up repeatedly with empirical moral codes; and, as in their presence
rational critique hushes for a second (or a century), one might feel
relieved from its unending pressure. Inevitably, there will be those
who blow up this temporary respite into the end of all struggles and
fears—who declare they have finally reached the objects that (for
them) defined their itinerary. And there will be no arguing with them
and convincing them otherwise, for there are no premises external to
the confrontation with them on which such an argument could be
based. But, just as inevitably (a Kantian *must* think), the hisses will be

heard again, our self-assurance will crumble, the task reason poses will come forcefully to the fore. The task that defines us, that constrains our being and yet, precisely in nailing it to "the sublimity of our nature (in its vocation)" (PR210 V 87), frees it from any empirical, "objective" fetters.

NOTES

Chapter 1

1. "The human will is free. This proposition is indispensable in morals. For if men could not act otherwise than they do act, then all laws would be in vain" (LL483 XXIV 749). At times, Kant suggests that, unless this challenge were successfully met, more than just ethics would vanish: that philosophy itself is at stake here. See, for example, TA413 XX 335: "In regard to theoretical problems of every kind, there is no need for any *analytic* and metaphysic at all, if the concept of freedom is but transformed into that of mechanical necessity." That is because philosophy in his sense (that is, transcendental philosophy, for which see the following chapter) is itself "autonomy, that is, a reason that determinately delineates its synthetic principles, scope, and limits, in a complete system" (O244 XXI 59; at O249 XXI 84 transcendental philosophy is also called "the self-creation (autocracy) of ideas"). So there is for him an intrinsic mutual connection between philosophy and freedom. I will return to this theme (and to the complications involved in reason's "delineation of synthetic principles") in the last chapter.

2. "If we follow up the determining grounds of human actions, they are linked to one another in a chain; if we go back to the source, the only possible outcome is that we must arrive at an external cause, a being that is outside the agent" (LE271 XXVII 505).

3. "Opposed to both, chance as well as destiny, are *nature* and *freedom*. These are the two explanatory grounds of the understanding, which are opposed to blind accident" (LM 23–24 XXVIII 200). See also note 1 of chapter 3.

4. That is, we want to remember that "all interest is ultimately practical and even that of speculative reason is only conditional and is complete in

practical use alone" (PR238 V 121). See also note 20 of chapter 6 and the attending text.

5. Kant himself, of course, had his own substantive ethical views, some of which will be mentioned in what follows. But they will not be our direct concern, nor will it matter that I or others would want to disassociate ourselves from them. For it is the very space where such disagreement can legitimately occur that I am interested in defending here; and it is to this defense that I find Kant's contribution to be of crucial relevance. In contemporary terminology, the discussion carried out in the present book belongs to metaethics, not to normative ethics.

Chapter 2

1. When a textual reference is made, in this chapter or in subsequent ones, in connection with a point established in the earlier book, it is intended less to provide additional support for my interpretation than to help the reader track its significance through the whole Kantian corpus. The references coming from the moral works are also intended to show how "every step one takes with pure reason, even in the practical field where one does not take subtle speculation into consideration, nevertheless fits with all the moments of the *Critique* of theoretical reason as closely, and indeed of itself, as if each step had been thought out with deliberate foresight merely to provide this confirmation" (PR225 V 106). (Consistency was, as we will see, a paramount concern for Kant, despite (or just because of) the fact that the complexity of his views made it anything but a straightforward objective.)

2. The Principle of Necessity invoked to prove this (allegedly) trivial consequence will become a main focus of attention in chapters 5 and 6.

3. Eventually, this characterization will prove too strong—or at least open to misunderstanding. For what the transcendental philosopher does may ultimately cause people to challenge their ordinary practices and attitudes. But such challenges will be consequences of the *fact* that people espouse (or antagonize) his views, which fact is compatible with those views being purely descriptive (as opposed to revisionary) of ordinary practices and attitudes. Similarly, people are often led to modifying their behavior when they hear it accurately characterized by, say, a health-care professional.

4. Thus, for example, "the deduction of the supreme principle of pure practical reason" is "the explanation of the possibility of such a cognition a priori" (PR215 V 93). At J161 V 280, the apparently stronger statement is made that a deduction is "the guarantee of the legitimacy . . . of a kind of judgment" (which "arises only if the judgment makes a claim to necessity"); but the "guarantee" is immediately accounted for in terms consistent with my reading when Kant redescribes his task as that of "explain[ing] how *it is possible* that something could please merely in the judging . . . and that . . . the satisfaction of one can also be announced as a rule for everyone else" (J161–62 V 281; italics

added). Which is confirmed later, when Kant says that by means of the relevant deduction "it may be comprehended how an aesthetic judgment *could* lay claim to necessity" (J168 V 288; italics added). A similar connection is also implicitly made at LM314 XXVIII 548, where the following two statements are juxtaposed: "The explanation of the possibility of pure concepts of the understanding we call *deduction*. . . . The deduction of the pure concepts of the understanding is a proof of the validity of the pure concepts of the understanding."

5. "How is the *metaphysician* different from the *transcendental philosopher*? In that the latter addresses merely what is formal, the former what is material (the object, the material)" (O246 XXI 78–79). "Transcendental philosophy is the (rational) principle of a system of *ideas*. . . . As ideas, they cannot contribute anything to the matter of knowledge (that is, to the confirmation of the existence of the object) but only to the principle of what is formal. . . . Whether there is a God, whether there are worlds or one absolute world-whole . . . , is not here decided" (O250 XXI 86–87). Therefore, transcendental philosophy is essentially transcendental *logic*: "Transcendental philosophy is in respect to metaphysics what logic [is] in respect to the whole of philosophy.—Logic contains the general rules of the use of the understanding and is to this extent an introduction to all philosophy. Transcendental philosophy is an introduction to pure philosophy. . . . In transcendental philosophy we consider not objects, but rather reason itself, just as in general logic we regard only the understanding and its rules. Thus transcendental philosophy could also be called transcendental logic" (LM116 XXIX 755–56). Transcendental logic differs from what Kant calls "general logic" (and we might call "formal logic") only because it "has a manifold of sensibility that lies before it a priori" (A76 B102)—that is, because it builds spatiotemporal constraints into its definitions (of knowledge, objects, or whatever). As I point out later, this does not mean that space and time have currency in transcendental logic (or philosophy), in the way they do (for example) in mathematics, but only that *their concepts* do. Note finally that, in a letter to Marcus Herz of May 11, 1781, Kant describes the first *Critique* as including "the *metaphysics of metaphysics*"—hence a second-order kind of philosophical inquiry with respect to traditional ones (C181 X 269).

6. It is also not for philosophy, insofar as it is, or it aims to be, a science, to decide on moral matters: "To pass judgment on morality, on right and wrong, . . . no science or learnedness is needed. . . . Here the common understanding is the judge of science" (LL11 XXIV 23–24).

7. In thus determining what (say) objects and knowledge are, transcendental philosophy will take an active stance, much as mathematics does: it will synthesize concepts and then inquire on their adequacy for the task at hand, instead of simply analyzing *given* concepts. As mentioned in note 1 of chapter 1, I will return to this issue in the last chapter. (There I will also explain how the synthesis I brought out here is in no contradiction with the following claim

that transcendental philosophy—like all philosophy—is entirely constituted of analytic judgments.)

8. "Many concepts ground other concepts. . . . The concept of time, motion, and measurement grounds the commonest concept of an hour. Whoever mentions the word 'friendship' relies on the concepts of love, honesty, etc. . . . One can call fundamental concepts *notiones fundamentales.* . . . Those fundamental concepts which do not in turn presuppose others are called *notiones primitivae* (first fundamental concepts)" (N79 XVII 250).

9. We will see shortly that philosophy can at best *aim at* cognition, but has no hope of attaining it. With this qualification, note that, in my characterization of it, transcendental philosophy aims at something more specific than just cognition from concepts: its objective is indeed the cognition *of* concepts. Kant occasionally makes exactly this kind of distinction: "Because cosmology borrows its principles not from experience, but rather from pure reason, it can be called *rational cosmology.* But because even the object as well, and not just the principles, is an object of pure reason and not experience, it is called transcendental cosmology" (LM19 XXVIII 195). "*Rational* physiology is the cognition of objects insofar as it is obtained not from experience, but rather from a concept of reason. The *object* is always an object of the senses and experience; only the *cognition* of it can be attained through pure concepts of reason, for thereby physiology is distinguished from transcendental philosophy, where the object is also borrowed not from experience, but rather from pure reason" (LM42 XXVIII 221–22). By using this terminology, we could say that, insofar as they used principles of pure reason to derive factual conclusions about ordinary objects, Descartes and Leibniz (for example) were involved in a *rational* but not in a *transcendental* inquiry.

10. Some Kantian statements, on the other hand (like the one I just quoted from the *Notes and Fragments*), make this point in a perfectly straightforward manner. See, for example, A47 B64–65: "it is clear that from mere concepts no synthetic cognition but only merely analytic cognition can be attained." Also, consider the following: In the *Opus Postumum*, Kant argues for the existence of ether (or caloric). The structure of his argument is a familiar one for readers of his published works: whereas experience would be able to prove such existence directly, he has to do it "*indirectly*: on the basis of the *subjective* principle of the *possibility* of experience." He then goes on to add: "[The proof] is not synthetic, through an ampliative judgment, but analytical, through an explicative one—that is, according to the principle of identity" (O79 XXI 548–49; see also O93 XXI 586 and O96 XXI 603). And I do not see how this proof is at all relevantly different from his many others where people have seen synthetic principles at work. Later in the *Opus Postumum* he says unmistakably: "Judgments through concepts are analytic (by the principle of identity), those through predicates of intuition are synthetic" (O174 XXII 33). And, again, "[s]ynthetic a priori propositions are only indirectly possible in philosophy, namely, in relation to objects of pure intuition in space and time" (O189 XXII

83)—"indirectly" because philosophy can only contain a discourse *about* such synthetic judgments, it does not *consist* of them. "Transcendental *philosophy* contains the principles of synthetic a priori judgments from concepts. That which contains synthetic a priori judgments from pure intuitions alone is not philosophy, but pure mathematics" (O188 XXII 81). What transcendental philosophy has to say about such judgments, of course, is how they are possible. (More about this later.)

11. "Metaphysics and transcendental philosophy differ from each other in the respect that the *former* contains already given a priori principles of natural science, the latter, on the other hand, such as hold within themselves the very possibility of metaphysics and of its synthetic a priori principles" (O187 XXII 79). So synthetic judgments belong to metaphysics; what belongs to transcendental philosophy is (say) the conjecture that nature is constituted of appearances, which allows one to understand the possibility of those very judgments. See also note 13 below.

12. Note Kant's defense of this modality at LL224 XXIV 278: "A judgment is expressed practically if it enunciates a possibly necessary action. This probably seems to be contradictory, that *something is possibly necessary*. But here it is completely correct, for the action is always necessary, to be sure, namely, if I want to bring the thing about[;] but the case is not necessary, but merely possible."

13. "[T]he concept of cause and effect is pure but not transcendental, but the consideration of the possibility of such a concept is transcendental.... Transcendental philosophy contains the principles of the possibility of a priori cognition" (LM141–42 XXIX 786).

14. As suggested in note 7 above, Kant complicates matters by using the same words to make *two* distinctions: between analytic and synthetic judgments and between an analytic and a synthetic *method*. And, again, I will return to this issue in chapter 6.

15. Kant also uses "*Erkenntnis*" for the activity that issues in cognitions, for the quality that distinguishes cognitions from non-cognitions, and for the collection of all cognitions—for all of which I typically use "knowledge." The Cambridge edition tries to reproduce this uniformity by using "cognition" as the most common translation of "*Erkenntnis*" (in all of its senses). But I see no reason to do so: once it is clear how "knowledge" and "cognition" are related, using the more common English term has the advantage of making Kant's views more immediately relevant—as indeed they are.

16. "[Contradictions] are *hidden*, where the contradiction can be cognized only through analysis" (LM148 XXIX 793). "[T]here can ... clearly be something possible in the concept, which shows itself as impossible as soon as one has become aware of the contradiction" (LM436 XXIX 965).

17. "[T]he thing of which the concept is possible is not on that account a possible thing. The first possibility may be called logical, the second, real possibility; the proof of the latter ... can never be furnished otherwise than by

presentation of the object corresponding to the concept" (TA406 XX 325).
"[T]he...principle of contradiction [which is the fundamental authority
within logical space]...can prove nothing but the possibility of thinking, not
that of the object which is thought" (J330 V 466). "Possibility must always
be given through experience" (LL336 XXIV 889). "We cannot assume any
object to be possible except that which we exhibit in intuition, thus whose
reality can be exhibited; for otherwise, if the representation does not contradict itself, the thought but not the thing is possible" (N295 XVIII 335).
(The intuition in which we exhibit objects can be pure, hence mathematics
can establish possibilities a priori: "Synthetic a priori propositions are only
possible in pure a priori intuition—space and time," O199 XXII 105. This, on
the one hand, accounts for Kant's hesitation, mentioned in *Kant's Copernican
Revolution*, in calling what mathematics provides *knowledge*, as no contact with
reality is made there: "in pure mathematics there can never be an issue of the
existence of things, but only of their possibility, namely the possibility of an
intuition corresponding to their concept," J239n V 366n. And, on the other,
it explains why, "since in any doctrine of nature there is only as much proper
science as there is a priori knowledge therein, a doctrine of nature will contain
only as much proper science as there is mathematics capable of application
there," TA186 IV 470.)

18. "[O]ne can clearly assume as correct: everything that contradicts itself
is impossible[,] but can deny the reverse: everything that does not contradict
itself is possible, because otherwise it would have to contradict itself.... It all
depends on whether I comprehend the contradiction, and that which I held as
possible will become impossible. Contradiction is only the means for cog-
nizing impossibility. But possibility corresponds to the existence of the object" (LM433–34 XXIX 962; text emended).

19. Ironically, there is a naturalistic *vulgata* of Kant's philosophy that reduces it pretty much to this point, turning transcendental reflection into
(something like) psychological inquiry. What is ironical about it is that the
(quasi-)empirical theories issuing therefrom (the uncertainty signaled by the
parentheses is not my own) are then offered as yet other universal rational
explanations of everything (including, presumably, themselves), making reason fall prey to the same misguided pretense that is described later in this
paragraph.

20. Kant himself, incidentally, is constantly *showing* this feature of reason
as well as *saying* it—which accounts for how he can at times naïvely claim
definitive completeness for his rational efforts while being at other times so
critical of rational claims as such. It is just as well, then, that he also shows how
aware he is of never attaining the completeness he had claimed: how, that is,
he continues to pursue that elusive prize to the very end of his life. See also
notes 35 and 37 of chapter 3 and the attending text.

21. Both limitations, in fact, mobilize the same kind of deferential attitude. For it is essential to what intuitions we can have that they be sensible,

that is, passive; hence to claim that our knowledge must involve intuitions amounts to claiming that it is not actively and independently generated by ourselves—that it is knowledge only insofar as our cognitive activity is applied to material that we *receive* as simply *given* from what is other than us. (But see note 54 below.)

22. At the end of the present section I will quote Kant expressing the hope that in the future philosophy can indeed be of assistance to rulers. But the "counseling" role he advocates there is the exact opposite of the "instruction" referred to here. According to Kant, philosophy can be useful because of the freedom with which it is conducted and which it can inspire, not because the truth allegedly attained by it is to constrain ordinary (ruling) practices. The connection between Kantian philosophy and freedom has already emerged above (see note 1 of chapter 1) and, as was indicated there, will be taken up in chapter 6.

23. This move is regarded by Kant as both inevitable to try and impossible to accomplish: "In the part of the philosophical science of nature ... entitled the metaphysical foundations thereof, there already lies a tendency toward *physics* as the goal to which it is directed—namely, to expound the empirical doctrine of material nature in a system" (O43 XXI 481–82). "[The task is] to classify the real objects of nature according to a principle, and to bring the empirical study of nature ever closer to a system—although it never attains such completeness, which cannot be expected from experience" (O41 XXI 477).

24. The main reason for this tendency (as indeed I explain in *Kant's Copernican Revolution*, and as I reiterated in the previous remark) is Kant's dissatisfaction with the vacuousness of a philosophy that turns entirely upon itself, thus abandoning all the richness of detail that can only come from proper attention to experience. See, for example, O39 XXI 474: "Metaphysical foundations of natural science yield something that is certain and a complete system; but their purpose—the only one which can be envisaged for them—is physics, for which they can give us no material. They are divisions for the concept which require to be filled; and mere forms without an underlying material can as little yield a system of experience, as richly distributed material without forms."

25. That is, since the synthesis that produces experience is "the mere effect of the imagination, . . . a blind though indispensable function of the soul" (A78 B103), the space in which only we can *imagine* (make images of, visualize) things. See C315 XI 53: "the circle is actually constructed by means of the definition, that is, it is exhibited in intuition, not actually on paper (empirically) but in the imagination (a priori)." And J5–6n XX 198n: "[The] pure and for that very reason sublime science [of geometry] seems to forgo some of its dignity if it concedes that, as elementary geometry, it needs *tools*, even if only two, for the construction of its concepts, namely the compass and the ruler. . . . But what is meant . . . is not the actual tools . . . , which can never give . . . shapes with mathematical precision, rather they are to signify only the

simplest kinds of exhibition of the imagination a priori, which cannot be matched by any instrument."

26. This issue will surface again occasionally in what follows and will be addressed in its most general form in the last chapter.

27. Thus (for example), in the Preface to *The Conflict of Faculties*, he characterizes his earlier *Religion Within the Boundaries of Mere Reason* as "an unintelligible, closed book [for the public], only a debate among scholars of the faculty, of which the people take no notice" (R241 VII 8).

28. He also thinks that practicing philosophy can have a beneficial effect on the practitioners' health: "*philosophizing*, in a sense that does not involve being a philosopher, is a means of warding off many disagreeable feelings and, besides, a *stimulant* to the mind that introduces an interest into its occupations— an interest which, just because it is independent of external contingencies, is powerful and sincere, though it is merely in the nature of a game, and keeps the vital force from running down. On the other hand *philosophy*, whose interest is the entire final end of reason (an absolute unity), brings with it a feeling of power which can well compensate to some degree for the physical weaknesses of old age by a rational estimate of life's value" (R317 VII 102).

29. Not every concept that is dependent on another is also definable in its terms. In TR, for example, one cannot understand what a property is without understanding what an object is (properties are what an object *has*, unless they are themselves taken to be (abstract) objects), but properties are not definable in terms of objects. The same relation (I point out below) holds in TI between representations, on the one hand, and their objects (and subjects), on the other.

30. "[T]he word 'representation' is understood with sufficient precision and employed with confidence, even though its meaning can never be analyzed by means of definition" (TB116 II 70). At TB252 II 280, Kant says that "there are many concepts which are scarcely capable of analysis at all," but then he gives only three examples of such concepts: "the concept of a *representation*, the concepts of *being next to each other* and *being after each other*." See also LL27 XXIV 40: "What representation is cannot really be explained. It is one of the simple concepts that we necessarily must have." LL440 XXIV 701: "*representation . . .* [is] a fundamental concept that cannot be explained." LL466 XXIV 730: "The word representation may not be explained at all." And LL485 XXIV 752: "representation is an elementary expression which cannot be further analyzed."

31. "The first judgment on a thing that is new always occurs according to the very prejudices that one wanted to root out from the matter. When one struggles against a prejudice, it defends itself, as it were" (LL318 XXIV 868).

32. As will surface later in this chapter, a representation always has a subject (as well as an object). But that is a feature of the representation, conceptually dependent on it; hence, to reiterate, the articulation of TI's logical space begins with representations, not with anyone (or anything) that they represent—or with any subject either.

33. In the second chapter of *Kant's Copernican Revolution* I argue that this regimenting project is not a promising one. But ultimately this is a problem for the supporters of TR to worry about.

34. In *Kant's Copernican Revolution* I give several examples of Kant's struggling to characterize the notion of an intentional object, which was not part of his received philosophical vocabulary (and conceptual framework). To those examples I can now add the following one, from the *Opus Postumum*: "The objects of... [a] representation [of things in space and time] are not existing things (*non sunt entia*), yet nor are they nonentities (*nonentia*). For they are not objects of perception, objectively outside the representing subject, but are our representation itself, that is, are only subjectively given *in* the subject's representation" (O186 XXII 77–78; last italics added). What are objects for him are neither things nor non-things, neither beings nor non-beings, as traditionally understood; and what being they have is to be found within the representation of which they are objects (that is, it is to be decided on that basis).

35. Thus understood, intentional objects could be also treated as providing an alternative foundation for TI's logical space (but see note 56 below), since they are nothing more (indeed, they are something less) than a linguistic variant of representations (and, as we will see shortly, generate no commitment to the *existence* of anything)—hence this reformulation would not amount to reinstating the conceptual primacy of objects. "The highest concept, under which all remaining elementary concepts are ordered, is the concept of an object in general, *which underlies representation*. . . . It seems striking to think of an object that comprises a nothing: but *a nothing* also *presupposes only a thought which then cancels itself*, {i.e., which contradicts itself} and therefore never has an existing object as ground" (LM431–32 XXIX 960–61; first italics added).

36. It might be worth pointing out explicitly that in TI one finds it natural to use two distinct sets of quantifiers, hence to say, for example (as I did here), that (a) when I think of a winged horse, I think of *something* while on the other hand (b) *there is* (or *exists*) no (such thing as a) winged horse. In TR, on the other hand, this distinction collapses: the notion of existence is as trivial (that is, as fundamental) as that of an object (between the two notions runs a very brief interdefinitional loop), and being is (no more than) being a value of a bound variable.

37. That such conditions are imposed on anything that is to count as an object allows Kant to explain how we can decide substantive matters about objects before having any experience of them—in his terminology, how synthetic a priori judgments are possible. But note that this "explanation," again, is to be understood as a transcendental one: as located at a conceptual level. If we wanted to provide an empirical variant of it, we would probably start out with objects (minds) constituted in certain ways and consequently imposing precisely those conditions on the (other) objects they experience. That is, we would proceed to elaborate an *empirically realist* theory of the kind

referred to in note 19 above. Which would be fine as long as the theory stays empirical, thereby proving its irrelevance to Kant's concerns (however inspired by Kant it might be).

38. "[T]he categories . . . always signify only an object in general" (PR249 V 136). As I point out in *Kant's Copernican Revolution*, these criteria are strict relatives of the empirical ones (mentioned above) we use in ordinary situations—and for good reason: it is for what generally happens (is done) in those situations that we are trying to provide a transcendental legitimation. The empirical criteria, however, have to go through the "torsion" required by the move from realism to idealism: what is ordinarily taken as empirical evidence that an object is present (hence as causally dependent on the object) will now be understood as definitional of objectivity (hence as conceptually prior to the object). That is: one defers to the ordinary person's practice, but not to the most obvious rationalization of it. I will return to this issue in chapter 6.

39. A suggestive statement of this criterion can be found at LE253 XXVII 481: "The laws produce the causality in actions, i.e., the property whereby the agent becomes the cause of the action." See also LM373 XXVIII 671: "Cause is that which, when it has been posited, something really distinct is posited, according to a universal rule." LM163 XXIX 809: "The criterion of a ground is not that something follows upon it but rather that something follows according to general rules." TA225 IV 514: "To attract one another immediately *means [heißt]* to approach one another in accordance with an invariable law" (italics added). And N221 XVIII 120: "That which is the condition under which we posit something in accordance with a rule is the cause." As these passages indicate, the rule-directedness of representations that matters here involves specifically their representational character: it is *what they represent* that is subject to rules. Representations, of course, are also objects—in the continuation of the passage from A108 cited above, Kant says: "and [representations] can themselves be objects of other representations in turn." As objects, they have properties: a representation, for example, can be vivid or dim, uplifting or depressing. And it is on these properties that a transcendental realist would focus, if the rule-directedness of representations became important for him (if, say, as Kant considers inevitable, he showed a tendency to become an empirical idealist); thus he might claim that vivid or uplifting representations always surface first in consciousness. In TI, on the other hand, it is the *intentionality* of representations that is rule-directed, which justifies our turning straight to their intentional objects as we bring up the next few definitional traits of a cognition.

40. That intellectual conditions must be translated into spatiotemporal terms holds for all categories, not only for those of quantity which are being referred to here. As I explain in *Kant's Copernican Revolution*, Kant replaces the unbridgeable chasm present in TR between the structure of objects and the structure of our knowledge of them with a chasm that turns out to be just

as unbridgeable between the conditions of intuition and the conditions of thought. As the realist cannot ultimately explain how our mental states can fit the outside world, the idealist Kant cannot ultimately explain how there can be objects that are *both* in space and time *and* obey categorial constraints. He repeatedly tries to avoid the problem by appealing to the *necessity* of both sets of conditions for us to be in contact with anything at all, including ourselves (that is, to a strategy I describe in my earlier book as his "making it too easy for himself"; see 116, 144 there), and by claiming that the ground of this necessity is a mystery "that of course lies wholly beyond the limits of human reason" (C314 XI 52); but he knows better—he knows that his self-appointed task is one of proving how certain matters are *possible*, not just how they could not be otherwise. So he proceeds painstakingly (and interminably) to articulate what it *means* for objects of experience to satisfy both sets of conditions (which, as I point out in *Kant's Copernican Revolution*, is most of what he does in the Analytic of the first *Critique* and much of what he continues to do in subsequent work). (A suggestive indication of the parallel nature of the two chasms mentioned above is the following: The transcendental realist Leibniz had appealed to pre-established harmony as providing a resolution of the chasm realists must worry about. Not surprisingly, Kant reinterprets pre-established harmony as providing a resolution of the chasm *he* must worry about. See TA335 VIII 250, C314 XI 52. Following the first of these two passages, he makes the remark that I used as an epigraph for the present book: true understanding of a previous philosopher can be obtained only through creative appropriation of his words, in the name of rational thought itself—hence not necessarily of what he did say, but rather of what he *ought to* have said. The history of philosophy is itself an intrinsically philosophical enterprise.)

41. Conversely, nothing can ever be learned about a fictional (hence unreal) object that is not already contained in the fiction from which it originates. Which, as we will see shortly, does not mean that such an object cannot have a useful or even an important role.

42. Or, more elaborately, that "that which makes cognition possible, which is its condition, that is also the condition of things" (LM57 XXVIII 239).

43. The notion of consistency has no immediate application to a set of representations. But, since there is not much riding on this issue, I will simply assume that the ordinary notion of consistency for sets of propositions can be extended to cover the present case: that a set of representations is consistent if it is not the case that obvious propositional descriptions of two of its members contradict one another. (For example, it is not the case that they are of the forms "The table at position p at time t is brown" and "The table at position p at time t is not brown.")

44. "[The form of a world] consists in the *coordination* . . . of substances. . . . This coordination is conceived of as *real* and objective, not as ideal and depending upon the subject's power of choice, by means of which any multiplicity

whatsoever may be fashioned into a whole by a process of adding together at will. For by taking several things together, you achieve without difficulty a *whole of representation* but you do not, in virtue of that, arrive at the *representation of a whole*. Accordingly, if there happened to be certain wholes consisting of substances, and if these wholes were not bound to one another by any connection, the bringing of these wholes together, a process by means of which the mind forces the multiplicity into an ideal unity, would signify nothing more than a plurality of worlds held together in a single thought" (TB380–81 II 390). "The principle of the form of the universe is that which contains the ground of the universal connection, in virtue of which all substances and their states belong to the same whole which is called *a world*" (TB391 II 398).

45. Conversely, "[c]oncepts of reason come about when one enlarges a concept of the understanding to infinity" (LM206 XXIX 848). But I continue to think that (as I said in *Kant's Copernican Revolution*) it is more illuminating to see understanding as a self-limitation of reason, rather than reason as an illegitimate extension of understanding.

46. Invoking a radical distinction between metaphysics and epistemology is, in fact, a typical ploy in TR—and is only possible there. In TI, as we have seen, what it is to know (the subject of epistemology) determines what it is to be (the subject of metaphysics).

47. "Were space and time properties of things in themselves then the infinity of the world would indeed be inconceivable, but not on that account impossible. But if space and time are not properties of things in themselves, then the impossibility of an infinite given world already flows from the inconceivability" (LM333 XXVIII 569). See also the letter to Christian Garve of August 7, 1783, where Kant says: "all objects that are given to us can be interpreted in two ways: *on the one hand*, as appearances, *on the other hand*, as things in themselves. If one takes appearances to be things in themselves and demands of those [appearances] the *absolutely unconditioned* in the series of conditions, one gets into nothing but contradictions. These contradictions, however, fall away when one shows that there cannot be anything wholly unconditioned among appearances; such a thing could only exist among things in themselves" (C199n X 341n; translation modified). After making the initial distinction, it would have been natural for him to claim that the interpretation of the objects given as things in themselves gives rise to contradictions, if indeed he wanted to use the antinomies as a refutation of TR. But that is not what he says: consistently with my reading in *Kant's Copernican Revolution*, he says rather that contradictions ensue if those objects are taken as *both* appearances *and* things in themselves—hence he uses the antinomies as a refutation of the claim that things in themselves can be found within the range of TI, where what is given is always to be construed as an appearance (that is, as the intentional object of a representation), though only after the antinomies it must be regarded as *only* an appearance.

48. This conclusion is complementary to the one mentioned in note 21 and the attending text: our knowledge must include *both* an active *and* a passive element.

49. That the act in question be referred to as a choice requires that a certain amount of violence be exercised on the ordinary notion of choice. In the real, empirical world, one faces a choice among a number of given objects or, if the choice is among a number of possible courses of action, each course is associated with moves to be made in a clearly identifiable objectual context. The "choice" we are talking about here, on the other hand, is one that founds the empirical world as such; before which, then, there are no objects whatsoever but only an undifferentiated manifold. Hence, one might say, it is really no choice at all because there is nothing *to choose from*. But I will argue later that a large part of what Kant does is explore the amount of meaning that can be retained when some of its ideal conditions are lost. The present situation is a case in point, which justifies my insistence on the use of the word "choice": while there is no question that this use differs from the ordinary one as noted above, it continues to be true that (as with ordinary choice) the act thus referred to is a spontaneous one, and one that amounts to privileging one of many possibilities—though none of these possibilities could even be described independently of the choice relevant to it.

50. Synthesis, of course, plays a major role in the first *Critique*. But only in the later essay on the progress of metaphysics do we find Kant's clearest statements that all that needs to be added to (passive) intuition in order to account for objectivity is the ability to synthesize, and all categories are but specifications of this ability: "the representation of a composite, as such, is not a mere intuition, but requires the concept of a compounding, so far as it is applied to the intuition in space and time. So this concept . . . is one that is not abstracted from intuitions, . . . but is a basic concept, and a priori at that—in the end the sole basic concept a priori, which is the original foundation in the understanding for all concepts of sensible objects. There will thus be as many a priori concepts resident in the understanding, to which objects given to the senses must be subordinated, as there are types of compounding (*synthesis*) with consciousness, i.e., as there are types of synthetic unity of apperception of the manifold given in intuition" (TA363 XX 271). "All representations which constitute an experience can be assigned to sensibility, with one solitary exception, namely that of the composite, as such. . . . [W]e require a priori the concept of a composite, and thus of the compounding (synthesis) of the manifold, and thus synthetic unity of apperception in combining this manifold; which unity of consciousness, in virtue of the diversity of intuitable representations of objects in space and time, requires different functions to combine them; these are called categories" (TA366–67 XX 275–76).

51. It will be worth insisting that this contribution or choice must not be understood as *my own*, or as *human*, or as *mental*—as empirical in any way. As suggested in note 37 above, one can be inspired by Kant's philosophy to the

construction of empirical theories, but must be careful not to reduce that philosophy to any such theory. It is the *concept* of a contribution or choice that is called upon here: activity or spontaneity as such, not *anyone's* activity or spontaneity. See also the following section.

52. "That which is perfect precedes in the idea a priori that which is imperfect, and the latter is only determinable in the former.... We would not have a concept of the imperfect if we did not conceive of that which is perfect" (N233 XVIII 202). "Human reason has need of an idea of highest perfection, to serve it as a standard according to which it can make determinations.... A concept of this kind, which is needed as a standard of lesser or greater degrees in this or that case, regardless of its reality, is called an idea. But are not these ideas (such as Plato's idea of a republic, for example) all mere figments of the brain? By no means. For I can set up this or that case so as to accord with my idea. Thus a ruler, for example, can set up his state to accord with the idea of the most perfect republic, in order to bring his state nearer to perfection" (R341 XXVIII 993). "Friendship is an idea, because it is not drawn from experience, but has its seat in the understanding; in experience it is very defective, but in morals it is a very necessary idea.... [N]o friendship ever matches the idea of friendship.... But the idea is true, nonetheless" (LE185 XXVII 423-24). "Absolute space is ... necessary, not as a concept of an actual object, but rather as an idea, which is to serve as a rule for considering all motion therein merely as relative" (TA265 IV 560).

53. See also N393 XVIII 685: "One cannot think of a kind of representation as *restricted* with regard to a certain principle without opposing it to another one that is general with respect to it. I.e., if I designate a cognition as being restricted to the sensibility of the subject then I must conceive of a cognition of the supersensible in opposition to this."

54. See also N387 XVIII 675: "Things considered as they are in themselves, not as appearances, are not qualified for any theoretical cognition, for they are mere ideas." Unquestionably, Kant's talk of passivity as a necessary condition for experience suggests more of a role for things in themselves than I allow. If (as I noted in the first section) we must conceive of our relation to the object of knowledge as one that is partly receptive, then what is at the other end of this receiving relation? Where are we receiving the material of experience from? In line with my general attitude toward Kant's project (suggested in note 49 above and articulated below in chapter 4), I believe that no direct, informative answers to such questions are possible: the receiving relation here is one for which there is no giver (other than in the empty, tautological sense in which I will speak of a "winner" for a race yet to be run); indeed, this is a receiving that (much like the "choice" discussed in that earlier note) lacks important features of ordinary receiving. Using other Kantian language, we might describe it by saying that it qualifies our experience as (necessarily) constituted *as if* it was receptive. Or, using yet other Kantian language, we might say that the ground at stake here is one that can never be *determinate*:

"[The] expression ['determinate'] must never be left out of the definition of 'ground.' For a *consequent* . . . is something that, if I posit it, I must at the same time think something else as posited, that is, a consequent always belongs to something or other that is its ground. But when I think something as consequent, I posit only *some* ground *or other, which* ground is undetermined" (C298n XI 35n).

55. Kant regards this (doubly) modal formulation as the only correct one; specifically, he does not think that the "I" is *in fact* mobilized in every representation. In his letter to Jacob Beck of December 4, 1792, commenting on Beck's explanatory account of the critical philosophy, he makes the following correction (among others): "Instead of . . . 'The *I think* must accompany all the representations in the synthesis' 'must *be capable of* accompanying' " (C445 XI 395). See also A117n: "the mere representation *I* in relation to all others . . . is the transcendental consciousness. Now it does not matter here whether this representation be clear (empirical consciousness) or obscure, even whether it be actual; but the possibility of the logical form of all cognition necessarily rests on the relationship to this apperception *as a faculty.*" (On the word "faculty," see note 30 of chapter 3.)

56. Expanding on the suggestion considered in note 35, we could reduce the concept of a representation to those of its subject and object, and define a representation as the *bearer* of both, much like in TR an object could be characterized as the bearer of properties. (In both cases, we would be exploiting brief and uninformative interdefinitional loops, hence not really rearranging the basic conceptual priorities that identify either framework.)

57. "One must distinguish pure (transcendental) apperception from empirical *apperception percipientis,* from *apperceptiva percepti.* The first merely asserts *I am.* The second that I was, I am, and I will be, i.e., I am a thing of past, present, and future time, where this consciousness that I am is common to all things as a determination of my existence as a magnitude. The latter is cosmological, the former purely psychological. The cosmological apperception which considers my existence as a magnitude in time sets me into relation with other things that are, that were, and that will be" (N365).

58. See also A350: "the I is, to be sure, in all thoughts; but not the least intuition is bound up with this representation, which would distinguish it from other objects of intuition. Therefore one can, to be sure, perceive that this representation continually recurs with every thought, but not that it is a standing and abiding intuition, in which thoughts (as variable) would change." TA250–51 IV 542–43: "The *I,* the general correlate of apperception, and itself merely a thought, designates, as a mere prefix, a thing of undetermined meaning—namely, the subject of all predicates—without any condition at all that would distinguish this representation of the subject from that of a something in general: a substance, therefore, of which, by this term, one has no concept of what it may be. . . . The thought *I* . . . is *no concept* at all, but only inner perception, and so nothing at all can be inferred from it . . . —including,

in particular, the persistence of the soul as substance." TA362 XX 270: "Of... the subject of apperception...it is absolutely impossible to know anything further as to what sort of being it is, or what its natural constitution may be." And see the following note.

59. "[T]he consciousness in itself is not even a representation distinguishing a particular object, but rather a form of representation in general, insofar as it is to be called a cognition" (A346 B404). "Because... the only condition accompanying all thinking is the I, in the universal proposition 'I think,' reason has to do with this condition insofar as it is itself unconditioned. But it is only the formal condition, namely the logical unity of every thought, in which I abstract from every object" (A398). "The consciousness of myself is not yet an act of self-determination for the knowledge of an object, but is only the modality of knowledge in general by which a subject makes itself into an object in general; it is what is formal in intuition in general" (O192 XXII 87).

60. Note that this connectedness brings about the unification of the spatiotemporal framework as well as of the world to be found in it. Individual representations may well come with their own spaces and times (for example, I can imagine a winged horse running through a forest, and later imagine Achilles crying over being slighted—and in both cases there will be a spatiotemporal dimension to my images); but it is only when representations are cognitive that we can "stitch together" their spaces and times into a single, *objective* spacetime ("In the Aesthetic I ascribed... [the] unity [of space] merely to sensibility, only in order to note that it precedes all concepts, though to be sure it presupposes a synthesis, which does not belong to the senses but through which all concepts of space and time first become possible," B160–61n). Or, rather (given the limitations we will be reminded of shortly), we make contact with a single, objective spacetime *to the extent that* representations are categorially connected.

61. There is a practical side to this issue. Humans do not necessarily have "a character," Kant thinks; they do only if their will "is determined to act according to firm principles" (AP203 VII 292). If it is not, they fall apart as much practically as they do theoretically, "shifting hither and yon like a swarm of gnats" (AP203 VII 292).

Chapter 3

1. And when "blind chance is assumed to be the explanation...nothing is explained" (J264 V 393), which is why "the blind chance that one might assume as the principle for judging nature" is "enraging to the human mind" (J323 V 458). Therefore, Kant occasionally points out, it is not appropriate to label his opponents "determinists"—thus suggesting that *he* believes that an action can occur without being determined. What is at stake is rather the *kind* of determination involved in the two cases. "[T]hat system or principle which previously was called determinism, must properly be called *predeterminism*. For

since it is absolutely necessary that every action must be determined by a ground, even that which a divinity performs, then determinism does not express what is of concern here, namely the principle according to which every action, even of a free being, is thought of as determined by its determining grounds in the previous time, and thus as not given in the control of the agent" (LM488 XXIX 1019). I will, however, stick to the more common label; and by "determinists" I will always mean "*hard* determinists"—that is, those who think that determinism amounts to a denial of freedom. For *soft* determinists must be seen not as opponents of Kant but as fighting on his side, that is, as admitting determinism while trying to find room for human freedom—except that, as we will see, Kant judges all other efforts in this direction as mere quibbling about words.

2. Kant is as much puzzled as Hume was by this notion of a thing *making another one be*, even when the first thing is God Himself: "How am I to understand *the fact that, because something is, something else is?* . . . The will of God is something. The world which exists is *something completely different.* Nonetheless, the one is posited by the other. . . . Nor am I willing to be fobbed off by the words 'cause' and 'effect,' 'cause' and 'action.' For if I already regard something as a cause of something else, or if I attach the concept of force to it, then I am already thinking of the cause as containing the relation of the real ground to its consequence, and then it is easy to understand that the consequence is posited in accordance with the rule of identity" (TB239– 40 II 202–3—see also TB356–57 II 370–71). No such mysterious "causal efficacy" is required in his own understanding of causality as regularity. See also LM224–25 XXIX 925–26, where destiny is defined as "a blind necessity without law" and Kant claims that "[d]estinies conflict with the interest of reason" because "that something should be without any grounds and causes, and yet be necessary, we have not the slightest concept" and "[t]o want to explain something by destiny is nonsensical, for calling upon destiny just means that I cannot explain something." Clearly, the ontological concept of a cause (of something that necessitates something else, period) is replaced for him by the concept of something that can *explain* the occurrence of something else, that can make rational sense of it, hence that is essentially related to the uncovering of a lawlike regularity.

3. "[I]n the case of freedom, the thing itself as cause . . . would nevertheless belong to the series of conditions, and only *its causality* would be thought as intelligible" (A561 B589).

4. See also TA89 IV 294: "*Nature* is the *existence* of things, insofar as that existence is determined according to universal laws." Even more clearly, "nature . . . in the *formal* sense" is said to be at TA111 IV 318 "the sum total of the rules to which all appearances must be subject if they are to be thought as connected in one experience." Still at TA111 IV 318 "nature in general" is "lawfulness in the connection of appearances" (see also N249 XVIII 248), and at TA112 IV 319 "nature . . . is fully identical with the mere universal lawfulness of experience." At TA184 IV 468–69 "the word nature already carries

with it the concept of laws" and "[the] necessity of laws is inseparably attached to the concept of nature." At LL527 IX 11 "[t]he whole of nature in general is really nothing but a connection of appearances according to rules; and there is *no absence of rules* anywhere."

5. "[T]he plurality of worlds ... signifies only the multiplicity of many systems, of which there may be an innumerable amount, together with their different forms and real relations (their effects in space and time)" (O234 XXI 30).

6. For a psychological explanation to be a natural one, according to Kant, it must refer to a *spatio*temporal framework. Therefore, "the mind's existence and action" cannot be detailed in terms of an immaterial soul: they must rather consist in the identification of behavioral patterns (typically different from the ones brought out by a physical explanation). Because the empirical psychology of his time had not yet taken this course, Kant's judgment of it is a scathing one: "one must admit that the situation of psychological explanations is quite pitiable compared to that of physical explanations, that they are endlessly hypothetical and that for three different grounds of explanation it is very easy to think up a fourth, equally plausible one, and that hence there is a host of so-called psychologists of this sort, who know how to propose causes for every affection or movement of the mind ... [and] yet fail to give a glimpse of even the ability let alone knowledge of how to explain scientifically the most common natural event in the corporeal world" (J38 XX 238). See also A848–49 B876–77, where after pointing out that "[e]mpirical psychology must ... be entirely banned from metaphysics, and is already excluded by the idea of it," he is willing to "concede it a little place ... in metaphysics," largely because of how modest its progress has been: "it is not yet rich enough to comprise a subject on its own."

7. As well as the related one between a mechanical and a teleological account: "we may confidently research the laws of nature (as far as the possibility of their product is cognizable from ... [either the mechanical or the teleological] principle of our understanding) in accordance with both of these principles, without being troubled by the apparent conflict between the two principles for judging this product" (J281–82 V 413). I will focus on teleology in chapter 5.

8. Somewhat inconsistently (see note 44 of the previous chapter and the attending text), at A418–19 B446–47 Kant distinguishes *world* as a mere spatiotemporal whole from *nature* as a causally connected (hence also a unitary) one. Still, in passages such as the one considered here, that distinction is not operative and the two terms ("*Welt*" and "*Natur*") appear virtually interchangeable (see also LM20 XXVIII 196: "the world is ... an absolute whole" and "all substances in the world stand in interaction, and thereby constitute a whole"); so I consider myself authorized, in what follows, to develop my account of this theme by using only the first term. Besides allowing us to bring out the relevance of contemporary semantical analysis to our concerns, this

policy will also free the term "nature" for another use it unmistakably has in Kant: that is, as equivalent to "sensible nature."

9. There are more complications and difficulties connected with this "identity through possible worlds" than I can discuss now. I will begin to focus on them in section 4 below. But it is important to note right away that the sensible and the supersensible (or, as Kant labels it elsewhere, the nonsensible) are radically distinct: we cannot expect them both to belong to the same connected whole. "The *Critique* always understands by the nonsensible only that which cannot at all, not even the least part, be contained in a sensory intuition, and it is a deliberate deception of the inexperienced reader to foist upon him in place of that something in the sensible object" (TA295 VIII 201). The direct reference of this passage is to the idea of the simple, which we should not think of as instantiated by the elements of spatiotemporal things: everything spatiotemporal, however minute and imperceptible, is still completely irrelevant to it. "No microscope has yet been able to detect Newton's *lamellae*, of which the colored particles of bodies consist, but the understanding recognizes (or assumes) not only their existence, but also that they really are represented, albeit without consciousness, in our empirical intuition. It has not, however, occurred to any of his followers to declare them on that account to be entirely nonsensible and moreover to be objects of understanding. . . . If the whole is to be an object of the senses, all of its parts would necessarily have to be so as well" (TA298 VIII 205). Similarly, (supersensible) freedom does not belong to the same field as spatiotemporal causal connections, if only imperceptibly so: recognizing it requires *another way of thinking altogether* (and it is an open question for now whether we can say that what we are doing then is thinking differently of *the same things*).

10. A clear statement of the overdetermination that is relevant to us can be found at LM488 XXIX 1019–20: "with a human being everything happens according to laws of natural necessity, and also everything happens according to the principle of freedom. As a natural being (phenomenon), every new action can be explained as determined according to laws of natural necessity. One also does this often in criminal cases. E.g., with the criminal one takes into consideration his education, external circumstances, inclinations or other motive grounds that are merely subjective, in order to derive from this the determination to the crime. As intelligence . . . , a human being is self-determining, independent of all laws of nature, takes from himself the ground for omitting the action that he can do, or should. . . . We are thus forced to assume, in his *selfhood*, an agreement of two, apparently wholly contradictory beings. . . . In consideration of his actions one can therefore also designate *freedom* (nominal definition): *the imputability of human beings.*" In what follows, we will see how far we can go in turning this nominal definition into a real one (see also note 31 below).

11. "[T]he critique of sensibility . . . would . . . not amount to anything if empiricism and predeterminism were not contrary to all morality. Thus in the

absence of critique morality runs into danger from speculative reason" (N368 XVIII 625–26).

12. "[W]e can explain nothing but what we can reduce to laws the object of which can be given in some possible experience" (G105 IV 459). At LE271 XXVII 505, Kant adds an interesting detail: "Freedom cannot . . . be made comprehensible, and so in itself there is no freedom; only the belief that we are free is capable of explanation." That we are free and that we believe ourselves to be free are two independent matters; but only the latter is a natural occurrence, hence only the latter can receive an explanation. Therefore, as will be pointed out later, determinists proceed to deny the former any status whatsoever, and to make do with the latter only.

13. As will become clear shortly, this original experience is not a *direct*, but an *inferential* experience of freedom. It is original because it establishes the reality of freedom once and for all, but its immediate object is not freedom. Kant makes this point (for example) at LE272 XXVII 506–7: "Just to become aware of freedom on its own, without acquaintance with duty, would be so utterly impossible that we would declare such freedom to be absurd; for in that case reason would determine something for which no determining cause would be present. . . . The position, then, is that freedom is known by an inference (namely from the moral law) and not immediately felt."

14. One passage among many (and an especially forceful one): "it is patently absurd, having granted . . . [the] concept of duty its authority, to want to say that one nevertheless *cannot* do it" (P338 VIII 370).

15. "Many have contended that conscience is a product of art and education, and that it judges and speaks in a merely habitual fashion. But if this were so, the person having no such training and education of his conscience could escape the pangs of it, which is not in fact the case" (LE134 XXVII 355–56).

16. At LE130 XXVII 351 Kant makes the distinction even clearer: "Conscience . . . is not a mere faculty, but an instinct, not to pass judgment on, but to direct oneself [according to moral laws]." And elsewhere he is clearer that the moral feeling does not judge either (though both it and conscience are consistent with moral judgment—indeed essential for giving that judgment any executive force): "One cannot judge . . . [truth] through a sense of truth— as little as one can judge duty through moral feeling. One can never judge through the senses but only through the understanding" (LL458 XXIV 721).

17. Kant clearly admits that we can be confused about conscience and mistake something else for it. See, for example, the following passage: "Everyone has an urge to award praise to himself for his good actions, according to rules of prudence. And conversely, he also reproaches himself for having acted imprudently. . . . This, however, is not yet conscience, but only an analogue of it, whereby a man apportions praise or blame to himself. People are often liable to confuse this analogue with conscience. A criminal in the condemned cell is angry, levels the severest reproaches at himself, and is

greatly agitated, but mostly over the fact that he has been so imprudent in his actions as to have been caught in them. These reproaches that he now levels at himself he confuses with the reproaches of conscience against his morality; but if only he had extricated himself without trouble, he would never have reproached himself at all, though had he a conscience, this would still have occurred. So the judgment by rules of prudence must assuredly be distinguished from the judgment of conscience" (LE131 XXVII 352; for a real-life application of this distinction by Kant himself, see his letter to Maria von Herbert of Spring 1792, C412 XI 333). See also LE328 XXVII 576: "The conscience must not be chimerical, i.e., it must not regard evil consequences, resulting by chance from *merita ed demerita fortunae*, as imputable *facta*; for example, when a loss at cards from want of prudence is confused with a want of morality; thus a delinquent often blames himself, not for his crime, but for his lack of dexterity in committing it; as a doctor does for the death of a patient to whom he has accidentally given the wrong medicine." In the immediately following paragraph, he also shows awareness of the possibility of a neurotic conscience: "The conscience must not be micrological, i.e., turn trifles into an important *casus conscientiae*; though that does not allow us to set aside all accounting in the matter, but merely bids us not to carry it to excess." Finally, Kant also admits that conscience is highly variable among humans: "the more virtuous a human being is, all the more harshly [conscientiousness] punishes him because of the slightest indiscretion frowned upon by the moral law in him. But...the depraved, if only he can escape the external floggings for his heinous deeds, laughs at the scrupulousness of the honest who inwardly plague themselves with self-inflicted rebukes" (R28–29 VIII 261).

18. This distinction between the (empirical) correctness of a particular claim and the (transcendental) legitimacy of the register in which the claim is formulated will be the subject of ample discussion in section 3 below.

19. It might be useful to cite another case in which Kant adopts the same strategy of defense. When considering whether "the human race is...to be conceived as progressing toward what is better with respect to the moral end of its existence," he considers himself "allowed to assume" that it is indeed to be so conceived because (a) any doubts one might have concerning this progress "cannot be made quite certain," and (b) he has the "innate duty...so to influence posterity that it becomes always better," hence to posit such improvement as possible. Once again, moral claims can assert themselves in an epistemic void: one "cannot exchange the duty (as something *liquidum*) for the rule of prudence not to attempt the impracticable (as something *illiquidum*, since it is merely hypothetical)"—and it does not matter that the favored option is just as epistemically uncertain as its opposite, since there faith can take the place of knowledge (see P306 VIII 308–9; the exact nature of this faith will be discussed in chapter 5).

20. See also N330 XVIII 443: "The freedom of the divine will does not consist in its having been able to choose something other than the best; for not

even human freedom consists in that, but in being necessarily determined by the idea of the best, which is lacking in the human being and thereby also restricts his freedom." The other main point made in this passage—that there is only freedom to do good—will become crucially relevant in chapter 4; hence the passage should be kept in mind when we get to that issue, in addition to what other textual evidence will be provided. (The same is true of other passages to follow—for example, the one from LE51 in the next paragraph.)

21. It is useful to point out that, as far as Kant is concerned, the origin of the word "maxim" is to be found in logic, and specifically in the theory of syllogism. "A rule . . . [is called] the *major*, sometimes, when it is the highest rule, it is called a *maxima*, or the rule of action" (LL390). Therefore, that there be a maxim to an action A of mine simply means that I can construct a series of syllogisms whose final conclusion is A and where the maxim is the very first major premise. And of course for any one action of mine I (or anyone else) can come up with indefinitely many such series, hence with indefinitely many maxims of the action; which proves nothing about what actually, *objectively*, caused it. (See also the following note.)

22. At PR153 V 19 Kant says that practical principles can be "subjective, or *maxims*, when the condition is regarded by the subject as holding only for his will," and "objective, or practical *laws*, when the condition is cognized as objective, that is, as holding for the will of every rational being." This passage brings out two elements of contrast between maxims and laws: the particularity of the former versus the universality of the latter, which is typically given most emphasis by commentators, and their different epistemic status ((mere) maxims are only "regarded [*angesehen*] . . . as holding" whereas laws are "cognized [*erkannt*] . . . as holding"). It is this second element that I consider basic, since the first one has no independent significance in a Kantian context: what the subject "regards" as holding only for herself is not necessarily so, given that self-consciousness is not a form of knowledge. For something to be known, one must prove it to be the case objectively, and here is where the universality comes in. I know that there is a brown table before me when I have established that everyone similarly positioned would have to see it; and that is the only knowledge in the vicinity. That it seems to me as if there were a brown table before me, far from being unfalsifiably the case (as would be in a Cartesian framework) is not even the sort of mental state that could be called knowledge—and much the same is true for what it seems to me my own goals are.

23. Hume distinguished this kind of freedom from freedom as indifference, which he regarded as a delusion. See *A Treatise of Human Nature*, 407ff. Kant would agree on Hume's negative judgment on indifference: "[F]reedom does not consist in the contingency of an action (in its not being determined through any ground at all)" (RR95n VI 50n). "One wants to prove, through the faculty for choosing between indifferent things, that freedom is a lawlessness from all incentives. But the freedom of indifference is a non-thing"

(LM268 XXIX 901). But, as I will now proceed to explain, he would strongly reject Hume's understanding of freedom as spontaneity.

24. "[T]here are cases where something is posited, and another thing is posited after, yet where the one is not a ground of the other. E.g., when the stork comes, good weather follows. But to posit does not mean something follows the other accidentally; for the stork could also be brought on the mail coach" (LM315 XXVIII 549). "If I arrange for a stork to fly in wintertime, it does not become warm. Hence this is not the cause" (N221 XVIII 120).

25. "[W]hat would one hold of a human being who, in order to demonstrate his freedom, danced in the gutter in fine clothes? The freedom of contrariety is merely a fabricated dream, for we will still find with all our actions that they happen from causes, and it would also be contradictory not to want that which satisfies me in the highest degree, but instead its opposite" (LM269 XXIX 903; this kind of behavior would have much greater significance, however, if the issue was, say, that of establishing one's independence of a natural attachment to one's fine clothes—see note 72 below and the attending text). A similar judgment is passed by Kant on the cases in which one must choose between equal things, hence again (it might seem) the choice is left entirely to one's arbitrary decision: "one leaves someone the choice between two {things} that are in themselves wholly equal. It is false to assure that he can choose in no other way than by a free self-determination of his own reason without concurrence of any natural causes: one can assume that previously he certainly inspects both {things} often and frequently, be it from mistrust, or because he expects an advantage with one, finally after fruitless bother, impatience overcomes him and he grabs one: is the latter not a determining ground that influences his reason, so that this finally decides for that which it demands of him?" (LM490–91 XXIX 1022–23).

26. Kant himself, at one point, did adopt this subterfuge: "*[S]pontaneity is action which issues from an inner principle. When this spontaneity is determined in conformity with the representation of what is best it is called freedom*" (TB25 I 402). "To act freely is to act in conformity with one's desire and to do so, indeed, with consciousness" (TB26 I 403). But note that, as we will see in section 4 below, the letter of some of these passages can be saved as long as one provides an appropriate articulation of the reference to "an inner [or internal] principle."

27. "*Willkür*" is used systematically only very late: before 1793, Kant often uses "*Wille*" instead. Unless we think that some dramatic change has occurred in his philosophy (a good strategy to hide interpretive confusion), this earlier practice (and the obvious common root of "*Willkür*" and "*Wille*") should make it clear that he has always been talking about two senses *of willing* and only getting clearer about distinguishing them, hence that "choice" is a misleading translation for "*Willkür*." (Besides, he routinely uses "*Wahl*" as an appropriate equivalent of "choice.") Rather than playing with words, we need to analyze the notion of will—and bring out that often *what is taken to be* a case of will exercising its power is not one.

28. Having this consciousness is not enough to determine *what* we are conscious of: what the *law* of freedom is. For such determination freedom must undergo the additional conceptual analysis to follow.

29. In addition to a passage quoted earlier (see note 13), consider the following: "Wholly incorrect . . . is the idea of some *philosophers* . . . , as if one could directly and immediately be conscious of absolute spontaneity or of the effectiveness of the law of freedom in our actions. . . . But this is impossible, we can indeed be aware that sensible impulses concur with the determination to act dutifully, but from that, that we are not conscious of their existence in a special case, we can in no way infer that they were also not all present in us and did not show themselves effective, for how is one supposed to be aware of their nonexistence?" (LM490 XXIX 1022). More about this constitutional opaqueness later.

30. Both "faculty" and "ability" in this passage translate the same German word "*Vermögen*" and, in a previous edition of the *Metaphysics of Morals*, the same translator (Mary J. Gregor) had translated the same word in both occurrences as "capacity." This terminological uncertainty is indicative of theoretical tension: scholars have a hard time resisting the temptation to reify Kant's "faculties"—whereas for him to have a faculty of X simply means to be able to do X. This point will become relevant later.

31. It will become apparent in the next chapter that, unless we did find something positive to say about freedom, what we have developed so far (freedom is *not* being determined by another) would be a purely *nominal* account, hence would provide no understanding—not even the limited kind the account to follow *can* provide. (Which will be the fate, as we will see, of the "freedom" to do evil.)

32. Therefore, "we cannot imagine another suitable form for a rational being than the form of man" (AP62 VII 172; see also AP68 VII 178). Nor can we expect to come up with an adequate definition of humans: "the problem of giving an account of the character of the human species is quite insoluble, because the problem could only be solved by comparing two species of rational beings on the basis of experience, but experience has not offered us a comparison between two species of rational beings" (AP238 VII 321).

33. And (to elaborate on a point made earlier) it is only when acting rationally (that is, morally) that humans can be said to really have *motives*: "A *motivum* is always a *moral causa impulsiva*, or a determining ground that determines man's *arbitrium tanquam liberum*, i.e. according to the laws of freedom, and thus treats him as a free being. . . . [M]otives occur only insofar as man is considered as a free being; they contain his activity, and are thus totally opposed to the state that depends on inclinations. They take their ground from the spontaneity of human willing, which is guided by rational conceptions, quite independently of all determining causes of nature, and thus solely by the moral law" (LE262 XXVII 493–94).

34. By the end of the present section, it will be clear that the unity of reason is a far more complex and unsettling condition than an obvious reading of these passages might suggest.

35. So it is not by chance that rational accounts are as self-contained as pointed out above—they would not count as rational otherwise; reason would not regard them as fulfilling its standards.

36. And, because philosophy is defined as rational cognition from concepts, this passage continues by saying: "philosophy is the only science that has a systematic connection, and it is that which makes all the other sciences systematic." Also, insofar as we are rational beings, *we* will not be satisfied by lack of systematicity either: "Mere manifoldness without unity cannot satisfy us" (LL549 IX 39).

37. It might go without saying that rational systematicity is not just unity (or totality), but *consistent* unity (or totality): "That which is required for the possibility of any use of reason as such . . . [is] that its principles and affirmations must not contradict one other. . . . [This] is . . . the condition of having reason at all" (PR236 V 120). And at J174–75 V 294–95 "[a]lways to think in accord with oneself" is called "[t]he maxim . . . of the *consistent* way of thinking" and "of reason." It is also the case, importantly, that reason is capable of establishing such consistency on its own, since it "can . . . draw inferences from given laws to conclusions" (J62 V 174–75). More precisely, reason subordinates cognitions to one another, bringing out their relations of logical dependency: "The senses sense, the understanding coordinates, but reason subordinates" (LL201 XXIV 251). "One cannot cognize any coordination at all through reason, for reason only subordinates" (LL184 XXIV 232). "[R]eason . . . is the height of subordination" (N83 XVII 261). "[T]he form of rational cognition is that of subordination" (N105 XVII 366). And it is precisely this subordination that brings about the systematic unity reason is looking for, whereas coordination only produces *aggregates*: "With an aggregate the parts precede the whole . . . ; with a system, the whole precedes the parts" (LL337 XXIV 891). "A system is where everything is subordinate to an idea that is concerned with the whole, and that has to determine the parts" (LL287 XXIV 831).

38. "The logical *actus* of the understanding, through which concepts are generated as to their form, are: 1. *comparison* of representations among one another in relation to the unity of consciousness; 2. *reflection* as to how various representations can be conceived in one consciousness; and finally 3. *abstraction* of everything else in which the given representations differ" (LL592 IX 94— the point is commonplace in Kant; see also, for example, LL204 XXIV 255, LL352–53 XXIV 909). Note that the acts involved here are *logical* ones; so they have nothing to do with the *psychological* operation of abstraction from empirical contents (nor is the "result" mentioned in my text to be read as related to any such operation). What is at issue is the logical relation between a concept and its instances—as Kant himself puts it, "universal logic does not have to investigate the *source* of concepts, not how concepts *arise as representations*, but

merely *how given representations become concepts in thought*; these concepts, more-over, may contain something that is derived from experience, or something invented, or borrowed from the nature of the understanding" (LL592 IX 94). "I concern myself not with the evolution of concepts, like Tetens (all actions by means of which concepts are produced), nor with their analysis, like Lambert, but solely with their objective validity. I am not in competition with these men.... *Tetens* investigates the concepts of pure reason merely subjectively (human nature), I investigate them objectively. The former analysis is empirical, the latter transcendental (N199 XVIII 23).

39. The case of chess is trickier, and for that very reason more interesting, than the case of mathematical proofs. For, to be sure, one can reduce chess to a mathematical model (which is why John von Neumann thought that it was not really a game in the sense of his game theory): that is, one can identify (besides a single initial position) a number of optimal end positions (for both the white and the black), and then judge a move optimal if it has the best mathematical chances of approaching one of those end positions. But, one could say, none of this would make any sense if we did not identify those optimal end positions as *winning* ones, and if we did not come to the game with the empirical goal of beating our opponents. Which in turn, one might continue, reconnects the game of chess with all the complexity (and the heteronomy) of empirical life; and that is just as well, because in the abstract space in which the mathematical model is situated there is no real currency for chess as we know it (or, von Neumann might add, for games in general). I agree with this diagnosis, which to me is but a vivid illustration of the systematic reversal of priorities issuing from Kant's Copernican revolution, and of the resulting quasi-hypothetico-deductive attitude we must assume with respect to empirical contents. Empirically we live among objects, whereas transcendentally we arrive at objects by imposing conceptual conditions on representations—and yet the objects we intend to arrive at should be the same as those among which we live. Empirically (as I will detail later) we are goal-directed beings, and identify our actions as ways of pursuing our goals, whereas transcendentally we define actions by their logical structure, in total independence of goals—and yet the actions we so define should fall within the range of the actions we empirically perform in the pursuance of goals. Empirically we play chess to win, and develop our understanding of optimal moves with that goal in mind, whereas in logical space we characterize an optimal move (at least for the purposes of our current example) with no reference to winning—and yet the optimal moves we so characterize must be the same ones we regard as conducive to winning. See also note 62 below.

40. At PR164 V 30 the law is given in a simpler form: "So act that the maxim of your will could always hold at the same time as a principle in a giving of universal law." Kant justifies the additional complication in the *Groundwork* by referring to the derivation of imperfect duties (see G75 IV 424), but it is instructive to consider the following alternative justification:

clearly, anyone can will, in the phenomenological sense, that his maxim should become a universal law. Hitler, say, can experience willing that everyone persecute Jews—even Jews themselves. But only when the will expresses a rational stance does it have true causal import, hence only then *can* one *in fact* will that his maxim should become a universal law.

41. A lot of fanciful moves have been made on the basis of the so-called "formula of humanity" in the obvious attempt to give credence to a "kinder, gentler Kant"—one more attuned to the current, largely eudaimonistic moral environment. None of these attempts, however, can make sense of Kant's clear statement that "[t]he . . . three ways of representing the principle of morality [including, then, the formula of humanity] are at bottom only so many formulae of the very same law" (G85 IV 436). In the interpretation I am articulating here, this statement is perfectly sensible; indeed analytical, as it should be. For the humanity referred to in it is but another name for rationality; and indeed, later in the *Groundwork*, Kant rephrases the same formula as follows: "so act with reference to every *rational being* (yourself and others) that in your maxim it holds at the same time as an end in itself" (G87 IV 437; italics added). This theme will surface again repeatedly in what follows.

42. Something is a rational law *if and only if* it applies to all rational beings (to argue from right to left, we can plausibly assume that the specific empirical circumstances of individual rational beings cancel each other out when *all of them* are taken into account, and hence only their rational character is left as a determining ground): between a practical law and a universal law, as we have seen (in the passage from PR161 V 27 quoted earlier), there is for Kant (not just an implication, but) an *identity*. So it makes sense for him occasionally to bring out universality (that something be a law for all) as the decisive factor; but we should always remember that the universality that matters here is universal applicability to *rational* beings.

43. For the time being, we will understand a duty as just a form of behavior that reason has proved *necessary*. The particular (deontic) necessity involved in it will be discussed later.

44. "[E]veryone must always feel that even when there are many adversities that one might not be pleased to shed at the risk of one's life, still in the choice between slavery and the risk of death one will have no reservation about preferring the latter" (N11). More generally, self-preservation becomes questionable when one's morality is at risk: "there is much in the world that is far higher than life. The observance of morality is far higher. It is better to sacrifice life than to forfeit morality. It is not necessary to live, but it is necessary that, so long as we live, we do so honorably; but he who can no longer live honorably is no longer worthy to live at all" (LE147 XXVII 373).

45. "One should not have the intention of speaking an untruth because, as one who can indicate his meaning, one must not destroy that significance. One should not kill himself because, when he does with himself as he pleases, he *considers* himself *as a thing* and loses the dignity of a human being. . . . The

suicide also displays freedom in the greatest opposition to itself, hence in the greatest breakdown of his delusion" (N436 XIX 165). More about the duty to tell the truth in the last section of this chapter.

46. Note that, with perfect (or strict, or narrow) duties, the arguments supporting them are all by *reductio*: what ought *not* to be done is conceptually prior to what ought to be. This conceptual relation is brought out clearly in the following passage: "If, when it is made into a universal rule, the intention is in agreement with itself, the action is morally possible; but if not, then it is morally impossible" (LE71 XXVII 1428). Moral impossibility is here given an explicit definition; moral *necessity* is supposed to just follow from it. See also N10: "That will must be good which does not cancel itself out if it is taken universally and reciprocally."

47. At times, Kant makes this fundamental point of his work absolutely clear, as when he says: "the special determination of duties as human duties . . . is possible only after the subject of this determination (the human being) is cognized as he is really constituted . . . ; this, however, does not belong to a *Critique of Practical Reason* as such, which has only to give a complete account of the principles of . . . [the] possibility [of duty], of its extent, and of its limits, without special reference to human nature" (PR143 V 8). But it is also the case (as I noted in the previous chapter) that he feels constantly tempted by the prospect of expanding his range in the direction of (rationalizing) empirical matters—of moving from the critique to the system.

48. Machiavelli is the first author who makes it clear that often our empirical choice is not between a good and an evil but between several evils, and that choosing none of them may issue in yet another evil worse than any of those. At a superficial level, his position can be made irrelevant to our present concerns by pointing out that "evil" in his case must typically be rewritten as "hurting some"; and it is quite possible that (what Kant would regard as) the rational, hence also good, choice in many situations be one that is evil in that sense. But there is more to this topic than such a simple resolution allows for: Machiavelli is also posing in bold, dramatic terms the problem of how evil (in Kant's sense as well as in his own) a "philosophical" attitude might turn out to be. (Transcendental) philosophy moves in conceptual space, which is to say: out of time. When projected onto a spatiotemporal dimension, the philosopher is inclined to take all the time it takes (which could be all the time) to resolve the issue before her; but that might mean refusing to act, hence perhaps acting in the worst possible way. So, by all means, proceeding philosophically gives no assurance of ending up with clean hands; at times it might be in order to interrupt the rational conversation—that course of action might be the least of evils (and the Sartre and Styron characters would not get off the hook by simply deliberating forever). Yet it is *still* an evil, unredeemed by its being the least one, as will be detailed later.

49. A powerful statement of this challenge, and of the relief provided against it by critical philosophy, is given by Heinrich Jung-Stilling in his letter

to Kant of March 1, 1789: "No foe was ever more horrible to me than determinism; it is the greatest despot of humanity, strangling every incipient attempt at goodness and every pious trust in God, and yet determinism is so reliable, so certainly true, so evident to every thinking mind, that the world is inescapably lost, religion and morality are destroyed, just as soon as we isolate our sense world and believe the world to be in itself exactly as we imagine it and think it to be. But who in the world even dreams that there is such a thing as a Kantian Transcendental Idealism?" (C287 XI 8).

50. These passages would be even clearer if the translators of the third *Critique* (Paul Guyer and Eric Matthews) had not chosen, with an inconsistency that is especially troubling in a general edition of Kant's works, to translate the German "*sollen*" as "should," whereas the same verb is commonly (and most notably in the moral works) translated as "ought to." The awkwardness thus generated culminates when we compare the third *Critique* with its *First Introduction* (translated by Matthews and probably not as thoroughly "revised . . . for stylistic uniformity" (Jxlvii) by Guyer), where we read passages making essentially the same point but using the more common auxiliary: "aesthetic judgments of reflection . . . lay claim to necessity and say, not that everyone does so judge—that would make their explanation a task for empirical psychology—but that everyone *ought* to [*solle*] so judge" (J39 XX 238–39). Note also that the auxiliary "will" can be used in these contexts as long as one is understood to be issuing not a prediction but a demand (or, which is the same, a condition for attributing taste to anyone): "One demands and presupposes that what we find beautiful as an object of taste, everyone else who has taste will, like us, also find beautiful" (LM480–81 XXIX 1011).

51. "[A]ll judgments of the same object must also agree with one another, and hence the objective validity of a judgment of experience signifies [*bedeutet*] nothing other than its necessary universal validity" (TA92 IV 298). "Objective validity and necessary universal validity (for everyone) are . . . interchangeable concepts" (TA93 IV 298).

52. "When . . . there is something to be found in my judgment . . . contrary to the judgments of others, then in respect of the truth of my judgment I am not very certain, and I must first of all be occupied with searching for an agreement of my judgment with the judgment of others" (LL73 XXIV 95).

53. The main point of this paragraph is that the logical form of a statement must be contrasted (not only with its truth-value but also) with its grammatical form (or structure). The latter reflects the way in which the statement is constructed out of its elements; the former reflects the relations of implication it has to other statements. "This painting is rectangular" and "This painting is beautiful" have the same grammatical form (they are both subject-predicate statements, and in both cases the predicate is a monadic one), as indeed do "I am a worthless man" and "I am a prudent man." But, because of their different logical forms, different kinds of statements will count as counterexamples to them (as implying their falsity)—and, to make this point apparent, it has been

common at least since Russell to proceed as I do in the text (and as Kant himself implicitly suggests): to replace them with statements of the same logical form but of a different grammatical form which makes that logical form more apparent.

54. Note that, because of their intrinsically normative character, judgments of taste can be falsified, whereas judgments expressing agreeableness cannot. See N526 XV 837.

55. At LM75-76 XXVIII 261-62 Kant makes an important distinction between a substance like the soul and its powers, and says that *"[p]ower is . . . not a separate principle, but rather a relation."* Therefore, he continues, from the unity of the soul we cannot infer that *"we are capable of deriving all actions of the soul, and its various powers and faculties, from one basic power"*—and indeed he eventually assumes "various basic powers" in it. The identity conditions of faculties are thus clearly distinguished from the identity conditions of objects. See also LM179 XXIX 771: "What . . . is the faculty of thinking? The relation of the soul to thought insofar as it contains the ground of its actuality." And LM182 XXIX 823-24: "The difference between power and faculty is difficult to determine. Faculty, insofar as it is determined with respect to an effect, is power, and insofar as it is undetermined, *becomes* faculty. Power contains the ground of the actuality of an action, faculty the ground of the possibility of an action."

56. "In the . . . [theoretical realm], if common reason ventures to depart from laws of experience and perceptions of the senses it falls into sheer incomprehensibilities and self-contradictions, at least into a chaos of uncertainty, obscurity, and instability. But in practical matters, it is just when common understanding excludes all sensible incentives from practical laws that its faculty of appraising first begins to show itself to advantage" (G59 IV 404).

57. How events should be conceived in TR is far from settled but is also of no concern to us. This explains my loosely running together events and things here: however TR supporters eventually resolve that issue, they will have to account for events in terms of things (that is, objects), hence it will be some conceptual constructions based on what it is to be a thing that belong to regular patterns.

58. Thus Hume's argument against miracles (in *An Enquiry concerning Human Understanding*) is an important step on the way from TR to TI—though one that, as always with Hume, stays on purely epistemological grounds, and hence fully within TR's scope. In Kant, rejecting miracles becomes a rational requirement, since "the maxim of healthy reason is this: *not to allow, but rather to reject all such experiences and appearances that are so constituted that, if I assume them, then they make the use of my reason impossible and suspend the conditions under which alone I can use my reason"* (LM106 XXVIII 300; see also LM 243 XXIX 873). And, of course, for him "objects must conform to our cognition"—hence, specifically, satisfy all such rational requirements.

59. And "[n]atural (*formaliter*) means what follows necessarily according to laws of a certain order of whatever sort, hence also the moral order (hence not always the physical order)" (R226n VIII 333n).

60. Or consider a more Kantian example: "There could be, if God so willed, a number of...substances, free from any connection with our universe, but, nonetheless, linked with each other by means of a certain connection of their determinations so as to produce place, position, and space: they would constitute a world banished beyond the limits of the world, of which we are parts, that is to say, they would constitute a solitary world. For this reason, the possibility that there might be, had it so pleased God, a number of worlds, even in the metaphysical sense, is not absurd" (TB42 I 414—once again, that objects, or "substances," constitute a world is equivalent to there being lawlike connections among them). Well, imagine one such world in addition to the actual one; what sense would it make (given that they have no common spatiotemporal coordinates) to ask which substance in the former is the same as which substance in the latter?

61. There is no need to think of this entity as having no spatiotemporal qualities at all (for example, of it not having a body). That it be non-spatiotemporal means here that it is not inserted in a system of spatiotemporal regularities, hence it is no part of a spatiotemporal, objective world. See note 60 of chapter 2.

62. So there is ample room within chess as an empirical game for suboptimal (but quite effective) strategies that take into account (say) the necessity to act under time pressure, the opponent's typical misconceptions or weaknesses, or any number of other environmental factors. Clearly, no discussion of such matters is relevant to my use of chess as an example of Kantian (perfect) rationality.

63. What gives my hope any substance it has in the case of rationality, and distinguishes it from mere wishful thinking (which is all it would be in the devil/shrub case), is the empirical rewriting to be discussed in the next section. And yet, there is no denying that, as was true before of choice and of receptivity (see notes 49 and 54 of chapter 2), this is a hope that is missing some of the characteristic features of ordinary hope: we can hope to win the lottery because someone will, but we cannot really hope to prove the rationality of our behavior because that is impossible. The best we can say is that we act *as if* we had such hope (what that kind of acting amounts to will be clearer in chapter 5). So we are faced once again by a recurring theme of this book: how much sense words still make when their ideal conditions of sense are not present. And, once again, this theme will be taken up in some detail in chapter 4.

64. "[T]he intelligible world...lies merely in the idea of reason" (TA334 VIII 248). "[T]he supersensible...is a mere idea" (TA396 XX 309). "[A]lthough an intelligible world, in which everything would be actual merely because it is (as something good) possible, and even freedom, as its formal condition, is a transcendent concept for us, which is not serviceable for any constitutive

principle for determining an object and its objective reality, still, in accordance with the constitution of our (partly sensible) nature, it can serve as a universal *regulative principle*" (J273–74 V 404).

65. See, for example, the following passage from the *Lectures on Ethics*: "We conceive of man first of all as an ideal, as he ought to be and can be, merely according to reason, and call this idea *homo noumenon*; this being is thought of in relation to another, as though the latter were restrained by him; this is man in the state of sensibility, who is called *homo phenomenon*. The latter is the person, and the former merely a personified idea; there, man is simply under the moral law, but here he is a phenomenon, affected by the feelings of pleasure and pain, and must be coerced by the noumenon into the performance of duty" (LE 341 XXVII 593). We are not yet prepared to discuss all the elements of this passage; specifically, the "ought" formulation of the rational law and its (related) coercive character have not yet surfaced here. But we can see in it a clear statement of the ideality (hence *un*reality) of the intelligible self, and of it being only *as though* there were a relation between this self and the sensible (that is, the actual) one.

66. Mary Gregor's translation of "*einsehen*" as "to see" is highly misleading (as she herself all but admits in footnotes on G58 and G94). "*Einsehen*" is a technical term for Kant, typically rendered as "to have insight": it means "to cognize something through reason. When I have insight into something, I cognize it through mediate marks, I infer, then, and thus search for a *nota notae*, a mark of the mark" (LL106 XXIV 135). (And, insofar as this is rational knowledge, it is also knowledge of *necessary* links: "to have insight a priori is to cognize not only that it is so . . . but that it must be so," LL466 XXIV 730.) It is trivially the case that what I cannot experience at all I cannot see; but Kant is not making this trivial point here. His claim is, rather, the highly significant one that of what I cannot experience I cannot have systematic, connected knowledge. Even less, then, can I comprehend (*begreifen*) it, that is, "have insight into . . . [it] sufficiently" (LL106 XXIV 135).

67. "[W]e always need a certain analogy with natural being in order to make supersensible characteristics comprehensible to us" (RR107n VI 65n). "[F]or the human being the invisible needs to be represented through something visible (sensible), indeed what is more, it must be accompanied by the visible for the sake of praxis and, though intellectual, made as it were an object of intuition (according to a certain analogy)" (RR208 VI 192). "[P]henomenal eternity or sempiternity . . . is to be distinguished from noumenal eternity; this I think of as not in time and can attribute it to God. Sempiternity is the boundlessness of an existence in time (LM199–200 XXIX 842). "*What is in time is everlasting* but not eternal" (XVII 429).

68. And which then is regarded by Kant elsewhere as an "irrational concept," which "can have no significance although . . . [it is], to be sure, free of contradiction," since "we cannot think of any magnitude of existence, i.e., a duration, except as in time" (N401 XVIII 715–16).

69. Additional examples of (what issues from) this purely negative stance come from (proper) thinking of God: "I will be able to determine the quality of divine predicates *via negationis*; that is, I can determine which predicates drawn from experience can be applied to my concept of God after all negations have been separated from them, but in this way I cannot come to cognize the quantity of reality in God; rather, the reality remaining in my concepts after all the limitations have been left out will be quite insignificant and small in degree" (R365–66 XXVIII 1022). "[I]t is the case in general that if we purify divine predicates of all negations, then we have no means of thinking them *in concreto*, since all sensible conditions have been taken away. Now just because this concept cannot be illustrated by an example, the suspicion might arise that the concept itself is obscure or even false; yet once a concept has been introduced a priori with apodictic certainty, then we need fear no error even if our incapacity or even all our reason forbids us to set up a case of it *in concreto*" (R402 XXVIII 1067). See also TB339 II 351–52: "the spirit-nature . . . can never be positively thought, for, in the entire range of our sensations, there are no *data* for such positive thought. One has to make do with negations if one is to think something which differs so much from anything of a sensible character."

70. "Natural science will never reveal to us the inside of things, *i.e.*, that which is not appearance but can nonetheless serve as the highest ground of explanation for the appearances" (TA142 IV 353; italics added).

71. When I do such rewriting, freedom as a purely intellectual condition (hence as something that either holds or does not) will be used as a standard to assess various empirical occurrences; hence it will make sense to say that one is *more or less* free depending on how closely she approximates the standard. And indeed, in the *Lectures on Ethics* Kant repeatedly refers to this empirical notion of freedom, and to the related (and similarly empirical) one of the degree to which behavior can be *imputed* to an agent: "It is strange: the more anyone can be compelled, in a moral sense, the more he is free. . . . His freedom increases with the degree of morality. . . . [T]he more he accedes to the moral ground of motivation, the more free he is. . . . The more a person practices self-compulsion, the freer he becomes" (LE60–62 XXVII 268–70). "The more a man is virtuous, the more he is free" (LE216 XXVII 464). "The more a man considers a moral act to be irresistible, and the more he is compelled to it by duty, the freer he is. For in that case he is employing the power he has, to rule over his strong inclinations. So freedom is all the more displayed, the greater the moral compulsion" (LE237 XXIX 617). "The degrees of imputation depend on the degree of freedom with which the action has come about; so the less free the agent is, the less the action can be attributed to him" (LE321 XXVII 567). This theme will be the object of renewed attention in chapter 5, when our discourse has made room for (the possibility of) moral education.

72. See also Kant's useful example at LM265 XXIX 898–99: "when someone writes a book, he commonly claims to be doing it out of love of

truth, although he is just as often doing it to earn money. The means that he uses, namely, writing a good book, is good. He must overcome considerable stimuli, such as the love of laziness, he can also serve the world, but his intention is still not intellectual, but rather sensible. A future life of comfort was his end; this was thus a cause which is impelling in some respect. But if someone writes a book simply from a love of truth and allows it to be made public only upon his death, when he cannot hope for any more profit from the world, then his end is good and the impelling cause intellectual. This depends on no other stimuli" (translation modified). How can one argue that the love of gain was not *really* a causal factor in the writing of the book? On the basis not of privileged access to any internal disposition of the agent, but of observable behavior (allowing publication only after death) that rules out the possibility of that factor being indeed operational (whatever may have gone through the agent's mind).

73. "Laws cannot be perceived, but rather presuppose principles in accordance with which perceptions must be able to be compared" (J17n XX 213n).

74. In fact, as we will see shortly, that is not enough either: counterfactual situations and behavior are also relevant.

75. In the *Lectures on Ethics* there are constant references to internal dispositions and to "the inner goodness of actions" (see, for example, LE90 XXVII 299). But they, too, should not be taken to suggest that one can thus establish independent criteria for evaluating behavior on the basis of the intentions behind it. For we can only know what our intentions are by looking at the behavior itself: "the observation of oneself... must not consist in eavesdropping on oneself; we have, rather, to observe ourselves through actions, and pay attention to them. The endeavor to know ourselves, and tell whether we are good or bad, must be carried on in life, and we have to examine our actions to see if they are good or bad.... So a man always has to get to know himself in a gradual fashion" (LE141 XXVII 365). "To be morally innocent is to give practical evidence, at every opportunity, of the purity of our dispositions" (LE193 XXVII 434). See also RR215 VI 201: "the teacher of the Gospel has himself put into our hands... external evidences of external experience as a touchstone by which we can recognize human beings, and each of them can recognize himself, by their fruits."

76. At A551n B579n Kant says that "[o]ur imputations can be referred only to the empirical character." But, as will become apparent below, such imputations are far from assured.

77. In the *Lectures on Ethics*, Kant appears to give an even stronger statement of this impossibility, that turns it from epistemic to factual: "it is impossible for man to perform a pure act of duty, merely from the idea thereof, since the natural inclination to deviate from the law prevents us, and the observance rests upon many collateral grounds of motivation that cannot always even be fathomed." But the continuation of the passage brings us back

to epistemic access: "How would a man ascertain whether his joy at the rescue of an unfortunate family stems from sympathetic, pathological fellow-feeling, or from pleasure at the fulfillment of his duty, or whether, in his action, the love of honor or advantage did not obscurely play a part?" (LE366 XXVII 624–25). On the other hand, such oscillation is hardly significant in TI, where (as we know) objects "must conform to our cognition."

78. Remember: Phalaris used to cook people he did not like inside an iron bull—a circumstance not many of us had to face, or are prepared to face. He also turns up at PR267 V 159, LM 384 XXVIII 683, and LM491 XXIX 1023.

79. Note how, in attempting to find an empirical equivalent for an intelligible state, we run into one more example of the recurring theme mentioned in note 63: we are forced to stretch and ultimately overcome the very conditions of empirical meaning. For real possibility, we know, must be based on actuality; hence what sense does it make to ask how *I*—this empirical object—would behave in situations in which I *cannot, really*, find myself, *because I never did*? Only logical possibility is left: something that only makes sense intellectually and that is awkwardly superimposed on empirical circumstances. Note also that what specifically creates the problem here is the counterfactual force of laws, which will come up again in chapter 5.

80. Kant's obsessive concern with the application of rational criteria to empirical circumstances underlies (for example) his doctrine of schematism and receives particular emphasis in the *Opus Postumum*. See, for example, O37 XXI 525–26: "The transition from one science to the other must have certain intermediary concepts, which are given in the one and are applied to the other, and which thus belong to both territories alike. Otherwise this advance is not a lawlike transition but a leap in which one neither knows where one is going, nor, in looking back, understands whence one has come. One might think that the transition from the metaphysical foundation of natural science to physics requires no bridge, for the former, as a system constituted by concepts a priori, exactly adjoins the ground of experience onto which it could alone be applied. But this very application creates doubts and contains difficulties which should be embarrassing for physics, as a particular system, separate from the former. For the admixture or insertion of the one into the other, as commonly occurs, is dangerous; not just to its elegance, but even to its thoroughness, because a priori and empirical principles might communicate with or make claims upon one another." And so, eight years after claiming, in the preface to the third *Critique*, that he had thus brought his "entire critical enterprise to an end" (J58 V 170), he announces in an October 19, 1798, letter to Kiesewetter that, with the new work, "the task of the critical philosophy will be completed and a gap that now stands open will be filled" (C553 XII 258). Except that, of course, that very new work *will never be completed*—because the task itself could not be. A suggestive passage that makes this impossibility especially conspicuous is the following: "It may seem that in this section we have greatly transgressed the boundary of the a priori concepts of

the moving forces of matter, which together are to form a system, and have drifted into physics as an empirical science (e.g. into chemistry); but one will surely notice that [*breaks off*]" (O50 XXII 149). See also note 40 of chapter 2; the chasm discussed there between conditions of intuition and of thought is obviously related to the "gap" brought out here between conceptual and empirical endeavors (and specifically, in the *Opus Postumum*, to the "gulf" between the metaphysics of nature and physics; see O39 XXI 475 and O40 XXI 476).

81. P611–15 VIII 425–30. See also, for example, TA459 VIII 422: "The *lie* . . . is the truly vile spot in human nature."

82. It is instructive to note how much more serious any damage done to our means of expression and communication looks from the perspective of TI. A realist may well conceive of language as an inessential (though quite convenient) reflection of the world—since he thinks of the latter as being what it is independently of how we think or talk about it. But for an idealist the structures of thought, hence also those of language (think of the metaphysical deduction in the first *Critique*—see also LM387 XXVIII 685: "When we think, we speak with ourselves"), are constitutive of the structures of being; therefore, any assault on the former may have devastating ontological consequences—it might make the world literally fall apart. Just because objects are appearances, in other words, it is much more important to preserve what makes for their feeble existence. Also, if the above is Kant's reason for unconditionally upholding the duty not to lie, it makes sense that he should have far less trouble with lack of candor—which, while it may give others the wrong impression of one's beliefs, does not directly damage language as a means of expression and communication, hence also of world-making. See, for example: "Although I am absolutely convinced of many things that I shall never have the courage to say, I shall never say anything I do not believe" (C90 X 69). "[I]t is the tenor of the times to sound an alarm where there is nothing but peace and quiet, so one has to have patience, be precisely obedient to the law, and put off censure of the abuses of the literary police establishment until gentler times" (C472 XI 476). "Since discussions of political and religious topics are currently subject to certain restrictions and there are hardly any other matters, at least at this time, that interest the general reading public, one must keep one's eye on this change of the weather, so as to conform prudently to the times" (C498 XII 11).

83. For a justification would require, paradoxically, the currency of the very (rational) level of discourse I have interrupted. Kant gives a clear description of the rational void in which one thus finds oneself (with specific reference to politics) at P300n VIII 302n: "Even if an actual contract of the people with the ruler has been violated, the people cannot react at once *as a commonwealth* but only as a mob. For the previously existing constitution has been torn up by the people, while their organization into a new commonwealth has not yet taken place."

84. I will argue in the last chapter that, from a Kantian point of view, ethics can be seen as the object-language counterpart of the essentially metalinguistic activity transcendental philosophy (which is to say, transcendental *logic*) consists of. So it is interesting to point out that both activities must be conducted with the same anxious attitude: "Since we cannot always maintain that our analysis is complete,... we must attend to our definition with fear and trembling" (LL364 XXIV 923).

85. "[A]s a human being... [one] is only the appearance of himself" (G104 IV 457).

Chapter 4

1. As is clear from this quote and the text around it, technical principles (also called *"technically practical"* at J60 V 172; why they are *imperatives* will be explained later) are the same as the hypothetical ones discussed in the last chapter. The two terms bring out two different (related) aspects of these principles: they belong to specific instrumental skills, and as such they have only conditional value.

2. "Propositions that in mathematics or physics are called *practical* should properly be called *technical*. For... they only point out the manifold of the possible action that is sufficient to produce a certain effect, and are thus as theoretical as any proposition that asserts the connection of a cause with an effect" (PR159n V 26n). Also, consistently with remarks made in the previous chapter (and with other remarks to follow), note that "[p]robabilities [which are implied in the references made in the text to the likelihood of certain outcomes] count for nothing... where judgments of pure reason are at stake" (J271 V 400)—what is at issue in the rational point of view is an absoluteness that is foreign to any empirical matters.

3. The impartial spectator turns up elsewhere in Kant, expressing the same viewpoint I highlight here. See, for example, R28n VIII 260n: "If it comes about (although it seldom happens) that an unjust, especially violent, villain does not escape unpunished from the world, then the impartial spectator rejoices, now reconciled with heaven.... Why? Because nature is here moral, solely of the kind we seldom can hope to perceive in the world." N352 XVIII 547: "The existence of a merely happy being without morality may well have its own value for this being, but not for a mere observer." And RR59 VI 5–6: "[A] human being... would... feel himself compelled by reason to acknowledge this judgment with complete impartiality, *as if rendered by somebody else yet at the same time his own*" (italics added). At TB113 II 67–68 impartiality is again characterized as the capacity to take the other's point of view, and the outcome of exercising it is (as will emerge later in my text) a higher degree of consensus: "If the judgments of unbiased reason held by different thoughtful people were examined with the frankness of an uncorrupted advocate—an advocate who so weighed the grounds of the two disputed positions that he

was able to imagine himself in the position of the two proponents, so as to be persuaded as strongly as possible of their respective views, and who only then decided to which side he wished to commit himself—if the judgments of unbiased reason were examined in this way, philosophers would disagree far less than they do. Unfeigned fairness in adopting as far as possible the opposite opinion would soon unite enquiring minds on a single path." See also TB336 II 349, where Kant applies this alienating strategy to himself: "I put myself in the position of someone else's reason, which is independent of myself and external to me, and regard my judgments, along with their most secret causes, from the point of view of other people. The comparison of the two observations yields, it is true, pronounced parallaxes, but it is also the only method for preventing optical deception, and the only means of placing the concepts in the true positions which they occupy relatively to the cognitive faculty of human nature." A similar point is made at C126 X 122: "You know very well that I am inclined not only to try to refute intelligent criticisms but that I always weave them together with my judgments and give them the right to overthrow all my previously cherished opinions. I hope that in that way I can achieve an unpartisan perspective, by seeing my judgments from the standpoint of others, so that a third opinion may emerge, superior to my previous ones." Finally, when setting up the antithetic of pure reason, Kant refers to the position he is going to occupy as one appropriate to "impartial referees" (A423 B451). See also note 39 below.

4. See note 41 in the previous chapter and the attending text. As the present chapter progresses, we will see that reason is more than uninterested in our biological identity: it downright opposes it. I explore the extremes this attitude can reach in "Kant's Sadism."

5. Conversely, being an end in himself establishes man's "unconditional equality" with all rational beings, and "even with higher beings; for even if the latter are incomparably superior to him in natural gifts, they do not have a right to use him as they please" (PW226 VIII 114).

6. We also know from the previous chapter that reason should not be put on a par with the inclinations, so we can only call it a "drive" in a metaphorical sense. I will return to this issue shortly.

7. We will see later that this reversal constitutes evil. When, on the other hand, priorities are kept straight, there is value to liking the outcome and disapproval for the sheer pursuance of pain: "The cynic's purism and the hermit's mortification of the flesh, without social good-living, are distorted interpretations of virtue and do not make virtue attractive; rather, being forsaken by the Graces, they can make no claim of humanity" (AP191 VII 282). So what is at issue here, again, is not empirical occurrences but their conceptual assessment.

8. "[R]eason demands to know the unconditioned, and therewith the totality of all conditions, for otherwise it does not cease to question, just as if nothing had yet been answered" (TA407 XX 326).

9. Rational choice theory is a specifically philosophical, not empirical, failure; it is a perversion of reason, not (just) of behavior. Thus Kant does not deny that people might take pleasure in performing their duty (for the sake of duty), but considers it conceptually confusing (as well as pragmatically self-serving) when the various sources of pleasure are as improperly lumped together as that theory does: "everything that pleases, just because it pleases, is agreeable. . . . But if this is conceded, then impressions of the senses, which determine inclination, or principles of reason, which determine the will, or merely reflected forms of intuition, which determine the power of judgment, are all entirely the same as far as the effect on the feeling of pleasure is concerned. For this would be the agreeableness in the sensation of one's state, and, since in the end all the effort of our faculties is directed to what is practical and must be united in it as their goal, one could not expect of them any other assessment of things and their value than that which consists in the gratification that they promise" (J91 V 206).

10. A relevant passage here is: "The revolution of a gifted people which we have seen unfolding in our day may succeed or miscarry; it may be filled with misery and atrocities to the point that a right-thinking human being, were he boldly to hope to execute it successfully the second time, would never resolve to make the experiment at such cost—this revolution, I say, nonetheless finds in the hearts of all spectators (who are not engaged in this game themselves) a wishful *participation* that borders closely on enthusiasm the very expression of which is fraught with danger; this sympathy, therefore, can have no other cause than a moral predisposition in the human race" (R302 VII 85). I have already discussed Kant's apparently ambivalent (but ultimately consistent) attitude toward revolutionary means, and I will return to it below; here I need only note that the "painful effort" mentioned in my text is not necessarily to include such extreme means.

11. Compare this example with Kant's own in the *Lectures on Ethics*: "the fact that a man is determined to action on grounds of reason and understanding does not yet release him from all mechanism of nature; a man, for example, is led from youth onward to have an eye to the main chance in every action; he will be covetous of the property of others; at first the difficulties and evil consequences restrain him, but he finds a plan for achieving his design unnoticed, and steals. The whole course of the matter in its linkage is natural mechanism, notwithstanding that the action depended on much use of rational grounds. The grounds of action lay in the past, and he was thereby led to the action itself. The grounds of action, which gradually determined him, obviously did not lie in his power, since he could not undo their occurrence; to that extent he was not acting freely, therefore, since he was simply subject to the mechanism of nature. The same must be assumed of the maxims on which the grounds of action are erected; he has witnessed stealing in his youth, for example, and has become handy in the use of tools" (LE270 XXVII 504).

12. "[A]ccording to his sensible character, man must be judged as being evil (by nature)" (AP241 VII 324).

13. This is not an empirical risk, from which we might think of being luckily exempt at times; it is a transcendental feature of the human form of life, a direct consequence of the internal fissure of human reason I brought out in chapter 3. For, as we will be reminded shortly, reason prizes consistency and agreement; hence can only disapprove of a condition where no ultimate agreement can be found or hoped for. Humans are radically evil to begin with, originally, because they are always already divided within themselves; and (as was pointed out in note 48 of chapter 3) empirically siding with reason provides no escape from this predicament. We must not lose sight of such troubling consequences of Kant's vindication of morality as we now proceed to argue that evil is intrinsically contentless, that there is no substantive logic to it. For none of that is going to make evil less real; specifically, that no articulation can be provided for the fundamental split in our experience, that *it just is that way* and we can only live with it, is not going to ease the agony with which reason does this living. As I point out in *Hegel's Dialectical Logic* and I detail in the last chapter below, the obvious alternative to Kant's stern recipe is a conciliatory view that has, however, no independent room for moral judgment. See also note 18 and the attending text.

14. So there is ultimately an empirical struggle going on here: between irrational inclinations and those other factors that reason can conceive as working for *its own* success. But (as I point out in the text) the very description of this struggle is open to the radical indeterminacy that haunts any rewriting of intelligible conditions in sensible terms.

15. So, conversely, agreement can be taken as evidence of rationality. In a letter to Lambert of December 31, 1765, Kant says: "It is no small pleasure for me that you have noticed the fortunate agreement of our methods, an agreement that I have often observed in your writings. It has served to increase my confidence, since it is a logical confirmation that shows that our methods satisfy the touchstone of universal human reason" (C81 X 55). And note that "the rational person must not be an eccentric; indeed he never will be, because he depends upon principles that are valid for everybody" (AP204 VII 293).

16. See also LE246 XXIX 629: "I can . . . picture a kingdom of purposes with autonomy, which is the kingdom of rational beings, who have a general system of ends in view."

17. The analogy with the students' case can be extended further, bringing out additional relevant detail. If all the students gave the correct solution, it would be legitimate to say that they all did *because* it was correct: an acceptable account of their behavior could be formulated entirely within rational discourse (by, say, enumerating the steps they must have taken)—though we might also want to provide a natural account of this behavior (on the basis, say, of the good instruction they received). If, on the other hand, they all

made the same mistake, we would think that a rational analysis of the situation is not adequate at all and that *only* empirical factors (such as: they copied from one another, the problem's formulation was misleading, . . .) could properly explain what happened. What is right can be understood at two independent levels; what is wrong can only be understood at one of them.

18. At TA373 XX 283, while criticizing Leibniz and Wolff, Kant says that "the principle . . . that all evil as ground = 0, i.e., mere limitation" is "at variance both with common sense and even with morality." And yet, consider the following passage: "evil in the world can be regarded as *incompleteness in the development of the germ toward the good.* Evil has *no special* germ; for it is *mere negation* and consists only in the *limitation of the good.* It is nothing beyond this, other than incompleteness in the development of the germ to the good out of uncultivatedness. *The good, however, has a germ; for it is self-sufficient.* . . . A *special germ toward evil cannot be thought*" (R411 XXVIII 1078). My understanding of such statements will become clear as we proceed: though it cannot be denied that evil is real, there is nothing (positive) to our *thought of* evil; we have (in contrast with the case of the rational, or the good) no notion of what its *law* might be; we can only think of it as what *denies* the law of rationality.

19. "For where the moral law speaks there is, objectively, no longer any free choice [*freie Wahl*] with regard to what is to be done" (J96 V 210). See also P288 VIII 287: "[One] feels . . . a revulsion merely at calculating the advantages he could gain by transgressing . . . [his duty], *as if he still had a choice [Wahl] in the matter*" (italics added). And P614 VIII 428: "[One] is not at all free to choose [*wählen*] in the matter, because truthfulness (if he must speak) is an unconditional duty." Hence the *Wahl* people "freely" exercise when they behave in opposition to reason can give no evidence of their manifesting what Kant has defined as "*freie Willkür*"—indeed it gives evidence to the contrary: though they might *seem* (to themselves) free, that is precisely when they are not. "If our power of choice [*Willkür*] were also to feel the objective necessitation subjectively as its own, that would not be opposed to freedom, and the capacity to act in opposition to objective necessitation does not demonstrate freedom" (N408 XV 457).

20. Kant has some relevant suggestions here: "To be unable to sleep at one's fixed and habitual time . . . is a kind of morbid feeling. . . . The only disciplinary advice is to turn away . . . [one's] attention as soon as he perceives or becomes conscious of any thought stirring. . . . This interruption of any thought that he is aware of gradually produces a confusion of ideas by which his awareness of his physical (external) situation is suspended" (R319–20 VII 105).

21. "[Human] actions are appearances and to that extent subject to the merely inner conditions of humanity. Punishments and rewards also belong among these" (N329 XVIII 439–40).

22. "If by nature we mean the principle that impels us to promote our *happiness*, and by grace the incomprehensible moral disposition in us—that is,

the principle of *pure morality*—then nature and grace not only differ from each other but often come into conflict. But if by nature (in the practical sense) we mean our ability to achieve certain ends by our own powers in general, then grace is none other than the nature of the human being insofar as he is determined to actions by a principle which is intrinsic to his own being, but supersensible (the thought of his duty)" (R268 VII 43).

23. It would be a perversion of philosophy analogous to the one discussed earlier (see note 9 and the attending text) if we tried to reduce this rational stance to the empirical one—if, say, we tried to base a rational account of judging and punishing practices on the "utility" of their outcomes, in any of the senses mentioned above (deterrence, rehabilitation, or whatever). See also note 33 and the attending text.

24. What he does says, however, is consistent with the present suggestion. Consider for example the following: "[T]here can be disgraceful punishments that dishonor humanity itself (such as quartering a man, having him torn by dogs, cutting off his nose and ears) . . . ; they . . . make a spectator blush with shame at belonging to a species that can be treated that way"(M580 VI 463). "[J]udges, in punishing crime, should not dishonor humanity; they must, indeed, penalize the evil-doer, but not violate his humanity by demeaning punishments; for if another dishonors a man's humanity, the man himself sets no value on it; it is as if the evil-doer had himself so demeaned his humanity, that he is no longer worthy of being a man, and must then be treated as a universal object of contempt" (LE181 XXVII 418–19).

25. "*[P]erpetual peace* . . . is indeed an unachievable idea. Still, the political principles directed toward perpetual peace, of entering into such alliances of states, which serve for continual *approximation* to it, are not unachievable. Instead, since continual approximation to it is a task based on duty and therefore on the right of human beings and of states, this can certainly be achieved" (M487 VI 350).

26. I will focus on how Kant understands respect in the next chapter.

27. More elaborately, "[o]ne must not immediately accuse someone of an obvious contradiction, *for* were it known to him, he would not contradict himself. . . . If one wants to accuse another of absurdity, . . . then he must change the hidden . . . into the evident, and if the opponent still persists in it, then he accepts an absurdity" (LM148 XXIX 793).

28. See also N5–6: "I can never convince another person except by means of his own thoughts. I must therefore presuppose that the other has a good and correct understanding, otherwise it is in vain to hope that he could be won over by my reasons. Likewise I cannot touch another morally except by his own sentiments; I must therefore presuppose that the other has a certain goodness of the heart, otherwise he will never feel abhorrence at my depictions of vice nor feel incentives in himself from my praises of virtue."

29. Also, as much as reason may approve the outcome of a revolution that has already happened (see note 10 above), it will not approve imitating its

example: "But this is not to say that a nation which has a monarchical constitution should therewith usurp the law, nor even only cherish the secret
wish of seeing it changed" (R302n VII 86n). "It is sweet . . . to imagine con-
stitutions corresponding to the requirements of reason . . . , but rash to propose
them and culpable to incite the populace to abolish what presently exists"
(R307n VII 92n).

30. In the next chapter this trust will turn out to be the basis of how we
are to understand the "postulates of practical reason."

31. That is, essentially, from the praise and blame we assess on others to the
ones we assess on ourselves. But the paradoxical character of this relation with
"oneself" must always be kept in mind. We know from early in the previous
chapter that our moral judgment of ourselves is based on the testimony of our
conscience, but we have also seen that testimony, however private it might
feel, gradually become (as we proceed to understand its significance) more and
more impersonal: "this original intellectual and . . . moral predisposition called
conscience is peculiar in that, although its business is a business of a human being
with himself, one constrained by his reason sees himself constrained to carry it
on as at the bidding *of another person*" (M560 VI 438).

32. One might object that a sunny day and the birth of a child are also
irrational sorts of events, hence that reason should necessarily disapprove of
them, too. But I would not agree: as will become clear in the next chapter, one
can think of the entire world as expression of a rational plan, so reason can
certainly pass positive (as well as negative) judgments on events other than
human actions. (What might create a problem here for some is the familiar
association of a "plan" with some kind of psychological state or performance.
But it should be clear from the discussion carried out in the previous chapter
that all there is to a plan, in the present context, is that events fall in a certain
pattern. Also, trusting in this rational plan must be compatible for Kant with
passing negative judgments on individual non-human events, much as in the
human case we can—indeed, we must—assume a moral progress of the species,
and even see revolutions as contributing to that progress, while continuing to
judge revolutions an evil.) For an extended passage in which Kant manifests
obvious rational approval of nonhuman, even inanimate, conditions and circumstances, consider P329–33 VIII 358–64: humans are forced to come together by the spherical shape of the earth, since "they cannot disperse infinitely
but must finally put up with being near one another"; and nature has made all
kinds of preparatory arrangements to ensure that they "should be able to live in
all regions of the earth. . . . That moss grows even in the cold wastes around the
Arctic Ocean, which the *reindeer* can scrape from under the snow in order to be
the nourishment, or also the draft animal, for the Ostiaks or Samoyeds; or that
the sandy wastes contain salt for the *camel*, which seems as if created for traveling in them, so as not to leave them unused, is already wonderful. But the end
shines forth even more clearly when we see that on the shore of the Arctic
Ocean there are, besides furbearing animals, also seals, walruses, and whales,

whose flesh gives the inhabitants food and whose blubber gives them warmth. But nature's foresight arouses most wonder by the driftwood it brings to these barren regions. . . ." It is still the case, however (as will be pointed out shortly), that only in the case of human actions can we expect to engage their originators rationally.

33. "[T]o look upon all punishments and rewards as mere machinery in the hands of a higher power, serving only to put rational beings into activity toward their final purpose (happiness) is so patently a mechanism which does away with the freedom of their will that it need not detain us here" (PR171 V 38).

34. At E83–84 IX 480, Kant points out that a level of exchange based on this mutual respect should be established as soon as possible in the life of a child, to the exclusion of more manipulative methods based on rewards and punishments: "Supposing a child tells a lie, for instance, he ought not to be punished, but treated with contempt, and told that he will not be believed in the future, and the like. If you punish a child for being naughty, and reward him for being good, he will do right merely for the sake of the reward." (See also E87–88 IX 482, E91 IX 484.) In fact, he goes so far as saying that "[i]f we wish to establish morality, we must abolish punishment. Morality is something so sacred and sublime that we must not degrade it by placing it in the same rank as discipline" (E84 IX 481; I will focus on the complex relation between morality and discipline in chapter 5).

35. The sentimentality Kant attributes to Cesare Beccaria (who then, he thinks, goes on to support it by a bad argument). See M475–76 VI 334–35.

36. This moral regard for the criminal is closely connected with the intellectual regard mentioned earlier (see notes 27 and 28 and the attending text): "[A] judge argued that he who draws real conclusions from false premises is insane. . . . On the basis of this argument it might easily be possible that all criminals be declared insane persons whom we should pity and cure, but never punish" (AP111n VII 214n).

37. "The principle, therefore, in regard to the frailty of human nature, is this, that in judging action I must not take this frailty into consideration" (LE86 XXVII 295).

38. "[O]ne can . . . consider . . . [a human being] as if he were not in time" (LM489 XXIX 1021). "[T]he relation of an action to the objective grounds of reason is not a temporal relation; here, that which determines the causality does not precede the action as regards time" (TA136 IV 346).

39. In general, any empirical act of judging must be distinguished from the nonempirical judgments reason itself issues. The latter are the ideal *standards* for the empirical acts; they cannot be experienced but only thought of; and they belong to the intelligible (not to the sensible, or actual) world ("a human being, considered in terms of his morality, is judged as a supersensible object by a supersensible judge, not under conditions of time," M601n VI 490n). To put it in equivalent terms, the "impartial rational spectator" is as much an

abstraction from any ordinary spectator as my noumenal self is from my ordinary, phenomenal self.

40. One can, of course, (re)appropriate evil behavior to oneself without any regret, indeed by proudly endorsing its evil quality. But this endorsement would no more belong to him as an agent than the behavior does (or did) in the first place. As with all behavior, only a judgment reason approves of can be free—whatever one thinks or says of it.

41. A central element in the analysis to be carried out then is that one behave *as if* one were free. So it is instructive to cite this additional passage, where the relevant connection is made explicit by Kant: "The human being acts according to the idea of freedom, he acts *as if he were free, and eo ipso he is free*" (R403 XXVIII 1068). Furthermore, the emphasis on actual features of one's behavior (such as could be observed by others, as well as by oneself), which will also be essential to that later analysis, is useful to dispel a possible misunderstanding of the current discussion. We are not to revert to thinking of the moral value of an action (in this case, the action of judging one's behavior to be free) as based entirely on the agent's intentions: the verbal, or silent, (re)appropriation one makes of one's behavior is going to have no moral significance unless it is inserted in a pattern that makes a moral difference— that actually shows the person ready to (re)institute the rational level of interaction.

42. "*Where* we do not at all comprehend the possibility because no experience is given to us, there we can still say we can do it because we *should* [*sollens*]" (LM379 XXVIII 677).

43. This apparent inconsistency can be resolved by noting that, though reason is intrinsically normative, in cognitive contexts it provides norms *from the outside*, norms to which *knowledge as a whole* must conform (and part of what these norms require is that knowledge be always articulated descriptively), whereas in moral contexts it considers *itself* practical—hence moves its norms from the metalanguage to the object-language.

44. In the next chapter, we will see that "practical belief" in the truth of this claim is a presupposition (a "postulate") of our acting. But note that there is enough already in Kant's philosophy to force the same conclusion. For, if the world must be conceived as originating from a free act of synthesis, and if our analysis of freedom shows it to be (the same as) rationality, then the world must be conceived as originating from a rational act.

45. In addition to passages already quoted, consider the following: "[T]he ground of evil cannot lie in any object *determining* the power of choice [*Willkür*] through inclination, not in any natural impulses, but in a rule that the power of choice itself produces for the exercise of its freedom" (RR70 VI 21). "Nothing is . . . morally (i.e. imputably) evil but that which is our own deed" (RR78–79 VI 31). "If the human being is to be a free creature and responsible for the development and cultivation of his abilities and predispositions, then it must also be within his power to follow or shun the laws of

morality" (R440 XXVIII 1113). "[A]ll moral evil arises from freedom, since otherwise it would not be *moral* evil, and however prone we may also be to this by nature, our evil actions still arise from freedom, on which account they are also debited to us as vices" (LE86 XXVII 295).

46. "[A] rational being can... rightly say of every unlawful action he performed that he could have omitted it even though as appearance it is sufficiently determined in the past and, so far, is inevitably necessary; for this action, with all the past which determines it, belongs to a single phenomenon of his character, which he gives to himself and in accordance with which he imputes to himself, as a cause independent of all sensibility, the causality of those appearances" (PR218 V 98).

47. Which is going to be crucial for the moral status of that very attitude; see note 41 above. For a powerful contrast (and a good example of a self-serving, cynical attitude) consider the following: "We must,... [politicians] say, take human beings as they are, not as pedants ignorant of the world or good-natured visionaries fancy they ought to be. But in place of that *as they are* it would be better to say what they *have made* them—stubborn and inclined to revolt—through unjust constraint, through perfidious plots placed in the hands of the government; obviously then, if the government allows the reins to relax a little, sad consequences ensue which verify the prophecy of those supposedly sagacious statesmen" (R298 VII 80). "[T]he politician... would willingly take the hope of the human being as the dreaming of an overstressed mind" (R307 VII 92). See also note 44 of chapter 5 and the attending text.

48. "The evil principle would be a subjective practical principle without a principle—to act against all principle, indeed; so it is a *contradictio in adjecto*. Hence merely *inclination* (instinct), that is, well-being..., to live for the day" (O204–5 XXII 123).

49. Kant was well aware of the fact that a nominal definition (which is to say, often, a negative one) only gives a deceptive impression of understanding the possibility of the thing defined. In his famous letter to Marcus Herz of February 21, 1772, he says: "In my dissertation I was content to explain the nature of intellectual representations in a merely negative way, namely, to state that they were not modifications of the soul brought about by the object. However, I silently passed over the further question of how a representation that refers to an object without being in any way affected by it can be possible" (C133 X 130–31). In the *Jäsche Logic* he makes the same point with absolute generality (and brings out its relevance to ethical matters): "Merely *negative* definitions cannot be called real definitions..., because negative marks can serve just as well as affirmative ones for distinguishing one thing from others, but not for cognition of the thing according to its inner possibility. In matters of morals real definitions must always be sought; all our striving must be directed toward this" (LL634 IX 144). And in the *Vienna Logic* he points out (with specific reference to freedom) that negative, nominal definitions provide no insight: "If the object itself is a lack, then I can only

have a negative concept. E.g., freedom is that the will not stand under the compulsion of men. . . . Through negation I have not extended the concept and cannot thereby have more distinct insight [*deutlicher einsehen*] into the concept. An affirmative concept must be added, and deeper distinctness must be provided. Through the latter we have insight [*sehen . . . ein*] into cognition, as to its content, more distinctly and with greater clarity. A negative mark is not used to increase our insight [*Einsicht*], then; rather, it serves only to exclude a concept from other things, in order to guard against errors" (LL291 XXIV 836).

50. "The depravity of human nature is . . . not to be named *malice*, if we take this word in the strict sense, namely as a disposition . . . to incorporate evil *qua evil* for incentive into one's maxim (since this is *diabolical*)" (RR84 VI 37).

51. And specifically one who questioned how "the world of ideas could be connected with the real world" (C280n).

52. "The principle of continuity forbade any leap in the series of appearances (alterations) (*in mundo non datur saltus*)" (A228–29 B281).

53. See also AP206 VII 294: "stability and persistence in principles can generally not be effected by education, examples, and instruction by degrees, but it can only be done by an explosion which suddenly occurs as a consequence of our disgust at the unsteady condition of instinct."

54. "[H]appening presupposes a time, consequently nothing happens in the noumenal world" (LM222 XXIX 923). "In the intelligible world nothing happens and nothing changes" (N253 XVIII 254).

55. Indeed, the very idea of evil has for Kant this purely tautological character: "We think of evil, when we think of the highest degree of it, as an immediate inclination to take satisfaction in evil with no remorse or enticement, and to carry it out with no consideration of profit or advantage, *merely because it is evil*. This idea we form in order to determine the intermediate degrees of evil according to it" (R341 XXVIII 994).

56. An additional passage bringing out the necessary connection between the concepts of a world and of lawlike regularities (hence implicitly arguing that we do not have a concept of a free, irrational world) is the following: "The concept of a world of understanding is . . . only a *standpoint* that reason sees itself constrained to take outside appearances *in order to think of itself as practical*, as would not be possible if the influences of sensibility were determining for the human being but is nevertheless necessary insofar as he is not to be denied consciousness of himself as an intelligence and consequently as a rational cause active by means of reason, that is, operating freely. This thought admittedly brings with it the idea of another order and another lawgiving than that of the mechanism of nature . . . ; and it makes necessary the concept of an intelligible world (i.e., the whole of rational beings as things in themselves)" (G104 IV 458).

57. "[An ethical community] can exist in the midst of a political community and even be made up of all the members of the latter (indeed, without

the foundation of a political community, it could never be brought into existence by human beings). It has however a special unifying principle of its own . . . and hence a form and constitution essentially distinct from those of the other" (RR130 VI 94). No such "special unifying principle" is forthcoming for a free, *un*ethical community. Intimations of this view of evil can be found quite early in Kant, for example in *Reflexion* 3856, from the 1760s (which the editors of the Cambridge edition of *Notes and Fragments* find "confusing," N555): "In the case of freedom, to be determined means not to be passive, either through the way in which objects affect or through a highest productive cause. I can say: at this moment I am free . . . and *unconstrained* to do what I prefer; yet it is unavoidably necessary that I act thus. It is a law of self-activity, which makes the opposite impossible. Even with regard to the morally evil one can be determined by just such a free resolve. No! one can be determined to that only passively or not at all, because the free will always remains and thus cannot be constrained at all, but does not always exercise its activity" (N89 XVII 314). See also N90–91 XVII 317–18, and especially the following suggestive statement: "Evil actions certainly stand under freedom, but do not happen through it" (N91 XVII 318). And N253 XVIII 254: "In the case of an evil will, . . . since it is still a will and not nature, all its actions are objectively impossible and subjectively contingent. For this contingency is the condition under which an objective law can be thought with respect to which an object can be represented as evil. An action that is evil in itself, that one should [*solte*] omit, is evil precisely because we act without an objectively sufficient ground; and the will is evil because it is not subjectively determined through this very rule."

58. We can even say that we *freely* choose not to behave *freely*. But it is important to insist that there are vastly different amounts of conceptual detail associated with these two occurrences of the word "freely." The first occurrence invokes an inarticulate gesture; the second one refers to freedom as rational autonomy.

59. We need to bring out explicitly the way in which the current summary qualifies, but does not contradict, the straightforward statement made on this topic in section 2 above. If freedom is a kind of causality, then there are indeed no three options concerning human behavior; specifically, it is impossible for it to be (conceivable as) evil and free. But there are three such options concerning what people can (indeed, must) *say* or *believe* about their behavior.

60. Even when he discusses boundaries within a purely speculative context (in the *Prolegomena*), Kant treats them as much more than simple, dimensionless lines: he suggests that we could be *inhabiting* a boundary and gather positive knowledge there. "[S]ince a boundary is itself something positive, which belongs as much to what is within it as to the space lying outside a given totality, reason therefore, merely by expanding up to this boundary, partakes of a real, positive cognition, provided that it does not try to go out beyond the boundary" (TA149 IV 361). The bottom line is: there is a lot of structure to

these boundaries and, by locating ourselves *on* them (TA146 IV 356–57), we can make cognitive claims about what is on "the other side" that, for being only relational and analogical, are not at all insignificant.

61. "It is commonly the case . . . that that which belongs to ordinary empirical concepts is usually regarded as if its possibility were also understood. . . . All matter offers a resistance in the space which it occupies; it is, for that reason, called impenetrable. . . . But, although the resistance which something exercises in the space which it occupies is thus *recognized*, to be sure, it is not for that reason *understood*. . . . [It] will, in respect of its possibility, . . . remain incomprehensible, even though its actuality presents itself to the senses" (TB310–11 II 322–23).

62. Conversely, it is "a not inconsiderable rule of prudence, not immediately to venture a definition and seek or pretend to completeness or precision in the determination of the concept if one can make do with one or another of its marks, without requiring a complete derivation of everything that constitutes the entire concept" (A241).

63. "[W]hatever conflicts with . . . [the] principle [of contradiction] is obviously nothing (not even a thought)" (TA290 VIII 195).

64. See also TA124 IV 332: "hyperbolical objects of this kind are what are called *noumena* or pure beings of the understanding (better: beings of thought)—such as, e.g., *substance*, but which is thought *without persistence* in time, or a *cause*, which would however *not* act in *time*, and so on—because such predicates are . . . deprived of all the conditions of intuition under which alone experience is possible, as a result of which the above concepts again lose all significance [*Bedeutung*]".

65. For additional examples of this "contentless" thinking, see TA301–2n VIII 209n: "The representation of an object as simple is a merely negative concept, which reason cannot avoid, because it alone contains the unconditioned for every composite (as a thing, not as mere form), the possibility of which is always conditioned. This concept does not, therefore, serve to extend our cognition, but merely designates a something, so far as it needs to be distinguished from objects of the senses (which all contain a composite)." And TA360 XX267: "we have no tenable concept of . . . an [intellectual] intuition, though we need to think of it, in order not to subject all beings that have powers of cognition to our own form of intuition."

66. Using a distinction from the lectures on logic, we can call such expressions *fruitless* while not *empty of sense*. "Identically tautological propositions are not *empty of sense*, but fruitless. . . . A judgment that does not produce a distinct concept is *empty*. . . . It is not empty of meaning, but logically empty. Through them nothing useful is attained, because they do not yield a distinct concept, and do not fulfill the understanding's ends" (LL376–77 XXIV 937). And, indeed, I pointed out above that, when we consider free, irrational choices (as when we consider tautologies), we are left totally inarticulate, and forced to a useless repetition of the identical.

Chapter 5

1. "[N]either a god nor an animal can act according to imperatives. God is not capable of a deviation from the law, he determines himself only by the law, i.e., by himself, with him there takes place no necessitation, no ought.... Animals, on the other hand, do not act according to rules because due to a lack of understanding they do not know them, but rather have only sensible impulses; therefore they also cannot observe imperatives and determine themselves thereby to an action, i.e., allow themselves to be necessitated" (LM485–86 XXIX 1017).

2. "Much is right, which no one does, and wrong, which everyone does" (LL203 XXIV 254).

3. An additional qualification is in order concerning the deontic character of the modalities relevant to moral discourse, consistently with the discussion in the previous chapter about (re)appropriating one's behavior. Insofar as I identify with reason, I will judge myself to be within the scope of rational principles even when I do not in fact obey them; even then, those principles will continue to be unconditionally applicable to me. Therefore, I cannot regard the very fact that I fell into irrational behavior as a justification (reason in me would approve of) for remaining stuck with it; it would be one more case of perversion on my part to tell myself or others, say, "it's clear I am only an animal; what I just did proves it; hence there is nothing else I can do."

4. When this theme first surfaced in the previous chapter, reason was seen to be needed for adjusting means to ends. Here we see another angle of the same issue: reason must be at work whenever a *necessary* link (for example, between means and ends) enters the picture. And, of course, it can be at work in a pure or in a perverted form. See also PR154 V 20–21: "Reason, from which alone can arise any rule that is to contain necessity, does indeed put necessity even into . . . [a prudential] precept (for otherwise it would not be an imperative), though it is only a subjectively conditioned necessity and cannot be presupposed in the same degree in all subjects. . . . [I]t is requisite to reason's lawgiving that it should need to presuppose only *itself*, because a rule is objectively and universally valid only when it holds without the contingent, subjective conditions that distinguish one rational being from another." Conversely, "[i]n the absence of reason everything seems to be accident" (N133 XVII 547).

5. In Kant's (most common) terms, between "general" and "universal" rules (PR169 V 36). See also P321n VIII 348n: "*general* laws . . . hold *on the whole* . . . [and] universal laws . . . hold *generally*"; and J98 V 213: "all empirical rules are . . . [only *general*], not *universal*." But see TA404 XX 323: "All bodies, so far as we know of them, are heavy, which universality we might call the empirical, as distinct from the rational, which as known a priori, is a *strict* universality."

6. "[I]n the absence of all reference to an end no determination of the will [*Willensbestimmung*] can take place in human beings at all, since no such determination can occur without an effect, and its representation, though not as the determining ground of the power of choice [*Willkür*] nor as an end that comes first in intention, must nonetheless be admissible as the consequence of that power's determination to an end through the law" (RR58 VI 4). More about this (empirical) dependence on goals in the next section.

7. At J81n V 196n, Kant notes that "[t]he resistance or the promotion is not between nature and freedom, but between the former as appearance and the *effects* of the latter as appearances in the sensible world." Which is another useful reminder of how words like "obstacle," "resistance," and "conflict" are to be understood here. For there to be a genuine conflict, it must take place in one and the same world; specifically, for there to be a *real* conflict (in the real world), it must involve a number of *real* factors. Hence no genuine (let alone real) conflict could arise between how we in fact are (in the phenomenal world) and how we can think of ourselves as possibly being (in a noumenal world). But there may be a conflict between natural inclinations and those other natural factors which, in any empirical situation, *we can think of* as acting consistently with reason's injunctions—as doing (in that situation) reason's work. This issue will be taken up again below.

8. See also PR201 V 75: "inasmuch as it moves resistance out of the way, in the judgment of reason... [the] removal of a hindrance is esteemed equivalent to a positive furthering of its causality." And J144 V 260, where we are given what might be regarded as the converse of these implications: "that which we strive to resist is an evil."

9. This humbling process must start early, Kant thinks, and restrain all manifestations of what is often mistakenly identified as freedom but is in fact only a natural instinct to have it one's own way: "The love of freedom is naturally so strong in man, that when once he has grown accustomed to freedom, he will sacrifice everything for its sake. For this very reason discipline must be brought into play very early; for when this has not been done, it is difficult to alter character later in life.... Men should therefore accustom themselves early to yield to the commands of reason, for if a man be allowed to follow his own will in his youth, without opposition, a certain lawlessness will cling to him throughout his life" (E4 IX 442). "Neglect of discipline is a greater evil than neglect of culture, for this last can be remedied later in life, but unruliness cannot be done away with, and a mistake in discipline can never be repaired" (E7 IX 444). More about the role of education and discipline later.

10. See also J133 V 249: "If... we say of an object absolutely that it is great,... we always combine a kind of respect with the representation, just as we combine contempt with that which we call absolutely small."

11. See G56n IV 401n; PR201 V 75.

12. Feeling is susceptibility to pleasure or displeasure (M373 VI 211).

13. "[In the second *Critique*] we did not actually derive this *feeling* [of respect] from the idea of the moral as cause, rather it was merely the determination of the will that was derived from the latter. The state of mind of a will determined by something, however, is in itself already a feeling of pleasure and is identical with it" (J107 V 222; see also J31 XX 229–30). The felt-like quality of the feeling is beyond the scope of this derivation; all we can do is describe it in general (conceptual) terms—that is, in terms of pleasure and displeasure.

14. If the person is taken to be the primary object of respect, one may end up encouraging moral enthusiasm: "a frivolous, high-flown, fantastic cast of mind, flattering ... [people] with a spontaneous goodness of heart" (PR208 V 85).

15. "[T]he humanity in our person remains undemeaned even though the human being must submit to ... [nature's] dominion" (J145 V 262). "We have reason to harbor a low opinion of our person, but in regard to our humanity we should think highly of ourselves" (LE129 XXVII 349). Note the structural similarity with the situation of speculative reason: "It is humiliating for human reason that it accomplishes nothing in its pure use, and even requires a discipline to check its extravagances and avoid the deceptions that come from them. But, on the other side, that reason can and must exercise this discipline itself, without allowing anything else to censor it, elevates it and gives it confidence in itself" (A795 B823). See also N125 XVII 495: "Metaphysics ... is strangely bitter, because it strikes down idle pride and removes imaginary knowledge."

16. "[W]e do wonder at our *ability* so to sacrifice our sensuous nature to morality that we *can* do what we quite readily and clearly conceive we *ought* to do. This ascendancy of the *supersensible* human being in us over the *sensible*, such that (when it comes to a conflict between them) the sensible is *nothing*, though in its own eyes it is *everything*, is an object of the greatest *wonder*; and our wonder at this moral predisposition in us, inseparable from our humanity, only increases the longer we contemplate this true (not fabricated) ideal" (R280 VII 58–59). So there is an obvious relation between the feeling of the sublime (or, indeed, of the beautiful) and the moral feeling: "both ... [the beautiful and the sublime] are purposive in relation to the moral feeling. The beautiful prepares us to love something, even nature, without interest; the sublime, to esteem it, even contrary to our (sensible) interest" (J151 V 267). And, conversely, "the true propaedeutic for the grounding of taste is the development of moral ideas and the cultivation of the moral feeling; for only when sensibility is brought into accord with this can genuine taste assume a determinate, unalterable form" (J230 V 356).

17. Note once again the distinction made in this passage between "the [rational] manner of thinking" and "its foundation in human nature." No direct relation can be established between reason's ideas and the natural world, but only between the latter and (what can be conceived as) the manifestation of the former within the latter.

18. This issue first surfaced for us at the end of chapter 3, when discussing revolutionary action. At LM345–46 XXVIII 584–86 Kant says that "[i]ntellectual pleasure is called moral feeling," that "[t]he discrimination of good and evil belongs to intellectual pleasure or displeasure," and that "[t]he feeling of the promotion of life is pleasure, and the feeling of the hindrance of life is displeasure." So one can say that the moral feeling, which is what does the actual work of making morality matter to me, *is* the feeling that certain kinds of behavior promote a life *of mine*: the one I (can think I) live as a rational being. See also LM63–66 XXVIII 247–50, where we are told that "[l]ife is threefold: 1. *animal*, 2. *human*, and 3. *spiritual*," and that "[t]here is thus a threefold pleasure." And J145 V 261–62, where Kant mentions "a self-preservation of quite another kind than that which can be threatened and endangered by nature outside us."

19. The straightforward contrast I am setting up here between moral injunctions and (a commonsensical view of) political ones is meant to be for the sake of illustration only (and to be external to my interpretation of Kant). It would also be possible, of course (and more in line with Kant's own views—see, for example, P614 VIII 429: "Right must never be accommodated to politics, but politics must always be accommodated to right"), to think of politics as part of morality, and hence of the claim politics has on me as falling within the second rather than the first horn of the present dilemma. Otherwise put, in the political arena we witness the same undecidable confrontation between sensible, positive laws and intelligible, rational ones as we do in the arena of individual behavior—and in both, of course, reason would regard only *its own* authority as final.

20. At N470–71 XIX 284 Kant makes an attempt to give a more substantial answer to the questions discussed here: "How can this *a priori principium* of the universal agreement of freedom with itself interest me? Freedom in accordance with principles of empirical ends has no thoroughgoing consensus with itself; from this I cannot represent anything reliable with regard to myself. It is not a unity of my will. Hence restricting conditions on the use of the will are absolutely necessary. Morality from the *principio* of unity. From the principle of truth." But, of course, one could immediately ask the same question about unity: What exactly is wrong about having no interest in it? (See also note 23 below.)

21. "[The] homage that every state pays the concept of right (at least verbally) nevertheless proves that there is to be found in the human being a still greater, though at present dormant, moral predisposition to eventually become master of the evil principle within him (which he cannot deny) and also to hope for this from others; for otherwise the word *right* would never be spoken by states wanting to attack one another" (P326–27 VIII 355).

22. The other side of the present coin is: No accumulation of natural factors will ever even approximate a moral conclusion. We could not regard

anything (natural) as relevant to morality unless we were already situated within moral discourse.

23. One might believe that this self-deception, for any member of the biological species *human*, will give rise to a variety of signs of discomfort: to neurotic symptoms of some sort. (Kant seems to believe that; see, for example, R413–14 XXVIII 1081 and TA453–54 VIII 414–15.) Two things should be noted about this possibility. First, it would provide no categorical, "external" justification of the "ought," but would still belong to the natural, conditional register ("What is good about not being neurotic?" "It is healthy." "What is good about health?" . . .). Second, we would tend to believe in it if we had the general, teleological attitude toward the ultimate agreement between reason and nature we will explore later.

24. But note that it is possible for the moral feeling to be refined and educated by philosophical training. See, for example, O83–84n XXII 545n: "One can be great in . . . [mathematics], yet, at the same time spiteful, envious and malevolent—it does not follow that one is a *good man* in all respects. To which philosophy, which cultivates the subject's original disposition [to goodness], gives direct guidance. So the latter stands beyond the former in the ordering of the incontestable inward advantages of human character." I will turn to some details of this "cultivation"—that is, of moral education—in the next section (see also note 26 below).

25. That nature be other than us depends on us taking the position of the noumenal self; and we have seen of course (and will be reminded shortly) that it is also possible to take the position of its phenomenal counterpart—in which case the noumenal self becomes the (alleged) counterpart of the empirical self and the struggle for identification must be conducted in the opposite direction. The unresolvable oscillation between the different registers of nature and freedom, in other words, involves an equally unresolvable oscillation between different options concerning *who I am to begin with.*

26. This discipline must not turn the human into an automaton, hence a difficult balance must be struck, when educating someone, between inducing obedience and promoting sheer mindlessness: "Discipline is compulsion; but as such it is contrary to freedom. Freedom, however, is the worth of man, and hence the young one must be subjected to compulsion by discipline in such a way that freedom is preserved; he must be disciplined by compulsion, but not of a slavish kind" (LE218 XXVII 467). "One of the greatest problems of education is how to unite submission to the necessary *restraint* with the child's capability of exercising his *freewill*. . . . I am to accustom my pupil to endure a restraint of his freedom, and at the same time I am to guide him to use his freedom aright. Without this all education is merely mechanical, and the child, when his education is over, will never be able to make a proper use of his freedom" (E27 IX 453). Here the conceptual space is opened for the skillful *empirical* operation, conducted in the wake of rational ideas (and further described below), of liberating ourselves and others to the largest extent

possible (see note 71 of chapter 3). Details about how this operation is to be concretely carried out are given by Kant throughout *Education* (for example, at E28–29 IX 454, E44–45 IX 463, E47–48 IX 464–65).

27. Among the most powerful factors for the promotion of moral behavior is the moral conscience. So it is especially significant for the argument I am developing here that Kant should repeatedly characterize conscience (as was pointed out in chapter 3—see note 16 there and the attending text) as an instinct, that is, as a natural and sensible agency, not an intellectual one.

28. Importantly, the moral feeling cannot be a feeling *of* morality, but only one that carries out morality's work in the phenomenal world. For "morality simply does not admit of being felt" (LE243 XXIX 625). "Moral feeling does not pertain to the giving of laws, but is the basis for their execution" (LE244 XXIX 626).

29. Note that habituation or training acquires a very different (both theoretical and practical) role depending on whether we believe that the ideal behavior or character can finally be attained or not. In the latter case (the one that applies to Kant), *all we ever have is training*—that is, an education of our sensible being by sensible means ("rewards and punishments can . . . serve . . . as means in the matter of moral training," LE80 XXVII 287), which may well be conducive to behavior that is judged positively by reason *but that will also never cease to be sensibly determined*.

30. In addition to passages quoted before (see notes 17 and 18 of chapter 2), consider the following: "Of course in the logical sense possibility always precedes actuality, and here I can think the possibility of a thing without actuality. Yet we have no concept of real possibility except through existence, and in the case of every possibility which we think *realiter* we always presuppose some existence. . . . Hence every possibility presupposes something actually given, . . . [the] ground of possibility must itself be given not merely as possible but also as actual" (R377 XXVIII 1036).

31. See also G63 IV 409: "examples serve only for encouragement, that is, they put beyond doubt the practicability of what the law commands and make intuitive what the practical rule expresses more generally." And LE117 XXVII 334: "Men like, in general, to have examples, and if none exists they are happy to excuse themselves, on the ground that everybody lives that way. But if examples are available, to which appeal can be made, then it encourages people to emulate them."

32. At PR202 V 77 Kant admits that such examples are fictionalized, while insisting on their significance: "I see observance of . . . [the moral] law and hence its *practicability* proved before me in fact. . . . [T]he law made intuitive by an example . . . strikes down my pride, the standard being furnished by the man I see before me whose impurity, such as it may be, is not so well known to me as is my own, who therefore appears to me in a purer light." At LE86 XXVII 294 he even explicitly chastises attempts to find (empirical) fault with them: "we must not seek out the flaws and weaknesses in the life of a

Socrates, for example, since it helps us not at all, and is actually harmful to us. For if we have examples of moral imperfection before us, we can flatter ourselves at our own moral imperfection. This desire to hunt for faults betrays something ill-natured and envious in seeing the morality that shines in others, when we do not possess it ourselves" (see also LE103 XXVII 316–17). And, since a sure way of bringing out empirical faults is by giving too detailed an account of such examples, Kant is quite negative about the moral significance of literary representations: "ideals . . . provide an indispensable standard for reason, which needs the concept of that which is entirely complete in its kind, in order to assess and measure the degree and the defects of what is incomplete. But to try to realize the ideal in an example, i.e., in appearance, such as that of the sage in a novel, is not feasible, and even has about it something nonsensical and not very edifying, since the natural limits which constantly impair the completeness in the idea render impossible every illusion in such an attempt, and thereby render even what is good in the idea suspect by making it similar to a mere fiction" (A569–70 B597–98). Along similar lines, Kant is also encouraging of maintaining the social semblance of virtue, however hypocritical it might be, since exploding it would have disheartening consequences: "Every human virtue in circulation is small change; only a child takes it for real gold. Nevertheless, it is better to circulate pocket pieces than nothing at all. . . . To pass them off as nothing but counters which have no value . . . is high treason perpetrated upon humanity. Even the appearance of the good in others must have value for us, because in the long run something serious can come from such a play with pretenses" (AP39 VII 152–53).

33. See also LE8 XXVII 13: "virtue entails, not just *morally good* actions, but at the same time a great possibility of the opposite, and thus incorporates an inner struggle. . . . [W]e can . . . ascribe *ethics*, but not virtue (properly speaking) to the angels and to God; for in them there is assuredly holiness but not virtue." At AP32 VII 147, Kant introduces an interesting qualification: "We cannot explain virtue by saying that it is readiness for free and lawful actions, because virtue would then be a mere mechanism of applying power. Virtue, on the contrary, is moral strength in pursuit of one's duty, a duty which should never be a matter of habit, but should always proceed, fresh and original, from one's mode of thought." A related point was made in the previous section about the role of discipline; see note 26 there. (As usual, these references to inner factors and to the influence of thought should not be taken to suggest an ethics of intentions. The point is rather that a purely mechanical recipe is going to break down morally sooner or later. No simple recipe can resolve the intrinsic ambiguity of human behavior—or exempt it once and for all from the relentless critical scrutiny that must be applied to it.)

34. The construction of such tales is clearly related to the drive toward the empirical in rational (pseudo)cognitive contexts (see note 23 of chapter 2): though reason will never, by Kant's lights, arrive at the definiteness of

empirical knowledge, he is constantly attempting to approximate the latter by adding more detail to his rational theorizing.

35. "There is no use of our powers at all, however free it might be, and even of reason . . . , which, if every subject always had to begin entirely from the raw predisposition of his own nature, would not fall into mistaken attempts if others had not preceded him with their own, not in order to make their successors into mere imitators, but rather by means of their method to put others on the right path for seeking out the principles in themselves and thus for following their own, often better, course" (J163–64 V 283).

36. At LM340 XXVIII 577 Kant adds further detail on this relation between examples and ideas (specifically, about the latter having not only moral, but also epistemic priority): "An *archetype* is actually an object of intuition, insofar as it is the ground of imitation. *Thus Christ is the archetype of all morality. But in order to regard something as an archetype, we must first have an idea according to which we can cognize the archetype*, in order to hold it for that; for otherwise we indeed would not be able to cognize the archetype, and thus could be deceived. But if we have an idea of something, e.g., of the highest morality, and now an object of intuition is given, someone is represented to us as being congruent with this idea, then we can say: this is the archetype, follow it! . . . The model is a ground of imitation. We can indeed realize actions and objects according to a model, also *without* an idea; but then they agree only *by mere chance* with the model. In morality we must assume no model, but rather follow the archetype which is equal to the idea of holiness."

37. In this regard, it is instructive to consider the following passage from LL140 XXIV 177–78: "One presents a great, famous learned man to the eye of the learned world and seeks to persuade all others firmly that they will always act in vain, irrespective of all the possible industry, work, and effort they can apply, since they could never be in a position to be equal to this great man, or to come near to him[;] indeed, since one regards the sayings of this great archetype as incontrovertible and unimprovable *oracula*, one simply rejects all their opinions, merely because they contradict, or seem to contradict, the judgment of the great man. One is afraid oneself, or seeks to make all others afraid, to try to strive ever to become equal to this learned man, just as if it would be a vain undertaking to strive after this. . . . There is actually nothing more harmful for the human race . . . than always to represent others as unattainable examples, and to take them, as it were, as models for imitation. One thereby copies more the errors than the good properties of the original that is set up, because everything in the world is imperfect, and thus even these models cannot be fully excluded from this." Here Kant makes two points complementary to the ones brought out in the text above: (a) examples should never be used to *discourage* people from trying their best behavior, and (b) painstaking imitation of all details of real examples is detrimental, since it makes people copy their imperfections as well. So, once again, examples must be used as vivid, object-based presentations of the behavioral features rationality demands of us, and

as arguing for the plausibility of those demands. Their historical character is irrelevant (or worse), and it would be a mistake to take *them* with excessive humility—we should only humble ourselves before the rational law.

38. "The ancients revealed this error openly by directing their moral investigation entirely to the determination of the concept of the *highest good*, and so of an object which they intended afterwards to make the determining ground of the will in the moral law" (PR192 V 64).

39. In addition to passages already quoted, consider the following: "Now it is indeed undeniable that every volition must . . . have an object and hence a matter; but the matter is not, just because of this, the determining ground and condition of the maxim" (PR167 V 34). As usual, a mere factual conjunction cannot settle priority issues: only conceptual analysis can.

40. Kant calls it a "paradox" that "*the concept of good and evil must not be determined before the moral law (for which, as it would seem, this concept would have to be made the basis) but only (as was done here) after it and by means of it*" (PR190 V 62–63). This paradox is but one of the many distortions created by the Copernican Revolution, and one of the many manifestations of the transcendental illusion that follows from it.

41. For the realist there would be no such reference: there being (before the race) no person who can be unambiguously identified as the winner, the definite description would (then) be an improper one—to be spirited away by some process of regimentation, or to be assigned a "conventional" reference. So whether in this case we can sensibly talk of reference, period, depends on one's transcendental position. On this matter, see my "Free from What?"

42. Kant does talk, in some cases, of *practical cognition* (see, for example, RR199 VI 181). What he means by that will be clear later, when I say more about how the cognitive register can be subordinated to the moral one.

43. Remember: the proper logic of this statement is "when I can think of what I do as a result of rewriting the moral (that is, rational, intelligible) law in sensible terms." An interpretive stance is embedded in this talk from the beginning, and will constantly surface in what follows ("come to the conclusion," "regard myself as," "make sense of," . . .).

44. Indeed, with such "exertions," "a human being often develops powers that were previously unknown to him" (LM483 XXIX 1014).

45. Though the analogy with objects of love, and in general of inclination, is useful in clarifying the kind of commitment relevant here, I hasten to add that in the case of inclination the commitment is entirely idiosyncratic, whereas the demands posed by reason are universally binding for all rational beings—hence Kant sees the two cases as radically different. See PR255n V 143–44n.

46. See also LM265 XXIX 898: "One may prove or also refute freedom in the theoretical sense, as one wants, nevertheless one will still always act according to ideas of freedom. There are many people who do not concede certain propositions in speculation, but still act according to them."

47. Kant would say that we *practically* believe it—or have practical faith in it (his "*Glaube*" is translated as both "belief" and "faith," as will be made clear by a number of subsequent quotes). Note also that at C155 X 180, as he refers to the relation one is to have to God's assistance in making things work out (discussed below in my text), Kant calls it "faith . . .[,] *that is*, an unconditional trust" (italics added).

48. That is, in the terms introduced in the previous chapter (see note 44 and the attending text), to trust that the synthetic act that (we must think) originates the world is indeed a free—or a rational—one.

49. The practical postulate of God's existence seems to be on a different level from those of freedom and immortality because in the latter I am committed to *my own* freedom and immortality whereas in the former I am invoking the presence of an Other. But this contrast fades when we remind ourselves of the ambiguous, paradoxical character of my relation to my rational counterpart. Reason is me insofar as I identify with something other than my empirical self, insofar as I take a point of view that does not come *naturally* to me ("My private will often fails to coincide with my will, taken as a universal rule," LE244 XXIX 627); hence invoking an omnipotent God (as indeed suggested in the text above) is not essentially different from invoking (my) reason. In some form or other, this point has been with us for a long time; it surfaced explicitly when, in chapter 3, we compared human with divine autonomy and when, in chapter 4, we talked about humans having to take the whole burden of world history on their shoulders. So, once again, the God that matters here is one within each of us—one that in a way *is* each of us. See R286–87 VII 67: "The God who speaks through our own (morally practical) reason is an infallible interpreter of His words in the Scriptures, whom everyone can understand. And it is quite impossible for there to be any other accredited interpreter of His words . . . ; for religion is a purely rational affair."

50. At times, Kant seems to be espousing the converse of this characterization: that practical postulates, that is, are theoretical propositions *from which* rational imperatives can be derived—and in this sense he opposes them to *speculative* propositions. "Cognitions can be theoretical and yet be either practical or speculative. For although they do not say what ought to happen, because they are theoretical, practical propositions can nonetheless be derived from them, and they are to this extent opposed to speculative propositions. E.g. That there is a God is a theoretical proposition, but it is *practical in potentia*[;] you must just act as if there is a highest legislator for your actions" (LL345–46 XXIV 901). "A *speculative* cognition is that which has no application practically. Practical propositions are either imperatives—then they are opposed to theoretical ones—or they are grounds for possible imperatives, and then they are opposed to merely speculative ones. E.g. There is a God[;] this is no merely speculative proposition but rather a practical one. For it contains grounds for possible imperatives" (LL485 XXIV 751). "Practical cognitions

are . . . either 1. *imperatives*, and are to this extent opposed to *theoretical* cognitions; or they contain 2. the *grounds for possible imperatives* and are to this extent opposed to *speculative* cognitions" (LL587 IX 86). But there is no conflict here: a practical postulate is a hypothesis that allows us to understand moral behavior, but the only point of the hypothesis, hence the only kind of strength it can have, it derives from the very behavior it presumes to explain.

51. Note the two distinct ways in which "from a practical point of view" is glossed in the last two quotes. As different elucidations of the same phrase, they must be taken as equivalent. Therefore, "to form a concept of the possibility of an end" is to be taken as equivalent to "to apply our powers to realize it," and the "possibility" referred to in the first quote is one whose "concept" we have whenever we work for the relevant end—whether or not we ever stop for a moment to even consider the theoretical problem of this possibility, indeed whether or not we even have a clear notion of the end that is supposed to be possible. I have been claiming that someone who did take this theoretical stance would have to regard us as committed to the possibility of the end we appear to be striving for—and that someone might of course be ourselves. But note that, even if as a result we did form the theoretical belief that God, freedom, and immortality are real (and I would expect this to often be the case), such a mental state would have no significance here: the controlling factor would continue to be how we behave, and what *practical* commitment (or belief) we manifest in our behavior. For, just as one can be theoretically cynical while acting as if one were free, one can be theoretically a believer while acting as if one were not free.

52. "A hypothesis is a proposition that one assumes for explaining certain phenomena, but which yet could well be explained through another hypothesis. But a practical postulate is the only possible thing that can explain certain appearances" (LM282 XXIX 918).

53. See also J316 V 450–51: "[The moral] proof . . . is not meant to say that it is just as necessary to assume the existence of God as it is to acknowledge the validity of the moral law." And J334–35 V 470–71: "the attainment of . . . [the] final end . . . is . . . not practically necessary like duty itself."

54. "[O]nce reason is in possession of this increment, it will, as speculative reason, go to work with these ideas in a negative way (really, only to secure its practical use), that is, not extending but purifying, so as . . . to ward off *anthropomorphism* . . . and . . . *fanaticism*" (PR249 V 135–36).

55. Which is why, "in spite of the diversity of religions, religion is everywhere the same" (E115 IX 496). See also P336n VIII 367n: "There can indeed be historically different *creeds* . . . and just as many different *religious books* . . . , but there can be only one single *religion* holding for all human beings and in all times. Those can therefore contain nothing more than the vehicle of religion, what is contingent and can differ according to differences of time and place." And R262 VII 36: "[the] distinction [of religion] from morality is a merely formal one. . . . This is why there is only one religion."

56. In this book I have argued that the first *Critique* can be regarded as a *theoretical* digression on the way to the legitimation of moral discourse; more precisely, as the elaborate construction of a main tool of defense for the tenability of that discourse. But it is also possible to provide some documentation of the fact that the first *Critique* was *historically* a digression Kant gradually convinced himself he had to take as he worked on the foundations of morality. His correspondence indicates that his main project late in 1770 was the writing of a metaphysics of morals (C108 X 97), and that people were hoping to see it completed soon (C121 X 112). Along the way the projected work turned into an examination of "the foundational principles and laws that determine the sensible world together with an outline of what is essential to the Doctrine of Taste, of Metaphysics, and of Moral Philosophy" (C127 X 123); and this change seemed to reassure Marcus Herz, who had been hearing that Kant had become totally disillusioned with, and even averse to, metaphysics (C128–29 X 124–25). Then comes the February 21, 1772, letter to Herz, in which the main question of the first *Critique* is finally and clearly formulated (C133–34 X 130–31) and indeed the very term "critique of pure reason" is introduced (C135 X 132). Even then, however, such a critique was supposed to provide (among other things) "the pure principles of morality" (C135 X 132), and what was to precede the working out of such principles was supposed to be completed quickly and published "within three months" (C135 X 132). So morality was constantly on the horizon of this whole operation, though getting there was going to take far longer than originally planned. (In a subsequent letter to Herz of November 24, 1776, Kant admits that "one major object . . . , like a dam," is blocking him, "an object with which I hope to make a lasting contribution and which I really think I have in my grasp" (C160 X 199). On August 20, 1777, always writing to Herz, he makes the "stone that lies in . . . [his] path" to be "the problem of presenting these ideas with total clarity, for I know that something can seem clear enough to an author himself and yet be misunderstood even by knowledgeable readers, if it departs entirely from their accustomed way of thinking" (C164 X 213–14).)

57. "I . . . climb even through difficult subtleties to the peak of principles, not so much as if the healthy understanding would not be able to get there without this detour, but rather in order to entirely rob of power all of the sophistical subtleties that are raised against it (N286 XVIII 313).

Chapter 6

1. He shows awareness of the possible confusion at TA73n IV 276n, while providing no justification for his use. There is a good reason for extending the two terms in this way, since the analytic method proceeds (as we will see) by drawing analytic consequences of given premises, and the synthetic one by positing synthetic connections in logical space (assumptions from which one

intends to draw certain desired conclusions). And yet the extension is still somewhat confusing because the "synthetic" method too is ultimately only constituted of analytic judgments (consistently with its application in philosophy). As I explain in *Kant's Copernican Revolution* and reiterate in chapter 2 above, all the connections posited "synthetically" are supposed to be within the scope of a possibility operator: the task is not proving that the desired conclusions are the case, but that they *can* be the case. (At PR183 V 53, describing the results of his efforts concerning the concept of cause in the first *Critique*, Kant claims that he "was able not only to prove . . . [its] objective reality . . . with respect to objects of experience but also to *deduce* it as an a priori concept because of the necessity of the connection that it brings with it," and then adds: "*that is*, to show its possibility from pure understanding without empirical sources" (last italics added). See also N217 XVIII 101: "Transcendental philosophy . . . is a science of the possibility of a synthetic a priori cognition.") And possibilities (as opposed to actualities) can be thought of as purely conceptual matters—when they do not require the mobilization of pure intuition, as mathematics does. (At TB134–35 II 91 Kant says: "The argument for the existence of God which we are presenting is based simply on the fact that something is possible. It is, accordingly, a proof which can be conducted entirely a priori.")

2. And one whose intimate resonance with TR will become apparent by the end of this chapter—thus also motivating its popularity.

3. This principle is equivalent to PN in the standard, realist view. Part of what can happen when PN is rejected is that the legitimacy of the inference from actuality to possibility be retained, hence the two principles *no longer* be equivalent. At LM320 XXVIII 555 Kant indeed claims that "[o]ne can infer to possibility from existence" and "to non-being from impossibility," but makes no mention of anything resembling PN. (See also TA288 VIII 193: "of what is true, we do not first have to ask if it is possible, and to that extent logic has the principle *ab esse ad posse valet consequentia* in common with metaphysics, or rather lends it to the latter." And LL69 XXIV 91: "Through the actuality of a thing, experience instructs us naturally of its possibility.") And later he adds: "Logical necessity does not prove the existence of a thing" (LM322 XXVIII 557). Real necessity might; but "[a]bsolute real necessity cannot be elucidated by any example. Only hypothetical necessity can be comprehended" (LM323 XXVIII 558). Even if we end up looking favorably upon the inference from actuality to possibility, however, actuality is not to acquire greater currency in transcendental philosophy; see the following note.

4. I pointed out in chapter 2 that the transcendental philosopher must account for the possibility of what is (ordinarily taken to be) the case; hence actuality is the starting point of her inquiry. But it is so only in an external way: as the source of motivation for initiating that inquiry. *Within* the inquiry itself, actuality should be taken to prove nothing of relevance, and indeed a revealing sign of the philosopher's having reached the end of what she can

contribute to a (transcendental philosophical) discussion is when she finally falls back on saying: "But that X be possible cannot be doubted, since it happens all the time." Cfr. TB331 II 344: "Nor shall I allow myself to be fobbed off with an answer which adduces other cases which have some kind of similarity with this kind of deception, and which occur, for example, in the state of fever. For whether the victim of the delusion be in a state of health or illness, what one wishes to know is not whether such deceptions also occur in other circumstances, but rather how the deception is possible." As this quote makes clear, Kant's crucial concern with *how* something is possible is not even addressed by the actuality of that thing, which is compatible with its remaining totally mysterious. See also TA238–39 IV 529: "how . . . rigid bodies are possible . . . is still an unsolved problem, no matter how easily the common doctrine of nature presumes to have settled it." (In the *Opus Postumum*, Kant returns repeatedly to this "unsolved problem.") And A209–10 B254–55: "[H]ow . . . [the law of continuity], which seems to amplify our cognition of nature so much, is possible completely a priori, very much requires our scrutiny, even though it is obvious that it is real and correct, and one might therefore believe oneself to be relieved of the question how it is possible. For there are so many unfounded presumptions of the amplification of our cognition through pure reason that it must be adopted as a general principle to be distrustful of them all and not to believe and accept even the clearest dogmatic proof of this sort of proposition without documents that could provide a well-grounded deduction."

5. At LM457 XXIX 988 Kant makes the curious statement that "necessity is a possibility, from which actuality can be inferred." Which suggests that actuality only follows from necessity *if possibility is also given*—a modified PN that does indeed make good sense in the Kantian framework.

6. This regressive procedure is also judged by many to be instantiated in the first *Critique*'s "transcendental arguments"—in contrast with Kant's explicit statement that his procedure there is synthetic, hence progressive. I discuss this matter in *Kant's Copernican Revolution*.

7. This is indeed an issue on which Kant waffles considerably—which, as I pointed out in *Kant's Copernican Revolution*, is evidence of hesitation on his part in accepting the most radical consequences of his philosophical practice. The uncertainty of his attitude is revealed most clearly in the *Lectures on Logic*. In the *Vienna Logic*, of the early 1780s, he says straightforwardly: "To make a distinct concept is the synthetic method, to make a concept distinct is the analytic one. . . . Mathematical distinctness is wholly synthetic. . . . The philosopher makes concepts distinct. . . . I cannot explain virtue synthetically. For I am supposed to say what we all think under the concept of virtue, not what I perhaps understand under this concept in accordance with my own caprice" (LL298–99 XXIV 844–45). But in the *Dohna-Wundlacken Logic*, of the early 1790s, the synthetic method is considered a possibility for philosophy, though, somewhat inconsistently, (a) this method is identified with the

mathematician's, and (b) it is judged a mistake for philosophy to imitate mathematics: "The first division [of methods] is into synthetic and analytic. The latter is where I go from consequences to grounds, the former where I go from grounds to consequences.... In philosophizing one can proceed synthetically or analytically. The mathematical method is a synthetic method" (LL511 XXIV 779). "[The mathematical method] is none other than the synthetic method, which proceeds from the first grounds of a cognition and stops at the last consequences. The first thing with this method, now, is definition, then axiom, theorem, problem, etc. {... Wolff expounded philosophy in accordance with this method, which cannot be done}" (LL515 XXIV 783). Finally, in the *Jäsche Logic*, published in 1800, Kant insists that "there is an essential difference between the two propositions: *to make a distinct concept* and *to make a concept distinct*" and that "[t]he philosopher only makes given concepts distinct," but then mysteriously adds: "Sometimes one proceeds synthetically even when the concept that one wants to make distinct in this way is already *given*. This is often the case with propositions based on experience, in case one is not yet satisfied with the marks already thought in a given concept" (LL568-69 IX 63-64). Does this mean that, if I am not satisfied with what is already thought in the concept of virtue, I can make up a different concept of it? (At times, Kant points out that moral concepts, being pure, are not constrained by deference to empirical archetypes: "[the concepts] of virtue, of right and wrong, of goodness, of legality and illegality, of actions, of the simple and the composite, and of the contingent and the necessary... do not arise at all from objects[;] therefore I cannot represent their determination just in part; rather, they are arbitrary. Reason is the creator of these concepts, and consequently the thing has no other determination than what reason has attached to it.... No one should venture to define empirical concepts, then, but one can well have correct *definitiones* of pure concepts of reason," LL97-98 XXIV 124-25. But, even if this point is granted, it will have no impact on the present issue: there is still a difference between the concepts of virtue, of right and wrong, etc., as "created" by human reason and as reconstructed by philosophy.) As I will argue below, a serious problem is lurking here, about the relevance of (transcendental) philosophical accounts to ordinary experience.

8. "In philosophy, the concept of a thing is always given, albeit confusedly or in an insufficiently determinate fashion. The concept has to be analyzed; the characteristic marks which have been separated out and the concept which has been given have to be compared with each other in all kinds of contexts; and this abstract thought must be rendered complete and determinate.... If,... [for example], I had tried to arrive at a definition of time synthetically, it would have had to have been a happy coincidence indeed if this concept, thus reached synthetically, had been exactly the same as that which completely expresses the idea of time which is given to us" (TB248-49 II 276-77). See also note 12 below.

9. See also (for example) PR168 V 35, where Kant claims that "[the conflict between morality and happiness] would ruin morality altogether were not the voice of reason in reference to the will so distinct, so irrepressible, and so audible even to the most common human beings; thus it can maintain itself only in the perplexing speculations of the schools, which are brazen enough to shut their ears to that heavenly voice in order to support a theory they need not break their heads over." At PR143n V 8n he is happy to accept the (unsympathetic) description a critic gave of the *Groundwork*, as a work where "no new principle of morality is set forth . . . but only a *new formula*," and asks rhetorically: "who would even want to introduce a new principle of all morality and, as it were, first invent it? Just as if, before him, the world had been ignorant of what duty is or in thoroughgoing error about it." Finally, at PR189 V 61, he claims that even someone who "finally gets a sound thrashing" for "vex[ing] and disturb[ing] peace-loving people" "must in his reason recognize that justice was done to him"; indeed, "[t]here is not one . . . [villain] unable to perceive or distinguish between good and evil, or who would not wish to be virtuous" (LE181 XXVII 418). Note however that the general agreement on what moral behavior is supposed to be is compatible for Kant with a highly infrequent realization of such behavior; therefore the agreement will often manifest itself in the form of self-reproach, and there will be ample room for the moral education which (as we saw in the previous chapter) is empirically indispensable to turn theory into practice. Also, given the role rationality plays in Kant's conceptual account of morality, his trust that all humans, whatever their behavior, must ultimately feel (what he considers) the moral call amounts to trusting that what are biologically human beings cannot but participate in that "humanity" which is a form of rationality—and in this regard it goes together with his trust that humans must feel the metaphysical "call" as well (see, for example, LM420 XXIX 947–48: "[it] is innate in every human being . . . [that they] found and still find an interest in [metaphysics]. . . . [N]o human being can be without metaphysics").

10. Kant's most sustained effort of proceeding analytically from ordinary morality to his own philosophical views is, of course, section I of the *Groundwork* (G49–60 IV 393–405). But it is hard to resist the impression, in reading this section, that there is little which is "common" about the strictness he imputes to the "innocent" judgment of ordinary people—and that others might well interpret the data in substantially different ways.

11. It might be worth noting that, despite the obvious influence Kant's early Pietist education had on him, his explicit references to Pietism are hardly laudatory. See, for example, the following: "Separatists and sectarians of every kind, clubbists, lodge-brothers, Herrenhuters and Pietists, are . . . destroyers of general goodwill and philanthropy" (LE406 XXVII 674). "[The Pietists make a] fantastic and—despite all their show of humility—proud claim to be marked out as supernaturally favored children of heaven, even though their

conduct, as far as we can see, is not the least bit better in moral terms than that of the people they call children of the world" (R279n VII 57n).

12. Kant was certainly sensitive to this issue. For he claimed that "[t]here are whole sciences whose philosophy differs from the common understanding not in matter but only in form, in distinctness[;] thus it is, e.g., with morals" (LL28 XXIV 40). So he would have regarded his "science" of morality as a failure if it validated a content different from what is assumed by "the common understanding."

13. "The usual scholastic and doctrinal methods of philosophy make one dumb, insofar as they operate with a mechanical thoroughness. They narrow the understanding and make it incapable of accepting instruction. By contrast, critique broadens the concepts and makes reason free. The scholastic philosophers operate like pirates who as soon as they arrive on an unoccupied coast fortify it" (N211 XVIII 84).

14. "[T]o bring... [psychological] principles into logic is just as absurd as to derive morals from life" (LL529 IX 14).

15. "The greatest difficulty in the right of nations has to do... with right during a war; it is difficult even to form a concept of this or to think of law in this lawless state without contradicting oneself (*inter arma silent leges*)" (M485 VI 347). That right during a war was our main metaphor in attempting to bring some level of consistency to the perplexing relation between freedom and evil in chapter 4 can then be seen as preparing the ground for the general point to be made here.

16. Alternatively (and, indeed, much more commonly), realist logic (here called "standard" because of the continuing prevalence of TR, in partial contrast with the practice of calling "nonstandard" such peripheral developments as relevance logic—which, from TI's viewpoint, can be seen as epicycles) simply changes the subject, moving from *monadic* to *dyadic* formal systems, hence in effect abandoning all treatment of categorical imperatives.

17. So the Stoics were wrong in thinking of holy behavior as really possible (and instantiated in the sage): in thus "[straining] the moral capacity of the *human being*" (PR242 V 127), they were still within the scope of that primacy of objects over norms which is definitional of TR. In Christianity, on the other hand, norms appear to be primary, precisely because what they require is unrealizable: "The moral law is holy (inflexible) and demands holiness of morals, although all the moral perfection that a human being can attain is still only virtue, that is, a disposition conformed with law *from respect* for law, and thus consciousness of a continuing propensity to transgression or at least impurity" (PR243 V 128).

18. That this be the case is especially clear (as is always the case with logical systems) from a semantical point of view, that is, when one considers that, in this case too, possible worlds *understood as domains of objects* are the starting point for any interpretations of the formalisms (and hence it should come as no surprise that the relevant "possible" worlds here be *deontically perfect* or *ideal* ones).

19. At A666 B692 Kant points out that what takes place between norms is not even a conflict, properly speaking. Each party will insist on the relevance of its requirements, but the various parties (and requirements) will not sufficiently engage with each other to produce real contradictions: "If merely regulative principles are considered as constitutive, then as objective principles they can be in conflict; but if one considers them merely as *maxims*, then it is not a true conflict, but it is merely a different interest of reason that causes a divorce between ways of thinking." Remember the similar point made in chapter 3 about the "conflict" between reason and the inclinations.

20. "[The final end] is nothing other than the entire vocation of human beings, and the philosophy of it is called moral philosophy. On account of the preeminence which moral philosophy had over all other applications of reason, the ancients understood by the name of 'philosopher' first and foremost the moralist" (A840 B868). In the preface to my *Hegel's Dialectical Logic* I point out that Kantian philosophy is "practical reason, ... deontic to the core, ... intrinsically normative" and, by implication, I suggest that Hegel's logic (and philosophy) be regarded as the most effective tool in the realist's hands. In the main body of that book, I go on to argue that Hegel's presence is vastly more dominant on the contemporary scene than many would imagine; the most obvious sign of this dominance, from the standpoint of the present book, is the reduction of morality (in various ways, occasionally mentioned above for purposes of illustration) to a cognitive register more akin to TR.

INDEX